The Editor

GRACE IOPPOLO is the founder and director of the Henslowe-Alleyn Digitisation Project and is Professor of Shakespearean and Early Modern Drama in the Department of English Literature at the University of Reading, England. She is the author of *Dramatists and Their Manuscripts in the Age of Shakespeare, Jonson, Middleton and Heywood: Authorship, Authority, and the Playhouse* and *Revising Shakespeare*. She has edited the Norton Critical Editions of *King Lear* and *Measure for Measure* and has published widely on textual transmission, the history of the book, and literary and historical manuscripts. She is the General Editor of *The Collected Works of Thomas Heywood*.

A NORTON CRITICAL EDITION

William Shakespeare
A MIDSUMMER NIGHT'S DREAM

AN AUTHORITATIVE TEXT
SOURCES
CRITICISM
ADAPTATIONS

Edited by

GRACE IOPPOLO
UNIVERSITY OF READING

W · W · NORTON & COMPANY · *New York* · *London*

W. W. Norton & Company has been independent since its founding in 1923, when William Warder Norton and Mary D. Herter Norton first published lectures delivered at the People's Institute, the adult education division of New York City's Cooper Union. The firm soon expanded its program beyond the Institute, publishing books by celebrated academics from America and abroad. By mid-century, the two major pillars of Norton's publishing program—trade books and college texts—were firmly established. In the 1950s, the Norton family transferred control of the company to its employees, and today—with a staff of four hundred and a comparable number of trade, college, and professional titles published each year—W. W. Norton & Company stands as the largest and oldest publishing house owned wholly by its employees.

ISBN: 978-0-393-92357-5 (pbk.)

W. W. Norton & Company, Inc., 500 Fifth Avenue, New York, N.Y. 10110
www.wwnorton.com

W. W. Norton & Company Ltd., 15 Carlisle Street, London W1D 3BS

1 2 3 4 5 6 7 8 9 0

Contents

Illustrations

Introduction

Only two of William Shakespeare's thirty-eight plays were completely reinterpreted and reenvisioned in the mid-twentieth century on both the page and the stage, and only as a result of theatrical productions directed by the Royal Shakespeare Company's cofounder Peter Brook. The first play was *King Lear* in 1962 and the second was *A Midsummer Night's Dream* in 1970. It is not surprising that *King Lear*, whose violence and cruelty remained so shocking that Shakespeare's version of the play was kept off the London stage from 1685 until almost 150 years later, could be made more comprehensible in the post–World War II and post-Holocaust age of the 1950s and 1960s. In a sense, the tragedy of *King Lear* became less tragic as the modern period became more tragic.[1] *A Midsummer Night's Dream*, a comedy, was cherished for almost three centuries for its joyous plot and silly characters, its celebration of courtship and marriage through language, and its representation of magical fairies as synonyms for love. Thus Algernon Swinburne could remark in 1909 that the play "is outside as well as above all possible imaginative criticism. It is probably or rather surely the most beautiful work of man." But in Peter Brook's hands in 1970 the play became more, rather than less, tragic and certainly less comic while remaining beautiful in different ways. Rather than being a dream, it became a nightmare. Brook was heavily influenced by the seminal book *Shakespeare Our Contemporary* by critic Jan Kott, who had lived under the repressive Soviet regime in Poland and who had argued that *A Midsummer Night's Dream* was "a most truthful, brutal and violent play" with "brutal and bitter poetry that every stylized theatre production is bound to annihilate and destroy."[2] Thus Brook, who envisioned theatre as a site in which "the life of a play begins and ends in the moment of performance,"[3] decided that this moment could be brutal, cruel, and unstylized.

Brook has not explained whether he reshaped *A Midsummer Night's Dream* because of his far-reaching success in reshaping *King Lear*, with the two plays signifying the beginning and end, and thus

---

1. See R. A. Foakes, *Hamlet versus Lear: Cultural Politics and Shakespeare's Art* (Cambridge, UK: Cambridge UP, 2004).
2. See Kott, "Titania and the Ass's Head," pp. 139–48 below.
3. See Brook, "A Cook and a Concept: Dreaming the *Dream*," pp. 163–68 below.

the entire range, of Shakespeare's career, or simply because Brook wanted to continue to redefine theatrical performance in the moment. But the plays can clearly be seen fifty years after their revolutionary performances as exemplars of how to stage and culturally value not only early and late, and comic and tragic, Shakespeare but also *all* of Shakespeare. It is difficult to find a review of any major stage, film, or television production of *A Midsummer Night's Dream* since 1970 that does not compare it in some way to Brook's production for the RSC. As this production toured around the world in the early 1970s, its influence and impact also spread widely to international audiences, including actors, directors, and critics still working today. Brook claims in *The Quality of Mercy* that "no form nor interpretation is for ever. A form has to become fixed for a short time, then it has to go. As the world changes, there will and must be new and totally unpredictable *Dreams*."[4] Yet no *Dream* has been as new or totally unpredictable as Brook's. The result of this play's place in modern culture being defined, both as literary and performance texts, since 1970 by this single production is that it has indeed become limited and fixed, certainly the antithesis of what Shakespeare himself envisioned for his play when he wrote it and what Brook planned when he reenvisioned it.

But even after four hundred years, scholars still cannot decide when and why Shakespeare wrote *A Midsummer Night's Dream* and whether it was originally performed as Swinburne came to define it or Kott or Brook later understood it. That it was written at least partly to commemorate a royal or aristocratic marriage, and perhaps was even performed at a particular wedding banquet, seems obvious from the triple wedding of the three couples in Act 5, shortly after the reconciliation of the long-married couple Oberon and Titania and immediately before the comic mockery of the tragic union of Pyramus and Thisbe. As Stanley Wells has noted, scholars have suggested at least eleven court weddings ranging in date from the mid-1590s as the occasion for the play's first performance.[5] The two strongest wedding contenders are that on January 26, 1595, between Elizabeth Vere and the Earl of Derby, who patronized his own acting company, the Earl of Derby's Men, with which Shakespeare may have been affiliated, and that on February 19, 1596, between Elizabeth Carey, the daughter of Sir George Carey and granddaughter of Lord Hunsdon, each of whom had served as Lord Chamberlain and patron of Shakespeare's acting company, and Thomas Berkeley.

Yet, as Wells notes, we never can establish that the play was written for a particular wedding, and such a myopic focus on its origin

---

4. See below, p. 166.
5. Wells, "*A Midsummer Night's Dream* Revisited," *Critical Survey* 3 (1991): 14–16.

disrupts our critical response to it as a whole,[6] particularly as the play repeatedly emphasizes the role of imagination in apprehending it, as Theseus reminds us at the beginning of Act 5. In fact, sixteenth- and seventeenth-century London professional acting companies were adept at moving plays performed at public theaters such as the Globe to various private spaces, including at court, stately homes, provincial town halls, and other temporary venues. For example, as R. A. Foakes has argued, the large cast, including four named fairies, implies a production in a private house in which extra resources were available.[7] Thus *A Midsummer Night's Dream* may have been later performed to celebrate a wedding without being specifically written for one.

Shakespeare most likely composed the play between 1595 and 1596, judging from the style of the writing, with 1598 as its latest possible date of composition, for in that year, Francis Meres stated in *Palladis Tamia* that

> *Shakespeare* among ye English is the most excellent in both kinds for the stage; for Comedy, witnes his *Gentlemen of Verona,* his *Errors,* his *Loue labors lost,* his *Loue labours wonne,* his *Midsummers night dreame,* & his *Merchant of Venice:* for Tragedy his *Richard the 2. Richard the 3. Henry the 4. King Iohn, Titus Andronicus* and his *Romeo* and *Iuliet.*[8]

Meres's list does not appear to be chronological, and *A Midsummer Night's Dream* was most certainly written after such early tragedies as *Titus Andronicus* and *Romeo and Juliet* (which the *Pyramus and Thisbe* play may satirize), and most likely in the mid-1590s when he wrote so many other romantic comedies with mismatched couples who straighten out their alliances in time for weddings in Act 5. As Geoffrey Bullough notes, no one source provides the plot and subplots of the play, which include the marriage of Theseus and Hippolyta, the courtships of Hermia and Lysander and of Helena and Demetrius, the fairy world of Oberon and Titania, the subplot of the rude mechanicals, and the *Pyramus and Thisbe* play-within-a-play.[9] As was not unusual in his career, Shakespeare blended a number of sources into the play, including histories of Theseus's life and romantic adventures in Chaucer's "The Knight's Tale" from *The Canterbury Tales* and Sir Thomas North's 1579 translation of Plutarch's *Lives of*

6. Wells, pp. 14–16.
7. R. A. Foakes, Introduction, *A Midsummer Night's Dream* (Cambridge, UK: Cambridge UP, 2003), p. 3.
8. Meres, *Palladis tamia Wits treasury being the second part of Wits common wealth* (London: P Short for Cuthbert Burbie), p. 282.
9. Bullough, *Narrative and Dramatic Sources of Shakespeare: Volume 1: Early Comedies, Poems, Romeo and Juliet* (London: Routledge and Kegan Paul, 1964), pp. 368ff.

the Noble Grecians and Romans, and the history of Oberon from a late-sixteenth-century translation of *The History of Huon of Bordeaux*, with Robin Goodfellow, or Puck, appearing in Reginald Scot's 1584 debunking of magic in *The Discoverie of Witchcraft*. The "translation" of Bottom into an ass and the figure of Titania appear to come directly from William Adlington's 1566 translation of Apuleius's *The Golden Ass*, and "the tragical history of Pyramus and Thisbe" from Arthur Golding's 1567 translation of Ovid's *Metamorphoses* as well as a con-temporary Latin copy of the story.[1] According to Kenneth Muir, in addition to Ovid's version, Shakespeare had read several general and particular versions of the Pyramus story, including in Sir Thomas More's *Dialoge of comfort and tribulacion*, J. Thomson's *A Handful of Pleasant Delites*, *The Gorgeous Gallery of Gallant Inventions*, and Thomas Mouffet's *Of the Silkewormes, and their Flies*, as well as Chaucer's version in *The Legend of Good Women* and John Gower's in *Confessio Amantis*.[2] Philip Henslowe's "Diary" or account book men-tions late December 1593 and early January 1594 performances of the play "hewen of burdoche," almost certainly based on the Huon of Bordeaux story, by the Earl of Sussex's Men,[3] of which Shakespeare was a member before joining the newly formed Lord Chamberlain's Men in 1594. So his sources for this play may have been not only those that he read but at least one in which he and his colleagues acted.

That *A Midsummer Night's Dream* was not immediately printed after its first performances suggests that the play was popular in pub-lic if not private performance, as once it went into print in an age without copyright, it could be performed by any acting company. Thus the Chamberlain's Men, of which Shakespeare became a sharer (that is, of profits and expenses) at its inception just outside London in 1594, appeared to want to keep the text of the play away from other actors and theatrical and literary audiences. Although no records of the play's original or later performances exist, if it was not written to be performed at a royal or aristocratic wedding, it may have pre-miered at the Theatre or the Curtain in Shoreditch before moving in 1599 or later to the newly built Globe (reconstituted from the Theatre) on the Bankside, and in which Shakespeare was also a sharer. The play probably remained in repertory with occasional performances, and its first publication in 1600 in Quarto 1 may have stemmed from its recent popularity at the Globe.

We know nothing of the original cast, although some scholars have argued that the Lord Chamberlain's leading actor, Richard Burbage,

---

1. See Bullough, pp. 367ff.
2. Muir, "Pyramus and Thisbe: A Study in Shakespeare's Method," *Shakespeare Quarterly* 5 (1954): 142.
3. See *Henslowe's Diary*, ed. R. A. Foakes (Cambridge: Cambridge UP, 1960; rpt 2002), p. 20.

would have played either Lysander or Demetrius, with Thomas Pope, or possibly Shakespeare, as the playwright and director Peter Quince, while an already famous clown in the company, Will Kemp, played Bottom.[4] At some later point an actor named Tawyer joined the cast, as he is named in a Folio stage direction at 5.1.125. *A Midsummer Night's Dream* seems a perfect example of effective doubling in casting, a practice that Shakespeare's company followed for financial, if not artistic, reasons. While the Lord Chamberlain's Men had a core of experienced actors, they would hire apprentices for smaller roles, and the fewer the number of paid actors, the more profitable their productions would be—so actors were accustomed to doubling or even tripling roles. One actor would have performed the roles of Theseus and Oberon, and another would have taken on the roles of Hippolyta and Titania, as the Greek monarchs are not on stage at the same time as the fairy monarchs. While modern productions exploit the two sets of monarchs representing the conscious and subconscious sides of the same character, this symbolic doubling may not be new but part of Shakespeare's original design.

The first record of the play's performance is that at Hampton Court in front of King James I and Queen Anne on New Year's Day, 1604, if this is the "play of Robin goode-fellow" noted by Dudley Carleton in a letter,[5] and the second recorded performance was on October 17, 1630, at Hampton Court in front of King Charles I.[6] The play almost certainly had moved many years before 1630 from a public to a private playhouse. As Jay Halio argues, the stage directions for Act 2, Scene 1 in the 1623 Folio text of the play, "*Enter a Fairie at one doore, and Robin goodfellow at another,*" probably refer to the use of two doors common in public playhouses, with Puck occasionally entering at other times through a trap door.[7] However, the unusual Folio stage direction at the end of Act 3, "*They sleepe all the Act,*" i.e., in the interval between acts, most likely refers to performance at a private, indoor playhouse such as the Blackfriars, leased by 1609 by Shakespeare and his company, which had become the King's Men in 1603.

The play was entered in the Stationers' Register on October 8, 1600, and first printed that year, probably by Richard Braddock,[8] for

---

4. See Jay Halio, "The Staging of *A Midsummer Night's Dream,*" in *Shakespeare's Universe: Renaissance Ideas and Conventions, Essays in Honour of W. R. Elton,* ed. John M. Mucciolo (Aldershot, UK: Scolar Press, 1996), pp. 155–72.
5. Cited by E. K. Chambers, *The Elizabethan Stage,* Volume III (Oxford: Clarendon P, 1974), p. 279.
6. See G. E. Bentley, *The Jacobean and Caroline Stage: Dramatic Companies and Players Volume I* (Oxford: Clarendon P, 1941), p. 27.
7. See Halio, pp. 156–59.
8. See Robert K. Turner, Jr, "Printing Methods and Textual Problems in *A Midsummer Night's Dream* Q1," *Studies in Bibliography* 15 (1962): 33. Also see W. W. Greg, *The Shakespeare First Folio: Its Bibliographical and Textual History* (Oxford: Clarendon P, 1955), pp. 240ff.

A Midſommer nights dreame.

As it hath beene ſundry times publickely acted, by the *Right* honourable, the Lord Chamberlaine his
ſeruants.

Written by William Shakeſpeare.

¶ Imprinted at London, for *Thomas Fiſher*, and are to
be ſoulde at his ſhoppe, at the Signe of the White Hart,
in *Fleeteſtreete.* 1600.

Figure 1. The title page of the first quarto (1600) of *A Midsummer Night's Dream.*
Reproduced by permission of The Folger Shakespeare Library. Call number STC
22302.

Thomas Fisher. Its Quarto 1 title page states, "A Midsommer nights dreame. As it hath been sundry times publickely acted, by the Right honourable, the Lord Chamberlaine his seruants. Written by William Shakespeare." Shakespeare's name first appeared on a title page of a play in 1598, by which time the author of a play appears to have begun to attract theatrical and literary audiences as much as the acting company performing it. Thus Shakespeare's name here emphasizes that he has acquired a reputation, and not just from Francis Meres, as a dramatist. But Shakespeare seemed to have spent a great deal of time rethinking his reputation, for he appears to have reworked this play in the heat of writing it and again sometime after its original performance. For instance, John Dover Wilson was the first to argue that the lines of Theseus's first speech of Act 5 as printed were hypermetrical because the compositor had printed them as he saw them, with Shakespeare's additions referring to the poet as of "imagination all compact" still in the margin and not clearly marked for insertion in the passage.[9] The speech apparently began with Shakespeare comparing the lover and the madman, but while composing the play, before it reached the playhouse, he added the poet to this list. As a result, the lines beginning "The lunatic" and ending with "strong imagination" (5.1.7–18) are mislined and have too many syllables for pentameter, the standard meter for iambic verse. The lineation has been partially corrected in the Folio text, although Shakespeare's lines on his own artistry, "The poet's eye . . . gives to airy nothing / A local habitation and a name," remained mislined.

Therefore, at some point before or after Shakespeare finished his foul papers (or first draft) or wrote them out as "fair copy" (or a copy of his foul papers), he revised the speech, Theseus's most powerful in the play. Perhaps Shakespeare's interlinear or marginal notations on how to adjust the lineation were ignored, illegible, or simply missing, but by the time the play was prepared for later performance, he or a scribe with whom he worked tried to fix the lineation, as reflected in the Folio text. However, Wilson's larger arguments both that the Quarto was printed from a theatrical "book," or prompt-book, in Shakespeare's handwriting (and thus an authorial fair copy), used in the theatre, and that it reflected a play written in 1592, and revised twice afterward in 1594 and 1598 to suit performance at particular aristocratic weddings, have been rejected by Robert W. Turner, Jr., among other textual critics.[1] In fact Quarto 1 appears to have been printed from Shakespeare's foul papers, showing his numerous revisions

---

9. See John Dover Wilson, "The Copy for *A Midsummer Night's Dream*," pp. 122–26 below.
1. Turner, pp. 46–47.

during composition. Such revision and his company's use of his foul papers as printers' copy were not unusual.[2]

This Quarto, as with Quartos of some other Shakespearean plays, was reprinted by William Jaggard for Thomas Pavier in 1619 with a false title page giving its publication date as 1600. Pavier appears to have printed the Quartos without any authority from the original printers, who still owned the rights to them, possibly after being prevented from attempting to put them together in the first collected edition of Shakespeare's plays. The minor alterations to the text introduced in Quarto 2 do not derive from Shakespeare, even when they correct printing errors in Quarto 1. Yet this Quarto 2 seems to have been used by Isaac Jaggard and Edward Blount and their compositors in the printing of the Folio text of the play, which differs in minor but consistent ways, including in expanded stage directions and the use of Act divisions, from the Quarto 1 text. Textual scholars generally now agree that the printers' copy for the Folio text was annotated with reference to a fair copy manuscript that served as the company's prompt-book, incorporating authorial additions, alterations, and cuts made at some point after the original composition and performance.[3] Most notably, the role of Egeus is expanded in the Folio. In Quarto 1, he appears only in Act 1, Scene 1, when he rebukes his daughter Hermia for rejecting Demetrius's offer of marriage and demands that Theseus intervene, and in Act 4, Scene 1. In the Folio, he appears in Act 5, Scene 1, replacing the role in Quarto 1 of Philostrate in announcing the possible entertainments offered to celebrate the three weddings. Although it may seem simply that the Folio shows a change in the problems of doubling the roles of Philostrate and Egeus, Barbara Hodgdon has argued that the Folio variants result from "Shakespeare's deliberate revisions," which "shape a sense of familial and community harmony that extends and strengthens the possibilities suggested in the Quarto."[4] Other signs in Act 5 of the Folio text also suggest that it was a later version by Shakespeare of the play as originally written and published in the 1600 Quarto 1. For example, the lines of Theseus in the Quarto reading out the possible plays to be performed to celebrate the three weddings are split between Theseus and Lysander in the Folio. The types of revision show a clear and cohesive pattern and thus indicate that an author, rather than actors or company personnel, reshaped the play in minor but deliberate ways for artistic and theatrical reasons.

The play's comic characters became the focus in the major adaptations of the play after the Restoration in 1660, when London

2. See Grace Ioppolo, *Revising Shakespeare* (Cambridge, MA: Harvard UP, 1991), pp. 104ff.
3. See Greg, pp. 243–47.
4. Hodgdon, "Gaining a Father: The Role of Egeus in the Quarto and the Folio," *Review of English Studies* ns 37 (1986): 541.

professional theaters that had been closed by the Puritan government in 1642 reopened. Despite the apparent success of the First
and the successive Folios of Shakespeare's works in the seventeenth
century, his plays were frequently rewritten to suit a Restoration
audience that wanted to forget the execution of King Charles I, the
suffering of the English Civil War (which took place partly on London streets), and the austerity of the Interregnum government of
Oliver Cromwell. So the genres of exaggerated farce and comedy
of manners replaced Elizabethan and Jacobean tragedy. Although
Thomas Killegrew and the newly reformed King's Men performed
some version of Shakespeare's *A Midsummer Night's Dream*, Restoration audiences were more interested in Bottom's foolish interac-
tion with the fairies than in Theseus's and Oberon's monarchies.
The first two adaptations of the play were *The Merry Conceits of
Bottom the Weaver*, printed in 1661 and evidently performed publicly and privately prior to that year, according to its title page, and
the comic opera *The Fairy Queen*, with a libretto by Elkanah Settle
and music by Henry Purcell, produced by Thomas Betterton in London in 1692 and printed in the same year.[5] In 1755, the great Shakespearean actor David Garrick also produced his own operatic
version, entitled *The Fairies*, and by 1763 he offered his own
adaptation of the play. In sum, heavily edited productions of the
play appeared on the London stage from the seventeenth to eighteenth centuries, with some notable critics such as Samuel Pepys
and William Hazlitt mistaking these adaptations for Shakespeare's
original play.[6] Beginning in 1826, Felix Mendelssohn wrote music,
including an overture and incidental music that includes the now-
famous "Wedding March," inspired by the play, and both pieces of
music were later inserted in an 1842 production of the play commis-
sioned by King Frederick William IV of Prussia. The music gained
immense popularity throughout the century, somewhat displacing
Shakespeare's text.

By the early twentieth century, directors attempted to return to celebrating the Shakespearean visual and poetic, and not the non-
Shakespearean musical, beauty of the play. For example, in 1914 the
noted theater director Harley Granville-Barker "reclaimed the play for
a Shakespearean-style stage. The fast, clear action was played out on an
apron stage with only two simple sets and the dexterous use of lighting and curtains to vary location." Unlike in the childlike productions
of the Victorian age, Oberon and Puck were played by male actors, yet
Puck "wore scarlet and a wild wig decorated with berries, while the
other fairies were painted in gold, like stiffly beautiful Cambodian

5. See pp. 188–228 below.
6. For a discussion of later adaptations of the play, see Halio, pp. 160–64.

Figure 2. Arthur Rackham's 1908 illustration of Demetrius's line "Are you sure that we are awake?" (4.1.182–83) as he, Helena, Hermia, and Lysander awake from their magical slumber in the woods. Reproduced by permission of The Folger Shakespeare Library. Call number ART Box R122 no. 5 (size L).

deities."[7] A more memorable and influential production, directed by Tyrone Guthrie at the Old Vic in London in 1937, presented Vivien Leigh's "ethereal Titania," who was "attended by 22 balletic fairies."[8] It may have been this production that Peter Brook recalled in stating, probably disdainfully, that he "had seen many charming productions with pretty scenery and enthusiastic girls pretending to be fairies."[9]

Shortly after the Royal Shakespeare Company asked Brook to stage the play, he saw the first visit to Europe of the Peking Circus, which revealed to him that "in the lightness of anonymous bodies performing astonishing acrobatics without exhibitionism, it was pure spirit revealed." For Brook, this was "a pointer to go beyond illustration to evocation." Soon afterward a ballet performance choreographed by Jerome Robbins that stripped away "the trappings of tutus, painted trees and moonlight" confirmed to Brook that there was "an unexpected form waiting to be discovered" for the play. Brook's production, inspired by Jan Kott's dark reinterpretation of the play, drew from the Peking Circus and the Robbins ballet, so that actors were poised on trapezes or swings and spinning dishes on long rods, with adult fairies celebrating Titania as her bower, a bed of feathers, descended from above. The set was a three-sided white box with no scenery but with a gallery across the top. After some failures in rehearsal, Brook notes, "We found a way of starting the play with a bang." Ignoring the opening stage directions, Brook had the composer offer "an explosion of percussion" as "the whole cast literally burst onto the stage, climbed up ladders and swarmed across the top level of the set with such joy and energy that they swept the audience along with them."[1] Brook insisted that the actors of the roles of Theseus and Hippolyta double the roles of Oberon and Titania to suggest that "the conflicts and erotic adventures of the nocturnal wood were the uncontrollable eruption of subconscious fears and desires."[2] But he also had all the actors watch the production from the gallery above when not performing, thus allowing the audience to watch this stage audience watch the play, adding another layer to the play-within-a-play of *Pyramus and Thisbe*.

Brook's RSC production was certainly not without controversy, especially as he had seized upon Kott's claim that *"The Dream* is the

7. See "The stage history of *A Midsummer Night's Dream* from the time Shakespeare wrote it to the present day," www.rsc.org.uk/a-midsummer-nights-dream/past-productions/stage-history.
8. See www.rsc.org.uk/a-midsummer-nights-dream/past-productions/stage-history.
9. See Brook, "A Cook and a Concept: Dreaming the *Dream*," p. 164 below.
1. See Brook, pp. 164–65 below.
2. See *Peter Brook's Production of William Shakespeare's 'A Midsummer Night's Dream' for the Royal Shakespeare Company: The Complete and Authorised Acting Edition* (Stratford-upon-Avon, 1974) and "Peter Brook 1970 Production": www.rsc.org.uk/a-midsummer-nights-dream/past-productions/peter-brook-1970-production.

Figure 3. Oberon (Alan Howard) enchants Titania (Sara Kestelman) while Puck (John Kane) looks on in Peter Brook's 1970 RSC production. Tom Holte Theatre Photographic Collection © Shakespeare Birthplace Trust.

Figure 4. Hermia (Mary Rutherford), Lysander (Christopher Gable), Helena (Frances De La Tour), and Demetrius (Ben Kingsley) sleep on trapezes, with Bottom (David Waller) sleeping on the ground, after Titania awakes from her dream, while Theseus watches two fairies spin plates in Peter Brook's 1970 RSC production. Joe Cocks Studio Collection © Shakespeare Birthplace Trust.

most erotic of Shakespeare's plays. In no other tragedy, or comedy, of his, except *Troilus and Cressida*, is the eroticism expressed so brutally."[3] For example, when Titania invited the fairies at the end of Act 3, Scene 1, to bring Bottom to her Bower, he was triumphantly carried on the shoulders of two adult male fairies, one of whom stuck his arm and clenched fist between Bottom's legs, so that he had an erect phallus.[4] The critic Benedict Nightingale found the entire production "perverse" and complained that "only a humourless man could have staged this. There are also times when one feels that only a cynical one could be in control." He added that Brook's "manic decoration has deprived it of suffering, fear, horror, and apart from one moment, when Bottom's phallus is crudely mimed by the fairies, even of lust."[5] John Russell Brown similarly argued that the "clean, stark gymnasium or circus for the setting of this production" allowed the actor and designer to ignore "many of the words of the text, especially the ambiguous, gentle and homely words in which the play abounds."[6] Yet, the production became so acclaimed that it went on a world tour from August 1972 to August 1973, travelling from central Europe to eastern Europe, Scandanavia, the United States, Japan, and Australia.[7] Although the only film of the production was destroyed at Brook's request, the Royal Shakespeare Company discusses the play's staging on its website.[8]

Later major productions of the play have been so burdened by Brook's innovations that directors have employed various other spectacular stage effects to impress audiences, with varying success. Ron Daniels's 1981 Royal Shakespeare Company production used small wooden hand puppets, operated by actors, to portray the fairies, although the physical beauty of the production was sometimes marred by the clacking noise of the puppets. Robert Lepage's 1992 production at England's National Theatre provided raincoats for audiences in the front rows to protect them from splashing mud and water, prompting critics to rename the play "A Mudsummer Night's Dream." Flashing lights, loud music, and other spectacular visual and auditory effects, as well as gender twists, have also been used to give productions their own identity. Productions in 2016 by the BBC and Shakespeare's Globe chose to comment on the play's sexuality by portraying same-sex couples: for the BBC, Theseus is conveniently killed off in

---

3. See Kott, p. 140 below.
4. At the performance of this production in Los Angeles in 1973 that I saw, the audience gasped and then laughed nervously at Bottom's exit in this scene.
5. Nightingale, "Review of *A Midsummer Night's Dream*," *New Statesman* (September 4, 1970): 281.
6. Brown, *Free Shakespeare* (London: Heinemann Educational, 1974), pp. 27–28.
7. See http://theatricalia.com/play/1e/a-midsummer-nights-dream/production/1ae.
8. See www.rsc.org.uk/a-midsummer-nights-dream/past-productions/peter-brook-1970 -production.

Act 5 so that Hippolyta and Titania can finally pair off, while for the Globe, Helena is played by a male actor, who happily settles with his beloved—a male Demetrius—who apparently dismisses his regard for the female Hermia under Oberon's magic spell, mistakenly applied by Puck.

As shown in the Criticism selections in this volume, the literary as well as the theatrical receptions of *A Midsummer Night's Dream* since its composition have focused primarily on the play's language and characters. Shakespeare's mastery of dramatic verse by 1595 or 1596, probably less than five years after he began a career as a playwright, gives the play not only its beauty but also its musicality. The long speeches especially of Titania and Oberon in Act 2 and of Theseus in Acts 4 and 5 resonate with elegant metaphors extolling the power of nature and art and the intersection of the mortal, physical world with the immortal, spiritual world. But Shakespeare also offers poetic debate on current philosophical ideas, for example in Helena's first soliloquy on Neoplatonic concepts of love as the pursuit of intellectual beauty:

> Things base and vile, holding no quantity,
> Love can transpose to form and dignity.
> Love looks not with the eyes, but with the mind,
> And therefore is winged Cupid painted blind. (1.1.232–35)

Here she offers a concise summary of the tradition of love handed down from Plato in *The Symposium* that true and transformative love springs only from the attraction of a lover to the beloved through the meeting of minds, not through sexual lust deriving from eyesight. By Shakespeare's time, this theory had been Christianized by the Italian Neoplatonists and exemplified by the speaker Pietro Bembo in Baldassare Castiglione's *The Book of the Courtier* and by Renaissance painters who depicted the true Cupid as blindfolded when he shot his arrow of love.[9] That Shakespeare gives this speech to a female character may be an ironic nod to the female speaker Diotima, who teaches Plato this theory in *The Symposium*, or to Neoplatonists such as Castiglione, Marsilio Ficino and Pico della Mirandola, who insisted that women, and not men, served as the beloved to a male lover.

But as Maurice Hunt notes, in addition to the elegant and intellectual verse of Helena and others, the play is also quite noisy, for "playgoers hear a chorus of frightened shrieks, brays, fairy songs, and lovers' lyrics and insults—to say nothing of winding horns, a huntsman's call and the worst kind of doggerel poetry."[1] Musical discord is

---

9. See Isabel Rivers, *Classical and Christian Ideas in English Renaissance Poetry* (London: Routledge, 1979), pp. 33ff.
1. Hunt, "The Voices of *A Midsummer Night's Dream*," *Texas Studies in Literature and Language* 34 (1992): 218.

indeed a feature of the play, as noted first by Hippolyta: "I never heard / So musical a discord, such sweet thunder" (4.1.114–15), and then by Theseus: "How shall we find the concord of this discord?" (5.1.60). Certainly Bottom's continually mangled language, for example in proclaiming, "The eye of man hath not heard, the ear of man hath not seen" (4.1.206), and his often unintentionally bawdy puns serve as a counterpoint to the more aristocratic characters who can easily command poetry. Yet all the mortals, even Theseus and Hippolyta, are occasionally or continually lost in the woods, so Bottom's confusion in words merely expresses the general befuddlement in an unknown space that leaves the four lovers so exhausted with fighting among themselves that "they sleep all the act."

Shakespeare's use of the pastoral fairy world beginning in Act 2 as an escape from the seeming harshness and control of the court offers him the opportunity to incorporate local English folklore into the classical philosophy and mythology of Act 1. For example, Shakespeare names the character of Puck after a "pouk," a type of mischievous spirit, as well as Robin Goodfellow, his full name.[2] Puck's long discussion at the beginning of Act 2 of his and other fairies' powers and antics would have been familiar to Elizabethan audiences, despite Reginald Scot's attempt in 1584 in his mammoth work *The Discoverie of Witchcraft* to prove that there were rational explanations for every possible occurrence of supposed magic, sorcery, and witchcraft. In essence, Scot argued that unexplainable events could be attributed to fraud and trickery, even going so far as to demonstrate how séances could be faked. Yet King James had written *Demonology* in 1597 when he was King of Scotland, and after his ascension to the English throne in 1603, the book was reprinted and found a much larger audience. James's complete belief in the existence of devils and witches was shared by many of his Scottish and English subjects. However, while the play *Macbeth*, eventually written to celebrate James's history, focuses on black magic, based on the worship of devils, *A Midsummer Night's Dream* and later *The Tempest* explore the use of white magic, based on the worship of the goddess Nature. When Puck discusses ghosts and other "[d]amnèd spirits all" that "consort with black-browed night," Oberon quickly responds, "But we are spirits of another sort" (3.2.382–88). Oberon's distinction is vitally important to the play's representations of the natural and spiritual worlds.

But this worship of the goddess Nature has not displaced the play's equivocal treatment of female characters. If Kott and Brook reshaped the theatrical representation and reception of the play as erotic and

2. See William Bell, *Shakespeare's Puck and his Folklore* (London: Richards, 1852), and Winfried Schleiner, "Imaginative Sources for Shakespeare's Puck," *Shakespeare Quarterly* 36 (1985): 65–68.

brutal, the rise of gender theory since the 1970s has continued to reex-
amine the theoretical interpretation of the play as misogynistic and
abusive. Gender critics have particularly focused on the layers of patriarchy in the play, first, in the mortal world ruled by Theseus, who tells
Hippolyta, "I wooed thee with my sword, / And won thy love doing
thee injuries" (1.1.16–17) and attempts to force Hermia to follow her
father's demand that she marry Demetrius, and second, in the supernatural world ruled by Oberon, who forces his wife Titania to fall in
love with the "vile" Bottom, "translated" into an ass, and has Puck
manipulate the love affairs of the two runaway couples in the woods.
Lynda E. Boose discusses the ways in which Shakespeare enforces
father-daughter bonds in his plays, often with the mother absent and
unmentioned, and particularly in A Midsummer Night's Dream, "a play
centered on marriage," in which "the intransigent father Egeus, supported by the king–father figure Theseus, poses a threat that must be
converted to a blessing to ensure a comic conclusion."[3] Similarly,
Marina Warner situates the relationship between Titania and Bottom
into "The Beauty and the Beast" myth, "a classic fairy tale of transformation, which, when told by a woman, places the male lover, the
Beast, in the position of the mysterious, threatening, possibly fatal
unknown, and Beauty, the heroine, as the questor who discovers his
true nature." This fairy tale "assumed a female audience on the whole
who fully expected to be given away by their fathers to men who might
well strike them as monstrous."[4] This may be why Hermia feels no
need to subject herself to the patriarchy of her father and her mon-
arch, as she immediately rejects their commands to marry Demetrius
or face "death, or to a vow of single life" (1.1.121) and agrees to run
away with Lysander without any fear of the consequences.

    Other women also disobey the commands of their male partners.
Helena refuses to accept Demetrius's rejection of her and instead follows him, offering to be his abused "spaniel," promising, "The more
you beat me, I will fawn on you" (2.1.204). Similarly, Titania chooses
to forswear, or forgo, the "bed and company" of the "jealous" Oberon
(2.1.61–62). However, at least Helena and Titania suffer humiliation
for their transgressive behavior, with Helena married to a man who
only loves her because he has been left under Oberon and Puck's
spell, and Titania becoming the beloved of an ass, or more harshly,
manipulated into a bestial rape by her voyeuristic husband.[5] Christy

---

3. See Boose, "The Father and Bride in Shakespeare," pp. 148–57 below.
4. See Marina Warner, "Reluctant Brides: Beauty and the Beast I," in From the Beast to the
   Blonde: On Fairy Tales and Their Tellers (London: Chatto & Windus, 1994), pp. 273–75,
   279–80.
5. See, for example, Laura Levine, "Rape, Repetition, and the Politics of Closure in A
   Midsummer Night's Dream," in Feminist Readings of Early Modern Culture: Emerging
   Subjects, ed. Valerie Traub, M. Lindsay Kaplan, and Dympna Callaghan (Cambridge,
   UK: Cambridge UP, 1996), pp. 210–28.

Figure 5. Louis Rhead's early-twentieth-century illustration of Helena's pursuit of Demetrius in 2.1. Reproduced by permission of The Folger Shakespeare Library. Call number ART Box R469 no. 79 (size S).

Desmet argues that such transgression can be seen primarily in language, for the play's women "usurp masculine rhetoric by speaking in the public sphere, disfiguring the patriarchal fictions that order erotic and social relationships in Shakespearean Athens." In addition, "they reconfigure that social rhetoric by offering alternative tropes for new ideals of love."[6] Yet, the heterosexual nature of this love has also been reconsidered by gender critics. Valerie Traub particularly argues that Shakespeare offers significant examination of homoeroticism, with the strongest bonds in the plays those between female characters and between male characters. But eventually women are punished for lesbian desire and men for homosexual desire when they attempt to fight the heterosexual norm by objecting to marriage. Both women and men must ultimately surrender to heterosexuality as society expects.[7] This type of theory can explain why

6. See Desmet, "Disfiguring Women with Masculine Tropes: A Rhetorical Reading of *A Midsummer Night's Dream*," in *A Midsummer Night's Dream: Critical Essays*, ed. Dorothea Kehler (Garland, 1998), p. 309.
7. See, for example, Valerie Traub, "The Homoerotics of Shakespearean Comedy," in *Shakespeare, Feminism and Gender*, ed. Kate Chedgzoy (Basingstoke, UK: Palgrave, 2001), pp. 135–60.

both Theseus and Demetrius seem so uncomfortable about marriage that they at first verbally abuse the women whom they had been expected to marry and why Lysander comes to believe that one woman, Hermia, is interchangeable with another, Helena.

Such pressure on gender also appears in the pressure on race mixed with gender, especially in Titania's preoccupation with her changeling, "a lovely boy, stol'n from an Indian king" (2.1.22). As she explains to Oberon, "His mother was a votress of my order / And, in the spicèd Indian air, by night / Full often hath she gossiped by my side. . . . / But she, being mortal, of that boy did die (2.1.123–24, 135). As Margo Hendricks states, the "simultaneity" of Athens and India "permits the articulation of a racial fantasy in *A Midsummer Night's Dream* where Amazons and fairies signify an alien yet domestic paradox in an otherwise stable, homogeneous world." The result is that "what we witness in India and fairyland is the fragmentation of patriarchal ideologies denoting race because women's erotic desires can displace and dispel the sexual continuum upon which race is constituted."[8] Such postcolonial discussion of the play can yield exciting new interpretations.

Whether in terms of race, gender, desire, magic, language, structure, plot, or characters, *A Midsummer Night's Dream* now serves as an exemplum of the ways in which a play can be endlessly reworked and reinterpreted on both the stage and the page. Shakespeare offers mocking examples of the poor, unimaginative acting by the "rude mechanicals" to comment on not just the imaginative responsibilities of his audience but also of his actors. Yet he also employs the standard theatrical device of a play-within-a-play, which he rarely uses in his career, of *Pyramus and Thisbe* to reconsider what happens when a heckling audience of three aristocratic couples watch a play while we watch them. This may be why Shakespeare needs to demand in Theseus's speech at the beginning of Act 5 that an audience use their imagination to endow the poet with the power to give form and substance to the intangible products of theatre. Although Theseus tells the mechanicals, "No epilogue, I pray you, for your play needs no excuse" (5.1.342–43), Shakespeare soon puts Puck into *A Midsummer Night's Dream*'s Epilogue, a standard theatrical device which he only occasionally uses that tries to convince us that the audience has the power to give meaning to the play. Yet even in this suggestion, Shakespeare manipulates us into assuming that he depends on us when in fact we will always have to depend on him. When Puck convinces us not to use the serpent's tongue (that is, to hiss) but to give him our hands (that is, to applaud) at

8. See Hendricks, "'Obscured by dreams': Race, Empire, and Shakespeare's *A Midsummer Night's Dream*, pp. 158–63 below.

the conclusion of *A Midsummer Night's Dream*, Shakespeare makes us complicit in the creation, production, and interpretation of his play. Whether we see it as a dream or a nightmare may remain up to us.

GRACE IOPPOLO

The Text of
A MIDSUMMER NIGHT'S
DREAM

Dramatis Personae

THESEUS, Duke of Athens
HIPPOLYTA, Queen of the Amazons
EGEUS, father of HERMIA
HERMIA, daughter of EGEUS, in love with LYSANDER
LYSANDER, in love with HERMIA
DEMETRIUS, suitor to HERMIA
HELENA, in love with DEMETRIUS
PHILOSTRATE, Master of the Revels to THESEUS
PETER QUINCE, a carpenter, who plays Prologue in *Pyramus and Thisbe*
NICK BOTTOM, a weaver, who plays Pyramus
FRANCIS FLUTE, a bellows-mender, who plays Thisbe
TOM SNOUT, a tinker, who plays Wall
ROBIN STARVELING, a tailor, who plays Moonshine
SNUG, a joiner, who plays Lion
OBERON, King of the Fairies
TITANIA, Queen of the Fairies
PUCK or ROBIN GOODFELLOW
PEASEBLOSSOM ⎤
COBWEB   ⎥
MOTH   ⎬ Fairies serving TITANIA
MUSTARDSEED ⎦
Other FAIRIES in service to TITANIA

LORDS and ATTENDANTS at the court of THESEUS

A Midsummer Night's Dream

Act 1, Scene 1

Enter THESEUS, HIPPOLYTA, PHILOSTRATE, *with others*

THESEUS   Now, fair Hippolyta, our nuptial hour
Draws on apace; our happy days bring in
Another moon—but O, methinks, how slow
This old moon wanes! She lingers my desires
Like to a step-dame or a dowager   5
Long withering out a young man's revenue.

HIPPOLYTA   Four days will quickly steep themselves in night;
Four nights will quickly dream away the time,
And then the moon, like to a silver bow
New-bent in heaven, shall behold the night   10
Of our solemnities.

THESEUS   Go, Philostrate,
Stir up the Athenian youth to merriments,
Awake the pert and nimble spirit of mirth,
Turn melancholy forth to funerals.
The pale companion is not for our pomp.   15

Exit PHILOSTRATE

Hippolyta, I wooed thee with my sword,
And won thy love doing thee injuries.
But I will wed thee in another key:
With pomp, with triumph and with revelling.

Enter EGEUS *and his daughter,* HERMIA, LYSANDER,
and DEMETRIUS

EGEUS   Happy be Theseus, our renownèd duke!   20

THESEUS   Thanks, good Egeus: what's the news with thee?

EGEUS   Full of vexation come I, with complaint
Against my child, my daughter Hermia.
Stand forth, Demetrius!—My noble lord,

1.1. Location: Theseus's palace in Athens
5. step-dame or a dowager: stepmother or widow, who continued to claim a husband's
    revenue
6. revenue: income, with pun on sexual prowess

This man hath my consent to marry her.   25
Stand forth, Lysander!—And, my gracious duke,
This man hath bewitched the bosom of my child.
Thou, thou, Lysander, thou hast given her rhymes,
And interchanged love-tokens with my child.
Thou hast by moonlight at her window sung   30
With feigning voice verses of feigning love,
And stolen the impression of her fantasy
With bracelets of thy hair, rings, gauds, conceits,
Knacks, trifles, nosegays, sweetmeats—messengers
Of strong prevailment in unhardened youth.   35
With cunning hast thou filched my daughter's heart,
Turned her obedience, which is due to me,
To stubborn harshness. And, my gracious Duke,
Be it so she will not here, before your grace,
Consent to marry with Demetrius.   40
I beg the ancient privilege of Athens:
As she is mine, I may dispose of her,
Which shall be either to this gentleman
Or to her death, according to our law
Immediately provided in that case.   45
THESEUS   What say you, Hermia? Be advised, fair maid:
To you your father should be as a god,
One that composed your beauties, yea, and one
To whom you are but as a form in wax,
By him imprinted, and within his power   50
To leave the figure or disfigure it.
Demetrius is a worthy gentleman.
HERMIA   So is Lysander.
THESEUS   In himself he is,
But in this kind, wanting your father's voice,
The other must be held the worthier.   55
HERMIA   I would my father looked but with my eyes.
THESEUS   Rather your eyes must with his judgment look.
HERMIA   I do entreat your grace to pardon me.
I know not by what power I am made bold,
Nor how it may concern my modesty   60
In such a presence here to plead my thoughts,
But I beseech your grace that I may know

---

28. **rhymes:** i.e., poetry
33. **gauds:** beads, i.e., jewelry
34. **Knacks:** knick-knacks, i.e., trinkets; **sweetmeats:** cakes or sweets
49. **form in wax:** i.e., something her father can shape
54. **wanting your father's voice:** i.e., lacking your father's consent

The worst that may befall me in this case,
If I refuse to wed Demetrius.
THESEUS   Either to die the death or to abjure   65
For ever the society of men.
Therefore, fair Hermia, question your desires,
Know of your youth, examine well your blood,
Whether, if you yield not to your father's choice,
You can endure the livery of a nun,   70
For aye to be in shady cloister mewed,
To live a barren sister all your life,
Chanting faint hymns to the cold fruitless moon.
Thrice-blessèd they that master so their blood
To undergo such maiden pilgrimage,   75
But earthlier happy is the rose distilled
Than that which, withering on the virgin thorn,
Grows, lives and dies in single blessedness.
HERMIA   So will I grow, so live, so die, my lord,
Ere I will yield my virgin patent up   80
Unto his lordship, whose unwishèd yoke
My soul consents not to give sovereignty.
THESEUS   Take time to pause, and, by the next new moon—
The sealing-day betwixt my love and me
For everlasting bond of fellowship—   85
Upon that day either prepare to die
For disobedience to your father's will,
Or else to wed Demetrius, as he would,
Or on Diana's altar to protest
For aye austerity and single life.   90
DEMETRIUS   Relent, sweet Hermia, and, Lysander, yield
Thy crazèd title to my certain right.
LYSANDER   You have her father's love, Demetrius;
Let me have Hermia's. Do you marry him.
EGEUS   Scornful Lysander! True, he hath my love,   95
And what is mine my love shall render him,
And she is mine, and all my right of her
I do estate unto Demetrius.
LYSANDER   I am, my lord, as well derived as he,
As well possessed; my love is more than his,   100

65. **abjure:** renounce
71. **in shady cloister mewed:** i.e., shut up in a convent
72. **sister:** nun
80. **virgin patent:** virginity
81. **yoke:** harness
84. **sealing-day:** wedding day
90. **aye:** perpetual
92. **crazèd:** flawed

My fortunes every way as fairly ranked,
If not with vantage, as Demetrius's,
And, which is more than all these boasts can be,
I am beloved of beauteous Hermia.
Why should not I then prosecute my right?   105
Demetrius, I'll avouch it to his head,
Made love to Nedar's daughter, Helena,
And won her soul, and she, sweet lady, dotes,
Devoutly dotes, dotes in idolatry,
Upon this spotted and inconstant man.   110
THESEUS   I must confess that I have heard so much,
And with Demetrius thought to have spoke thereof,
But, being over-full of self-affairs,
My mind did lose it. But, Demetrius, come,
And come, Egeus. You shall go with me;   115
I have some private schooling for you both.
For you, fair Hermia, look you arm yourself
To fit your fancies to your father's will,
Or else the law of Athens yields you up—
Which by no means we may extenuate—   120
To death, or to a vow of single life.
Come, my Hippolyta; what cheer, my love?
Demetrius and Egeus, go along;
I must employ you in some business
Against our nuptial and confer with you   125
Of something nearly that concerns yourselves.
EGEUS   With duty and desire we follow you.
                          Exeunt all but LYSANDER *and* HERMIA
LYSANDER   How now, my love! Why is your cheek so pale?
How chance the roses there do fade so fast?
HERMIA   Belike for want of rain, which I could well   130
Beteem them from the tempest of my eyes.
LYSANDER   Ay me! For aught that I could ever read,
Could ever hear by tale or history,
The course of true love never did run smooth,
But, either it was different in blood—   135
HERMIA   O cross! Too high to be enthralled to low.
LYSANDER   Or else misgraffèd in respect of years—

---

102. **vantage:** advantage
107. **Made love to:** i.e., courted
110. **spotted:** i.e., unfaithful
125. **Against:** pertaining to
130. **rain:** i.e., tears
131. **Beteem:** cover
137. **misgraffèd:** mismatched

HERMIA O spite! Too old to be engaged to young.
LYSANDER   Or else it stood upon the choice of friends—
HERMIA O hell! To choose love by another's eyes!   140
LYSANDER   Or, if there were a sympathy in choice,
　　War, death, or sickness did lay siege to it,
　　Making it momentary as a sound,
　　Swift as a shadow, short as any dream,
　　Brief as the lightning in the collied night,   145
　　That, in a spleen, unfolds both heaven and earth,
　　And ere a man hath power to say "Behold!",
　　The jaws of darkness do devour it up.
　　So quick bright things come to confusion.
HERMIA   If then true lovers have been ever crossed,   150
　　It stands as an edict in destiny.
　　Then let us teach our trial patience,
　　Because it is a customary cross,
　　As due to love as thoughts and dreams and sighs,
　　Wishes and tears: poor fancy's followers.   155
LYSANDER   A good persuasion. Therefore, hear me, Hermia:
　　I have a widow aunt, a dowager
　　Of great revenue, and she hath no child.
　　From Athens is her house remote seven leagues,
　　And she respects me as her only son.   160
　　There, gentle Hermia, may I marry thee,
　　And to that place the sharp Athenian law
　　Cannot pursue us. If thou lovest me, then
　　Steal forth thy father's house to-morrow night,
　　And in the wood, a league without the town,   165
　　Where I did meet thee once with Helena
　　To do observance to a morn of May,
　　There will I stay for thee.
HERMIA　　　　　　　　　　My good Lysander!
　　I swear to thee, by Cupid's strongest bow,
　　By his best arrow with the golden head,   170
　　By the simplicity of Venus's doves,
　　By that which knitteth souls and prospers loves,

---

145. collied: i.e., darkened with coal dust
146. spleen: i.e., angry
150. crossed: thwarted
155. fancy's: delusion's, i.e., love's
159. leagues: measurements of three miles each
167. morn of May: i.e., May 1, May Day, the spring festival
168. stay: wait
171. Venus's doves: In Roman mythology, Venus, goddess of love, was often depicted with doves.
172. knitteth: unites

And by that fire which burned the Carthage queen
When the false Troyan under sail was seen,
By all the vows that ever men have broke,   175
In number more than ever women spoke,
In that same place thou hast appointed me,
Tomorrow truly will I meet with thee.
LYSANDER   Keep promise, love. Look, here comes Helena.
        Enter HELENA
HERMIA   God speed, fair Helena! Whither away?   180
HELENA   Call you me fair? That "fair" again unsay.
  Demetrius loves your fair: O happy fair!
  Your eyes are lodestars, and your tongue's sweet air
  More tuneable than lark to shepherd's ear
  When wheat is green, when hawthorn buds appear.   185
  Sickness is catching. O, were favor so,
  Yours would I catch, fair Hermia, ere I go;
  My ear should catch your voice, my eye your eye;
  My tongue should catch your tongue's sweet melody.
  Were the world mine, Demetrius being bated,   190
  The rest I'll give to be to you translated.
  O, teach me how you look, and with what art
  You sway the motion of Demetrius's heart.
HERMIA   I frown upon him, yet he loves me still.
HELENA   O that your frowns would teach my smiles such skill! 195
HERMIA   I give him curses, yet he gives me love.
HELENA   O that my prayers could such affection move!
HERMIA   The more I hate, the more he follows me.
HELENA   The more I love, the more he hateth me.
HERMIA   His folly, Helena, is no fault of mine.   200
HELENA   None, but your beauty: would that fault were mine!
HERMIA   Take comfort; he no more shall see my face.
  Lysander and myself will fly this place.
  Before the time I did Lysander see,
  Seemed Athens as a paradise to me.   205
  O, then, what graces in my love do dwell
  That he hath turned a heaven unto a hell!
LYSANDER   Helen, to you our minds we will unfold:

173. **Carthage queen:** Dido, first Queen of Carthage
174. **false Troyan:** In Vergil's *Aeneid,* Dido committed suicide after the Trojan prince
    Aeneas abandoned her.
180. **fair:** beautiful
183. **lodestars:** guiding stars
185. **green:** unripe
190. **bated:** subdued
191. **translated:** transformed
193. **motion:** power

Tomorrow night, when Phoebe doth behold
Her silver visage in the wat'ry glass,   210
Decking with liquid pearl the bladed grass,
A time that lovers' flights doth still conceal,
Through Athens' gates have we devised to steal.
HERMIA   And in the wood, where often you and I
Upon faint primrose-beds were wont to lie,   215
Emptying our bosoms of their counsel sweet,
There my Lysander and myself shall meet
And thence from Athens turn away our eye
To seek new friends and strange companions.
Farewell, sweet playfellow: pray thou for us,   220
And good luck grant thee thy Demetrius!
Keep word, Lysander, we must starve our sight
From lovers' food till morrow deep midnight.
LYSANDER   I will, my Hermia.

>   *Exit* HERMIA
>   Helena, adieu!
As you on him, Demetrius dote on you!   *Exit* LYSANDER   225
HELENA   How happy some o'er other some can be!
Through Athens I am thought as fair as she.
But what of that? Demetrius thinks not so;
He will not know what all but he do know,
And as he errs, doting on Hermia's eyes,   230
So I, admiring of his qualities.
Things base and vile, holding no quantity,
Love can transpose to form and dignity.
Love looks not with the eyes, but with the mind,
And therefore is winged Cupid painted blind.   235
Nor hath Love's mind of any judgment taste;
Wings and no eyes figure unheedy haste,
And therefore is Love said to be a child,
Because in choice he is so oft beguiled.
As waggish boys in game themselves forswear,   240
So the boy Love is perjured everywhere;
For, ere Demetrius looked on Hermia's eyne,

---

209. Phoebe: in Greek mythology, a member of the Titan deities, associated with the
  moon
210. wat'ry glass: watery reflection
216. sweet: pleasant
232. quantity: value
235–37. winged Cupid . . . unheedy haste: In Renaissance Neoplatonism, Cupid, son of
  Venus, had two natures in shooting his arrow of love: blind, and unbiased, producing
  intellectual love, and sighted, and biased, producing physical love.
237. unheedy: careless
240. waggish: mischievous; **forswear:** renounce
242. eyne: eyes

He hailed down oaths that he was only mine,
And when this hail some heat from Hermia felt,
So he dissolved, and showers of oaths did melt.   245
I will go tell him of fair Hermia's flight,
Then to the wood will he, tomorrow night,
Pursue her, and for this intelligence
If I have thanks, it is a dear expense.
But herein mean I to enrich my pain,   250
To have his sight thither, and back again.   *Exit*

Act 1, Scene 2

Enter QUINCE, *the Carpenter, and* SNUG, *the Joiner, and*
BOTTOM, *the Weaver, and* FLUTE, *the Bellows-mender, and*
SNOUT, *the Tinker, and* STARVELING, *the Tailor*

QUINCE   Is all our company here?

BOTTOM   You were best to call them generally, man by man,
according to the scrip.

QUINCE   Here is the scroll of every man's name which is
thought fit through all Athens to play in our interlude before   5
the Duke and the Duchess, on his wedding-day at night.

BOTTOM   First, good Peter Quince, say what the play treats on;
then read the names of the actors, and so grow to a point.

QUINCE   Marry, our play is, "The most lamentable comedy and
most cruel death of Pyramus and Thisbe."   10

BOTTOM   A very good piece of work, I assure you, and a merry.
Now, good Peter Quince, call forth your actors by the scroll.
Masters, spread yourselves.

QUINCE   Answer as I call you. Nick Bottom, the weaver?

BOTTOM   Ready. Name what part I am for, and proceed.   15

QUINCE   You, Nick Bottom, are set down for Pyramus.

BOTTOM   What is Pyramus? A lover, or a tyrant?

QUINCE   A lover, that kills himself most gallant for love.

BOTTOM   That will ask some tears in the true performing of it.
If I do it, let the audience look to their eyes: I will move storms,   20

---

249. **dear expense:** expensive sacrifice
1.2. **Location:** the forest outside Athens
SD. **Joiner:** a craftsman who joins pieces of wood, for example, to make furniture; **Bottom, the Weaver:** puns on "bottom" as buttocks and as a spool on which thread would be wound; **Bellows-mender:** bellows were used to start or fan fires; **Tinker:** a craftsman who repairs metal household items
2. **generally:** Bottom's error for "individually"
3. **scrip:** script
5. **interlude:** short comic entertainment usually shown between the acts of a play
7. **Quince:** with pun on quince as a sour fruit and as slang for "carve" or "cut up"
8. **point:** conclusion
13. **spread yourselves:** i.e., spread out

I will condole, in some measure. To the rest—yet my chief
humor is for a tyrant. I could play Ercles rarely, or a part to
tear a cat in, to make all split.

The raging rocks

And shivering shocks   25

Shall break the locks

   Of prison gates;

And Phibbus' car

Shall shine from far

And make and mar   30

   The foolish Fates.

This was lofty! Now name the rest of the players. This is
Ercles's vein, a tyrant's vein; a lover is more condoling.

QUINCE   Francis Flute, the bellows-mender?

FLUTE   Here, Peter Quince.   35

QUINCE   Flute, you must take Thisbe on you.

FLUTE   What is Thisbe? A wandering knight?

QUINCE   It is the lady that Pyramus must love.

FLUTE   Nay, faith, let me not play a woman! I have a beard
coming.   40

QUINCE   That's all one: you shall play it in a mask, and you may
speak as small as you will.

BOTTOM   An I may hide my face, let me play Thisbe too. I'll
speak in a monstrous little voice: "Thisne, Thisne!" "Ah,
Pyramus, lover dear! Thy Thisbe dear, and lady dear!"   45

QUINCE   No, no; you must play Pyramus, and, Flute, you
Thisbe.

BOTTOM   Well, proceed.

QUINCE   Robin Starveling, the tailor?

STARVELING   Here, Peter Quince.   50

QUINCE   Robin Starveling, you must play Thisbe's mother. Tom
Snout, the tinker?

SNOUT   Here, Peter Quince.

QUINCE   You, Pyramus's father; myself, Thisbe's father. Snug, the
joiner: you, the lion's part, and, I hope, here is a play fitted.   55

SNUG   Have you the lion's part written? Pray you, if it be, give
it me, for I am slow of study.

---

21. **condole:** lament
22. **Ercles:** In Roman mythology, Hercules (known as Heracles in Greek), son of the god
   Jupiter (Zeus in Greek), was renowned for his strength.
28. **Phibbus' car:** chariot of the Roman god of the sun Phoebus (known as Apollo in
   Greek).
31. **Fates:** three goddesses in classical mythology who controlled human destiny
39–40. **beard coming:** i.e., he's about to grow facial hair after a much-delayed puberty
48. **Starveling:** i.e., his name suggests that he is very thin
55. **fitted:** i.e., with a full cast

QUINCE You may do it extempore, for it is nothing but roaring.

BOTTOM   Let me play the lion too. I will roar that I will do any
man's heart good to hear me. I will roar that I will make the   60
Duke say, "Let him roar again! Let him roar again!"

QUINCE And you should do it too terribly, you would fright
the Duchess and the ladies that they would shriek, and that
were enough to hang us all.

ALL   That would hang us, every mother's son.   65

BOTTOM   I grant you, friends, if that you should fright the ladies
out of their wits, they would have no more discretion but to
hang us, but I will aggravate my voice so that I will roar you
as gently as any sucking dove. I will roar you and 'twere any
nightingale.   70

QUINCE You can play no part but Pyramus, for Pyramus is a
sweet-faced man, a proper man as one shall see in a summer's
day, a most lovely gentleman-like man. Therefore you must
needs play Pyramus.

BOTTOM   Well, I will undertake it. What beard were I best to   75
play it in?

QUINCE Why, what you will.

BOTTOM   I will discharge it in either your straw-color beard,
your orange-tawny beard, your purple-in-grain beard, or
your French-crown-color beard, your perfect yellow.   80

QUINCE Some of your French crowns have no hair at all, and
then you will play bare-faced. But, masters, here are your
parts, and I am to entreat you, request you and desire you to
con them by tomorrow night, and meet me in the palace wood,
a mile without the town, by moonlight. There will we rehearse,   85
for if we meet in the city, we shall be dogged with company, and
our devices known. In the meantime I will draw a bill of properties, such as our play wants. I pray you, fail me not.

BOTTOM   We will meet, and there we may rehearse most
obscenely and courageously. Take pains; be perfect! Adieu.   90

QUINCE At the Duke's oak we meet.

BOTTOM   Enough; hold, or cut bow-strings.   *Exeunt*

---

58. **extempore:** i.e., without a script
68. **aggravate:** Bottom's error for "moderate"
69. **sucking:** Bottom's confusion of the proverbial expression about "sucking lambs" and "sitting doves"
81. **French crowns:** French coins, with pun on "syphilis," known as "the French disease," causing the loss of hair on the head or "crown" and body
90. **obscenely:** Bottom's error for "seemly"

Act 2, Scene 1

Enter, a FAIRY *at one door, and* PUCK, *or* ROBIN GOODFELLOW, *at another.*

PUCK How now, spirit! Whither wander you?

FAIRY Over hill, over dale,
 Thorough bush, thorough briar,
 Over park, over pale,
  Thorough flood, thorough fire,   5
 I do wander everywhere,
 Swifter than the moon's sphere,
 And I serve the Fairy Queen,
 To dew her orbs upon the green.
 The cowslips tall her pensioners be;   10
 In their gold coats spots you see—
 Those be rubies, fairy favors,
 In those freckles live their savors.
 I must go seek some dewdrops here
 And hang a pearl in every cowslip's ear.   15
 Farewell, thou lob of spirits; I'll be gone;
 Our Queen and all our elves come here anon.

PUCK The king doth keep his revels here tonight.
 Take heed the queen come not within his sight,
 For Oberon is passing fell and wrath   20
 Because that she as her attendant hath
 A lovely boy, stol'n from an Indian king.
 She never had so sweet a changeling,
 And jealous Oberon would have the child
 Knight of his train, to trace the forests wild. 25
 But she perforce withholds the lovèd boy,
 Crowns him with flowers and makes him all her joy,
 And now they never meet in grove or green,
 By fountain clear, or spangled starlight sheen,
 But they do square, that all their elves for fear 30
 Creep into acorn-cups and hide them there.

FAIRY Either I mistake your shape and making quite,
 Or else you are that shrewd and knavish sprite
 Called Robin Goodfellow. Are not you he

2.1. **Location:** another part of the forest outside Athens
9. **orbs:** planets or spheres
10. **cowslips:** primulas, yellow wildflowers
16. **lob:** clown
20. **passing fell and wrath:** exceedingly fierce and angry
23. **changeling:** a child stolen or exchanged by fairies
30. **square:** fight

That frights the maidens of the villagery,   35
Skim milk, and sometimes labor in the quern
And bootless make the breathless housewife churn,
And sometime make the drink to bear no barm,
Mislead night-wanderers, laughing at their harm?
Those that "Hobgoblin" call you, and "sweet Puck,"   40
You do their work, and they shall have good luck:
Are not you he?
PUCK   Thou speakest aright:
I am that merry wanderer of the night.
I jest to Oberon and make him smile
When I a fat and bean-fed horse beguile,   45
Neighing in likeness of a filly foal,
And sometime lurk I in a gossip's bowl,
In very likeness of a roasted crab,
And when she drinks, against her lips I bob
And on her withered dewlap pour the ale.   50
The wisest aunt, telling the saddest tale,
Sometime for three-foot stool mistaketh me;
Then slip I from her bum, down topples she,
And "tailor" cries, and falls into a cough,
And then the whole quire hold their hips and laugh,   55
And waxen in their mirth and 'neeze and swear
A merrier hour was never wasted there.
But, room, fairy! Here comes Oberon.
FAIRY   And here my mistress. Would that he were gone!
          Enter OBERON, *the King of Fairies, at one door, with his*
          train, and TITANIA, *the Queen at another, with hers*
OBERON   Ill met by moonlight, proud Titania.   60
TITANIA   What, jealous Oberon? Fairies, skip hence.
I have forsworn his bed and company.
OBERON   Tarry, rash wanton! Am not I thy lord?
TITANIA   Then I must be thy lady. But I know
When thou hast stol'n away from fairy land,   65

36. **quern:** device for grinding corn
37. **bootless:** useless
40. **"Hobgoblin" . . . "Puck":** common names for a mischievous spirit haunting the countryside
47. **gossip's:** i.e., an old woman's
50. **dewlap:** folds of skin under the throat
53. **bum:** buttocks
54. **"tailor":** Crying "tailor" after a fall seems to have been proverbial.
55. **quire:** group
56. **waxen:** louder; **'neeze:** sneeze
62. **forsworn:** renounced
63. **rash wanton:** i.e., lustful woman

And in the shape of Corin sat all day,
Playing on pipes of corn and versing love
To amorous Phillida. Why art thou here,
Come from the farthest steppe of India,
But that, forsooth, the bouncing Amazon,   70
Your buskined mistress and your warrior love,
To Theseus must be wedded, and you come
To give their bed joy and prosperity?
OBERON   How canst thou thus for shame, Titania,
Glance at my credit with Hippolyta,   75
Knowing I know thy love to Theseus?
Didst thou not lead him through the glimmering night
From Perigenia, whom he ravished,
And make him with fair Aegle break his faith,
With Ariadne and Antiopa?   80
TITANIA   These are the forgeries of jealousy:
And never, since the middle summer's spring,
Met we on hill, in dale, forest or mead,
By pavèd fountain or by rushy brook,
Or in the beached margent of the sea,   85
To dance our ringlets to the whistling wind,
But with thy brawls thou hast disturbed our sport.
Therefore the winds, piping to us in vain,
As in revenge, have sucked up from the sea
Contagious fogs, which falling in the land   90
Have every pelting river made so proud
That they have overborne their continents.
The ox hath therefore stretched his yoke in vain,
The ploughman lost his sweat, and the green corn

66–68. **Corin . . . Phillida:** generic names in the pastoral genre for a shepherd, who plays
    on his pipe all day, and his beloved
69. **steppe:** plain
70. **bouncing:** brash or strapping (Amazon women were famed for their physical
    prowess)
71. **buskined:** wearing a type of leather boot
75. **credit:** i.e., romantic history
78–80. **Perigenia, Aegle, Ariadne, Antiopa:** names of women in Greek myth abandoned
    by Theseus, as noted in Thomas North's translation of *Plutarch's Lives of the Noble
    Grecians and Romans* (1579 and 1595). For example, Theseus rejected Ariadne,
    daughter of the King of Minos, after she helped him escape from the Labyrinth.
81. **forgeries:** delusions
83. **mead:** meadow
84. **rushy brook:** brook full of rushes, i.e., plants
85. **beached margent:** river bank with a beach area
86. **ringlets:** circular dances
87. **brawls:** angry arguments
88. **piping:** playing on a pipe or flute
92. **continents:** boundaries

Hath rotted ere his youth attained a beard.   95
The fold stands empty in the drowned field,
And crows are fatted with the murrion flock;
The nine men's morris is filled up with mud,
And the quaint mazes in the wanton green
For lack of tread are undistinguishable.   100
The human mortals want their winter here;
No night is now with hymn or carol blest.
Therefore the moon, the governess of floods,
Pale in her anger, washes all the air,
That rheumatic diseases do abound,   105
And thorough this distemperature we see
The seasons alter. Hoary-headed frosts
Fall in the fresh lap of the crimson rose,
And on old Hiems' thin and icy crown
An odorous chaplet of sweet summer buds   110
Is, as in mockery, set. The spring, the summer,
The childing autumn, angry winter change
Their wonted liveries, and the mazèd world
By their increase now knows not which is which,
And this same progeny of evils comes   115
From our debate, from our dissension.
We are their parents and original.
OBERON   Do you amend it then; it lies in you.
Why should Titania cross her Oberon?
I do but beg a little changeling boy   120
To be my henchman.
TITANIA   Set your heart at rest:
The fairy land buys not the child of me.
His mother was a votress of my order,
And, in the spicèd Indian air, by night
Full often hath she gossiped by my side   125

95. **youth . . . beard:** i.e., came to maturity
96. **fold:** enclosure for domestic animals
97. **murrion:** dead flesh of animals
98. **nine men's morris:** the board on which the strategy game of nine men's morris is played
99–100. **quaint . . . undistinguishable:** i.e., old mazes cut into the lawn are overgrown with no footprints
101. **want:** lack
106. **distemperature:** intemperate or disturbed condition
107. **Hoary-headed:** grey-haired
109. **Hiems':** Winter's
110. **odorous chaplet:** scented garland of flowers
112. **childing:** fertile
113. **wonted liveries:** customary clothing
115. **progeny:** offspring
121. **henchman:** squire or servant of a nobleman
123. **votress:** votaress, a woman devoted to religious service

And sat with me on Neptune's yellow sands,
Marking th'embarkèd traders on the flood,
When we have laughed to see the sails conceive
And grow big-bellied with the wanton wind,
Which she, with pretty and with swimming gait   130
Following (her womb then rich with my young squire),
Would imitate, and sail upon the land,
To fetch me trifles, and return again,
As from a voyage, rich with merchandise.
But she, being mortal, of that boy did die,   135
And for her sake do I rear up her boy,
And for her sake I will not part with him.

OBERON   How long within this wood intend you stay?

TITANIA   Perchance till after Theseus' wedding-day.
If you will patiently dance in our round   140
And see our moonlight revels, go with us;
If not, shun me, and I will spare your haunts.

OBERON   Give me that boy, and I will go with thee.

TITANIA   Not for thy fairy kingdom! Fairies, away!
We shall chide downright if I longer stay.   145

                    Exeunt TITANIA *with her train*

OBERON   Well, go thy way: thou shalt not from this grove
Till I torment thee for this injury.
My gentle Puck, come hither. Thou rememb'rest
Since once I sat upon a promontory
And heard a mermaid on a dolphin's back   150
Uttering such dulcet and harmonious breath
That the rude sea grew civil at her song,
And certain stars shot madly from their spheres
To hear the sea-maid's music?

PUCK   I remember.

OBERON   That very time I saw, but thou couldst not,   155
Flying between the cold moon and the earth,
Cupid all armed: a certain aim he took
At a fair vestal thronèd by the west
And loosed his love-shaft smartly from his bow
As it should pierce a hundred thousand hearts.   160
But I might see young Cupid's fiery shaft

---

126. **Neptune's**: belonging to the Roman god of the sea (known as Poseidon in Greek)
127. **th'embarkèd traders**: traders already on board ships
140. **round**: roundel, or round dance
145. **chide**: argue
151. **dulcet**: sweet
158. **vestal**: vestal virgin, a priestess devoted to the Roman goddess Vesta; possibly a flattery of Queen Elizabeth I

Quenched in the chaste beams of the watery moon,
And the imperial votress passèd on,
In maiden meditation, fancy-free.
Yet marked I where the bolt of Cupid fell: 165
It fell upon a little western flower,
Before milk-white, now purple with love's wound,
And maidens call it "love-in-idleness."
Fetch me that flower, the herb I showed thee once;
The juice of it on sleeping eye-lids laid   170
Will make or man or woman madly dote
Upon the next live creature that it sees.
Fetch me this herb, and be thou here again
Ere the leviathan can swim a league.
PUCK   I'll put a girdle round about the earth   175
  In forty minutes.   *Exit*
OBERON   Having once this juice,
  I'll watch Titania when she is asleep,
  And drop the liquor of it in her eyes.
  The next thing then she waking looks upon,
  Be it on lion, bear, or wolf, or bull,   180
  On meddling monkey, or on busy ape,
  She shall pursue it with the soul of love,
  And ere I take this charm from off her sight,
  As I can take it with another herb,
  I'll make her render up her page to me.   185
  But who comes here? I am invisible,
  And I will overhear their conference.
        Enter DEMETRIUS, HELENA, *following him*
DEMETRIUS   I love thee not, therefore pursue me not.
  Where is Lysander and fair Hermia?
  The one I'll slay, the other slayeth me.   190
  Thou told'st me they were stolen unto this wood,
  And here am I, and wode within this wood,
  Because I cannot meet my Hermia.
  Hence, get thee gone, and follow me no more.
HELENA   You draw me, you hard-hearted adamant,   195
  But yet you draw not iron, for my heart
  Is true as steel. Keave you your power to draw,
  And I shall have no power to follow you.

---

168. **love-in-idleness:** viola, a type of flower
174. **leviathan:** enormous sea creature
185. **page:** servant, i.e., the changeling boy
192. **wode:** made crazy
195. **adamant:** a man who attracts affection
197. **Keave:** overturn

DEMETRIUS   Do I entice you? Do I speak you fair?
  Or, rather, do I not in plainest truth   200
  Tell you, I do not, nor I cannot, love you?
HELENA   And even for that do I love you the more.
  I am your spaniel, and, Demetrius,
  The more you beat me, I will fawn on you.
  Use me but as your spaniel, spurn me, strike me,   205
  Neglect me, lose me; only give me leave,
  Unworthy as I am, to follow you.
  What worser place can I beg in your love
  (And yet a place of high respect with me)
  Than to be used as you use your dog?   210
DEMETRIUS   Tempt not too much the hatred of my spirit,
  For I am sick when I do look on thee.
HELENA   And I am sick when I look not on you.
DEMETRIUS   You do impeach your modesty too much
  To leave the city and commit yourself   215
  Into the hands of one that loves you not,
  To trust the opportunity of night
  And the ill counsel of a desert place
  With the rich worth of your virginity.
HELENA   Your virtue is my privilege: for that   220
  It is not night when I do see your face,
  Therefore I think I am not in the night;
  Nor doth this wood lack worlds of company,
  For you in my respect are all the world.
  Then how can it be said I am alone,   225
  When all the world is here to look on me?
DEMETRIUS   I'll run from thee and hide me in the brakes,
  And leave thee to the mercy of wild beasts.
HELENA   The wildest hath not such a heart as you.
  Run when you will, the story shall be changed: 230
  Apollo flies, and Daphne holds the chase;
  The dove pursues the griffin; the mild hind
  Makes speed to catch the tiger—bootless speed,
  When cowardice pursues and valour flies.
DEMETRIUS   I will not stay thy questions. Let me go: 235
  Or, if thou follow me, do not believe
  But I shall do thee mischief in the wood.

227. **brakes:** bushes
231. **Apollo . . . Daphne**: When the Greek god Apollo pursued an unwilling Daphne, she
    asked her father Peneus for help, and he turned her into a laurel tree.
232. **griffin:** a mythical creature with the head and wings of an eagle and the body and
    hindquarters of a lion

HELENA   Ay, in the temple, in the town, the field,
   You do me mischief. Fie, Demetrius!
   Your wrongs do set a scandal on my sex: 240
   We cannot fight for love, as men may do;
   We should be wooed and were not made to woo.
                           Exit DEMETRIUS
   I'll follow thee and make a heaven of hell,
   To die upon the hand I love so well.   *Exit*
OBERON   Fare thee well, nymph: ere he do leave this grove,   245
   Thou shalt fly him and he shall seek thy love.
     Enter PUCK
   Hast thou the flower there? Welcome, wanderer.
PUCK   Ay, there it is.
OBERON   I pray thee, give it me.
   I know a bank where the wild thyme blows,
   Where oxlips and the nodding violet grows,   250
   Quite over-canopied with luscious woodbine,
   With sweet musk-roses and with eglantine.
   There sleeps Titania sometime of the night,
   Lulled in these flowers with dances and delight,
   And there the snake throws her enamelled skin,   255
   Weed wide enough to wrap a fairy in,
   And with the juice of this I'll streak her eyes,
   And make her full of hateful fantasies.
   Take thou some of it, and seek through this grove:
   A sweet Athenian lady is in love   260
   With a disdainful youth: anoint his eyes.
   But do it when the next thing he espies
   May be the lady. Thou shalt know the man
   By the Athenian garments he hath on.
   Effect it with some care, that he may prove   265
   More fond on her than she upon her love,
   And look thou meet me ere the first cock crow.
PUCK   Fear not, my lord, your servant shall do so.   *Exeunt*

---

250. **oxlips**: a primula plant with yellow flowers
251. **woodbine**: honeysuckle, a climbing plant
252. **eglantine**: sweet-briar plant

Act 2, Scene 2

Enter TITANIA, *Queen of Fairies, with her train*

TITANIA   Come, now a roundel and a fairy song,
Then for the third part of a minute, hence—
Some to kill cankers in the musk-rose buds,
Some war with rere-mice for their leathern wings
To make my small elves coats, and some keep back   5
The clamorous owl that nightly hoots and wonders
At our quaint spirits. Sing me now asleep,
Then to your offices and let me rest.
   Fairies sing.
FIRST FAIRY   You spotted snakes with double tongue,
      Thorny hedgehogs, be not seen.   10
      Newts and blind-worms, do no wrong,
      Come not near our Fairy Queen.
[CHORUS] Philomel, with melody
      Sing in our sweet lullaby;
   Lulla, lulla, lullaby, lulla, lulla, lullaby.   15
      Never harm,
      Nor spell nor charm
   Come our lovely lady nigh.
   So, good night, with lullaby.
FIRST FAIRY   Weaving spiders, come not here;   20
      Hence, you long-legged spinners, hence!
      Beetles black, approach not near;
      Worm nor snail, do no offence.
[CHORUS] Philomel, with melody,
      Sing in our sweet lullaby;   25
   Lulla, lulla, lullaby, lulla, lulla, lullaby:
      Never harm,
      Nor spell nor charm
   Come our lovely lady nigh.
   So, good night, with lullaby.   30
SECOND FAIRY   Hence, away! Now all is well:
   One aloof stand sentinel.
               Exeunt Fairies. TITANIA *sleeps.*
   Enter OBERON [*who squeezes the flower on* TITANIA's
   eyelids]

2.2. **Location:** another part of the forest outside Athens
1.   **roundel:** a round dance
3.   **cankers:** i.e., lesions
4.   **rere-mice:** mice who are running away; **leathern:** leather
13. **Philomel:** mythological Greek princess who turned into a nightingale after her rape
   and mutilation by her brother-in-law Tereus

OBERON   What thou seest when thou dost wake,
    Do it for thy true-love take;
    Love and languish for his sake,   35
    Be it ounce, or cat, or bear,
    Pard, or boar with bristled hair
    In thy eye that shall appear
    When thou wak'st, it is thy dear.
    Wake when some vile thing is near!   *Exit*   40
     Enter LYSANDER *and* HERMIA

LYSANDER   Fair love, you faint with wandering in the wood,
    And, to speak troth, I have forgot our way.
    We'll rest us, Hermia, if you think it good,
    And tarry for the comfort of the day.

HERMIA   Be it so, Lysander; find you out a bed,   45
    For I upon this bank will rest my head.

LYSANDER   One turf shall serve as pillow for us both:
    One heart, one bed, two bosoms and one troth.

HERMIA   Nay, good Lysander, for my sake, my dear,
    Lie further off yet; do not lie so near.   50

LYSANDER   O, take the sense, sweet, of my innocence!
    Love takes the meaning in love's conference.
    I mean that my heart unto yours is knit,
    So that but one heart we can make of it:
    Two bosoms interchainèd with an oath,   55
    So then two bosoms and a single troth.
    Then by your side no bedroom me deny,
    For lying so, Hermia, I do not lie.

HERMIA   Lysander riddles very prettily.
    Now much beshrew my manners and my pride   60
    If Hermia meant to say Lysander lied.
    But, gentle friend, for love and courtesy
    Lie further off; in human modesty,
    Such separation as may well be said
    Becomes a virtuous bachelor and a maid;   65
    So far be distant, and, good night, sweet friend.
    Thy love ne'er alter till thy sweet life end!

LYSANDER   Amen, amen, to that fair prayer say I;
    And then end life when I end loyalty!
    Here is my bed; sleep give thee all his rest!   70

HERMIA   With half that wish the wisher's eyes be pressed!
                   They sleep

---

37. **Pard:** leopard
56. **troth:** pledge of faith or loyalty
60. **beshrew:** i.e., corrupt or abuse

Enter PUCK

PUCK   Through the forest have I gone,
          But Athenian found I none
          On whose eyes I might approve
          This flower's force in stirring love.   75
          Night and silence—Who is here?
          Weeds of Athens he doth wear.
          This is he, my master said
          Despised the Athenian maid,
          And here the maiden, sleeping sound,   80
          On the dank and dirty ground.
          Pretty soul! She durst not lie
          Near this lack-love, this kill-courtesy.
          Churl, upon thy eyes I throw
          All the power this charm doth owe.   85
          [*He squeezes the juice on* LYSANDER's *eyes.*]
          When thou wak'st, let love forbid
          Sleep his seat on thy eyelid.
          So awake when I am gone,
          For I must now to Oberon.   *Exit*

          Enter DEMETRIUS *and* HELENA, *running*

HELENA   Stay, though thou kill me, sweet Demetrius!   90
DEMETRIUS   I charge thee, hence, and do not haunt me thus.
HELENA   O, wilt thou darkling leave me? Do not so!
DEMETRIUS   Stay, on thy peril: I alone will go.   *Exit* DEMETRIUS
HELENA   O, I am out of breath in this fond chase!
          The more my prayer, the lesser is my grace.   95
          Happy is Hermia, wheresoe'er she lies,
          For she hath blessèd and attractive eyes.
          How came her eyes so bright? Not with salt tears—
          If so, my eyes are oftener washed than hers.
          No, no, I am as ugly as a bear,   100
          For beasts that meet me run away for fear.
          Therefore no marvel though Demetrius
          Do as a monster fly my presence thus.
          What wicked and dissembling glass of mine
          Made me compare with Hermia's sphery eyne?   105
          But who is here? Lysander—on the ground?
          Dead, or asleep? I see no blood, no wound.
          Lysander if you live, good sir, awake!

77. **Weeds:** clothing
84. **Churl:** peasant or rude person
92. **darkling:** in darkness
104. **dissembling:** deceptive
105. **eyne:** eyes

LYSANDER [*waking*]   And run through fire I will for thy sweet
  sake.
  Transparent Helena! Nature shows art   110
  That through thy bosom makes me see thy heart.
  Where is Demetrius? O, how fit a word
  Is that vile name to perish on my sword!
HELENA   Do not say so, Lysander; say not so.
  What though he love your Hermia? Lord, what though?   115
  Yet Hermia still loves you; then be content.
LYSANDER   Content with Hermia! No, I do repent
  The tedious minutes I with her have spent.
  Not Hermia, but Helena I love.
  Who will not change a raven for a dove?   120
  The will of man is by his reason swayed,
  And reason says you are the worthier maid.
  Things growing are not ripe until their season,
  So I, being young, till now ripe not to reason,
  And touching now the point of human skill,   125
  Reason becomes the marshal to my will,
  And leads me to your eyes, where I o'erlook
  Love's stories written in love's richest book.
HELENA   Wherefore was I to this keen mockery born?
  When, at your hands, did I deserve this scorn?   130
  Is't not enough, is't not enough, young man,
  That I did never, no, nor never can
  Deserve a sweet look from Demetrius' eye,
  But you must flout my insufficiency?
  Good troth, you do me wrong, good sooth, you do,   135
  In such disdainful manner me to woo.
  But fare you well; perforce I must confess
  I thought you lord of more true gentleness.
  O, that a lady of one man refused
  Should of another therefore be abused!   *Exit*   140
LYSANDER   She sees not Hermia. Hermia, sleep thou there,
  And never may'st thou come Lysander near!
  For as a surfeit of the sweetest things
  The deepest loathing to the stomach brings,
  Or as the heresies that men do leave   145
  Are hated most of those they did deceive,
  So thou, my surfeit and my heresy,
  Of all be hated, but the most of me,

---

120. **change:** exchange
135. **Good troth:** i.e., truly; **sooth:** truth

And, all my powers, address your love and might
To honor Helen and to be her knight!   *Exit*   150
HERMIA [*waking*]   Help me, Lysander, help me! Do thy best
   To pluck this crawling serpent from my breast!
   Ay me, for pity! What a dream was here!
   Lysander, look how I do quake with fear:
   Methought a serpent eat my heart away,   155
   And you sat smiling at his cruel prey.
   Lysander! What, removed? Lysander! Lord!
   What, out of hearing? Gone? No sound, no word?
   Alack, where are you? Speak, and if you hear,
   Speak, of all loves! I swoon almost with fear.   160
   No? Then I well perceive you all not nigh.
   Either death or you I'll find immediately.   *Exit*

Act 3, Scene 1

Enter the Clowns, QUINCE, SNUG, BOTTOM, FLUTE, SNOUT,
and STARVELING

BOTTOM   Are we all met?
QUINCE   Pat, pat, and here's a marvelous convenient place for
   our rehearsal. This green plot shall be our stage, this hawthorn-
   brake our tiring-house, and we will do it in action as we will do
   it before the duke.   5
BOTTOM   Peter Quince—
QUINCE   What sayest thou, bully Bottom?
BOTTOM   There are things in this comedy of Pyramus and Thisbe
   that will never please. First, Pyramus must draw a sword to kill
   himself, which the ladies cannot abide. How answer you that?   10
SNOUT   By'r lakin, a parlous fear.
STARVELING   I believe we must leave the killing out, when all
   is done.
BOTTOM   Not a whit. I have a device to make all well. Write me
   a prologue, and let the prologue seem to say we will do no   15
   harm with our swords, and that Pyramus is not killed indeed,
   and, for the more better assurance, tell them that I, Pyramus,
   am not Pyramus, but Bottom the weaver. This will put them
   out of fear.

3.1. Location: another part of the forest outside Athens
2.   Pat, pat: ready, ready
3–4. hawthorn-brake: hawthorn bush
4.   tiring-house: theatrical dressing room
11. By'r . . . fear: by Our Lady Mary, a harmful fear
14. whit: bit

QUINCE   Well, we will have such a prologue, and it shall be   20
written in eight and six.

BOTTOM   No, make it two more: let it be written in eight and
eight.

SNOUT   Will not the ladies be afeard of the lion?

STARVELING   I fear it, I promise you.   25

BOTTOM   Masters, you ought to consider with yourselves, to
bring in—God shield us!—a lion among ladies is a most
dreadful thing, for there is not a more fearful wild-fowl than
your lion living, and we ought to look to't.

SNOUT   Therefore another prologue must tell he is not a lion.   30

BOTTOM   Nay, you must name his name, and half his face must
be seen through the lion's neck, and he himself must speak
through, saying thus, or to the same defect: "Ladies," or
"Fair-ladies, I would wish you," or "I would request you," or
"I would entreat you not to fear, not to tremble: my life for   35
yours. If you think I come hither as a lion, it were pity of my
life. No, I am no such thing; I am a man as other men are,"
and there indeed let him name his name, and tell them
plainly he is Snug the joiner.

QUINCE   Well it shall be so. But there is two hard things: that   40
is, to bring the moonlight into a chamber, for, you know,
Pyramus and Thisbe meet by moonlight.

SNOUT   Doth the moon shine that night we play our play?

BOTTOM   A calendar, a calendar! Look in the almanac: find
out moonshine, find out moonshine!   45

QUINCE   Yes, it doth shine that night.

BOTTOM   Why, then may you leave a casement of the great
chamber window, where we play, open, and the moon may
shine in at the casement.

QUINCE   Ay, or else one must come in with a bush of thorns and   50
a lanthorn, and say he comes to disfigure, or to present, the
person of Moonshine. Then, there is another thing: we must
have a wall in the great chamber, for Pyramus and Thisbe,
says the story, did talk through the chink of a wall.

SNOUT   You can never bring in a wall. What say you, Bottom?   55

---

21. **eight and six:** the usual meter of a ballad: alternating lines of eight and six syllables
22–23. **eight and eight:** Bottom proposes a non-sensical meter
28. **wild-fowl:** Bottom's error for "wild-beast"
33. **defect:** Bottom's error for "effect"
47. **casement:** window frame
50. **bush of thorns:** conventional accompaniment of the man in the moon
51. **lanthorn:** archaic form of "lantern"; **disfigure:** Quince's error for "figure"
54. **chink:** gap

BOTTOM   Some man or other must present Wall, and let him
   have some plaster, or some loam, or some rough-cast about
   him, to signify Wall, or let him hold his fingers thus, and
   through that cranny shall Pyramus and Thisbe whisper.
QUINCE   If that may be, then all is well. Come, sit down, every   60
   mother's son, and rehearse your parts. Pyramus, you begin.
   When you have spoken your speech, enter into that brake,
   and so every one according to his cue.
      Enter PUCK
PUCK   What hempen home-spuns have we swaggering here,
So near the cradle of the fairy queen?   65
What, a play toward! I'll be an auditor,
An actor too, perhaps, if I see cause.
QUINCE   Speak, Pyramus. Thisbe, stand forth.
BOTTOM [*as Pyramus*]   Thisbe, the flowers of odious savors
      sweet,—
QUINCE   Odors, odors!   70
BOTTOM [*as Pyramus*]   —odors savors sweet:
      So hath thy breath, my dearest Thisbe dear.
   But hark, a voice! Stay thou but here awhile,
      And by and by I will to thee appear.   *Exit*
PUCK   A stranger Pyramus than e'er played here.   *Exit*   75
FLUTE   Must I speak now?
QUINCE   Ay, marry, must you, for you must understand he
   goes but to see a noise that he heard, and is to come again.
FLUTE [*as Thisbe*]   Most radiant Pyramus, most lily-white of hue,
      Of color like the red rose on triumphant briar,   80
   Most brisky Juvenal and eke most lovely Jew,
      As true as truest horse that yet would never tire,
   I'll meet thee, Pyramus, at Ninny's tomb—
QUINCE   "Ninus' tomb," man! Why, you must not speak that
   yet; that you answer to Pyramus. You speak all your part at   85
   once, cues and all. Pyramus, enter—your cue is past. It is
   "never tire."
FLUTE   O—[*as Thisbe*]   —As true as truest horse, that yet would
      never tire.
      Enter PUCK, *and* BOTTOM [*with*] *the ass's head on*

---

57. **loam:** a mixture of clay and sand used for bricks and other building material;
   rough-cast: plastering material composed of lime, water, and gravel
62. **brake:** bush
64. **hempen home-spuns:** homemade items created from hemp, here meaning "fools"
65. **cradle:** i.e., bed, possibly on rockers or a swing
66. **auditor:** listener
81. **Juvenal:** classical Roman poet, author of the *Satires*
83. **Ninny's:** Bottom's confusion of "ninny" or fool for "Ninus"
84. **Ninus':** Ninus was the founder of Nineveh, capital of ancient Syria

BOTTOM [*as Pyramus*]   If I were fair, Thisbe, I were only thine.
QUINCE   O monstrous! O strange! We are haunted! Pray,   90
   masters! Fly, masters! Help!

              The Clowns, QUINCE, SNUG, FLUTE, SNOUT, *and*
                                STARVELING, *all exit*

PUCK   I'll follow you: I'll lead you about a round,
   Through bog, through bush, through brake, through briar;
   Sometime a horse I'll be, sometime a hound,
   A hog, a headless bear, sometime a fire;   95
   And neigh, and bark, and grunt, and roar, and burn,
   Like horse, hound, hog, bear, fire, at every turn.   *Exit*

BOTTOM   Why do they run away? This is a knavery of them to
   make me afeard!

       Enter SNOUT

SNOUT   O Bottom, thou art changed! What do I see on thee?   100
BOTTOM   What do you see? You see an ass head of your own,
   do you?

                             Exit SNOUT

       Enter QUINCE

QUINCE   Bless thee, Bottom! Bless thee! Thou art translated.

                                   Exit

BOTTOM   I see their knavery. This is to make an ass of me, to
   fright me, if they could. But I will not stir from this place,   105
   do what they can: I will walk up and down here, and I will
   sing, that they shall hear I am not afraid.
     [*Sings*]   The ousel cock so black of hue,
   With orange-tawny bill,
   The throstle with his note so true,   110
     The wren with little quill—
TITANIA [*waking*]   What angel wakes me from my flow'ry
   bed?
BOTTOM [*sings*]   The finch, the sparrow and the lark,
   The plain-song cuckoo gray,
   Whose note full many a man doth mark,   115
     And dares not answer nay—
   for, indeed, who would set his wit to so foolish a bird?
   Who would give a bird the lie, though he cry "Cuckoo"
   never so?
TITANIA   I pray thee, gentle mortal, sing again!   120

---

93. **brake:** bush
98. **knavery:** trickery
103. **translated:** transformed
108. **ousel cock:** male blackbird
110. **throstle:** thrush, a kind of songbird

Mine ear is much enamored of thy note;
So is mine eye enthrallèd to thy shape,
And thy fair virtue's force, perforce, doth move me
On the first view to say, to swear, I love thee.

BOTTOM   Methinks, mistress, you should have little reason   125
for that, and yet, to say the truth, reason and love keep little
company together nowadays; the more the pity that some
honest neighbours will not make them friends. Nay, I can
gleek upon occasion.

TITANIA   Thou art as wise as thou art beautiful.   130

BOTTOM   Not so, neither, but if I had wit enough to get out of
this wood, I have enough to serve mine own turn.

TITANIA   Out of this wood do not desire to go;
Thou shalt remain here, whether thou wilt or no.
I am a spirit of no common rate;   135
The summer still doth tend upon my state,
And I do love thee. Therefore, go with me;
I'll give thee fairies to attend on thee,
And they shall fetch thee jewels from the deep,
And sing while thou on pressed flowers dost sleep,   140
And I will purge thy mortal grossness so
That thou shalt like an airy spirit go.
Peaseblossom! Cobweb! Moth! And Mustardseed!

Enter PEASEBLOSSOM, COBWEB, MOTH, *and* MUSTARDSEED

PEASEBLOSSOM   Ready.

COBWEB   And I.   145

MOTH   And I.

MUSTARDSEED   And I.

ALL   Where shall we go?

TITANIA   Be kind and courteous to this gentleman:
Hop in his walks and gambol in his eyes;   150
Feed him with apricocks and dewberries,
With purple grapes, green figs, and mulberries;
The honey-bags steal from the humble-bees,
And for night-tapers crop their waxen thighs
And light them at the fiery glow-worm's eyes   155
To have my love to bed and to arise,
And pluck the wings from painted butterflies
To fan the moonbeams from his sleeping eyes.
Nod to him, elves, and do him courtesies.

PEASEBLOSSOM   Hail, mortal!   160

---

129. **gleek:** i.e., joke
135. **rate:** value or rank
150. **gambol:** bound or leap
154. **night-tapers:** evening candles

COBWEB   Hail!
MOTH   Hail!
MUSTARDSEED   Hail!
BOTTOM   I cry your worship's mercy. Heartily, I beseech your
  worship's name.   165
COBWEB   Cobweb.
BOTTOM   I shall desire you of more acquaintance, good
  Master Cobweb. If I cut my finger, I shall make bold with
  you. Your name, honest gentleman?
PEASEBLOSSOM   Peaseblossom.   170
BOTTOM   I pray you, commend me to Mistress Squash, your
  mother, and to Master Peascod, your father. Good Master
  Peaseblossom, I shall desire you of more acquaintance too.
  Your name, I beseech you, sir?
MUSTARDSEED   Mustardseed.   175
BOTTOM   Good Master Mustardseed, I know your patience
  well; that same cowardly, giant-like ox-beef hath devoured
  many a gentleman of your house. I promise you your
  kindred had made my eyes water ere now. I desire your
  more acquaintance, good Master Mustardseed.   180
TITANIA   Come, wait upon him; lead him to my bower.
  The moon methinks looks with a wat'ry eye,
  And when she weeps, weeps every little flower,
  Lamenting some enforcèd chastity.
  Tie up my love's tongue bring him silently.   *Exeunt*   185

Act 3, Scene 2

Enter OBERON, *King of Fairies*
OBERON   I wonder if Titania be awaked,
  Then, what it was that next came in her eye,
  Which she must dote on in extremity.
    Enter PUCK
  Here comes my messenger. How now, mad spirit!
  What night-rule now about this haunted grove?   5
PUCK   My mistress with a monster is in love!
  Near to her close and consecrated bower,
  While she was in her dull and sleeping hour,
  A crew of patches, rude mechanicals,
  That work for bread upon Athenian stalls,   10
  Were met together to rehearse a play

3.2. Location: another part of the forest outside Athens
9.   **rude mechanicals:** uneducated laborers
10. **stalls:** i.e., market-stalls (rather than shops)

Intended for great Theseus' nuptial-day.
The shallowest thick-skin of that barren sort,
Who Pyramus presented, in their sport
Forsook his scene and entered in a brake,   15
When I did him at this advantage take,
An ass's nole I fixèd on his head.
Anon his Thisbe must be answerèd,
And forth my mimic comes. When they him spy—
As wild geese that the creeping fowler eye,   20
Or russet-pated choughs, many in sort,
Rising and cawing at the gun's report,
Sever themselves and madly sweep the sky—
So, at his sight, away his fellows fly,
And, at our stamp, here o'er and o'er one falls.   25
He "Murder!" cries and help from Athens calls.
Their sense thus weak, lost with their fears thus strong,
Made senseless things begin to do them wrong,
For briars and thorns at their apparel snatch:
Some sleeves, some hats, from yielders all things catch.   30
I led them on in this distracted fear,
And left sweet Pyramus translated there:
When in that moment, so it came to pass,
Titania waked and straightway loved an ass!

OBERON   This falls out better than I could devise.   35
  But hast thou yet latched the Athenian's eyes
  With the love-juice, as I did bid thee do?

PUCK   I took him sleeping—that is finished too—
  And the Athenian woman by his side
  That, when he waked, of force she must be eyed.   40

          Enter DEMETRIUS *and* HERMIA

OBERON   Stand close: this is the same Athenian.

PUCK   This is the woman, but not this the man.

DEMETRIUS   O, why rebuke you him that loves you so?
  Lay breath so bitter on your bitter foe.

HERMIA   Now I but chide, but I should use thee worse,   45
  For thou, I fear, hast given me cause to curse.
  If thou hast slain Lysander in his sleep,
  Being o'er shoes in blood, plunge in the deep,

---

15. **Forsook:** left
17. **nole:** head
20. **fowler:** bird-catcher
21. **russet-pated choughs:** crows or jackdaws with reddish-brown heads
22. **cawing:** crying of crows
36. **latched:** covered
40. **eyed:** seen
48. **o'er:** covering

And kill me too.
The sun was not so true unto the day   50
As he to me. Would he have stolen away
From sleeping Hermia? I'll believe as soon
This whole earth may be bored and that the moon
May through the center creep and so displease
Her brother's noontide with Antipodes.   55
It cannot be but thou hast murdered him;
So should a murderer look: so dead, so grim.
DEMETRIUS   So should the murdered look, and so should I,
Pierced through the heart with your stern cruelty.
Yet you, the murderer, look as bright, as clear,   60
As yonder Venus in her glimmering sphere.
HERMIA   What's this to my Lysander? Where is he?
Ah, good Demetrius, wilt thou give him me?
DEMETRIUS   I had rather give his carcass to my hounds.
HERMIA   Out, dog! Out, cur! Thou driv'st me past the bounds   65
Of maiden's patience. Hast thou slain him, then?
Henceforth be never numbered among men!
O, once tell true, tell true, even for my sake!
Durst thou have looked upon him being awake,
And hast thou killed him sleeping? O brave touch!   70
Could not a worm, an adder, do so much?
An adder did it, for with doubler tongue
Than thine, thou serpent, never adder stung.
DEMETRIUS   You spend your passion on a misprised mood.
I am not guilty of Lysander's blood,   75
Nor is he dead, for aught that I can tell.
HERMIA   I pray thee, tell me then that he is well.
DEMETRIUS   And if I could, what should I get therefore?
HERMIA   A privilege never to see me more,
And from thy hated presence part I so.   80
See me no more, whether he be dead or no   *Exit*
DEMETRIUS   There is no following her in this fierce vein;
Here therefore for a while I will remain.
So sorrow's heaviness doth heavier grow
For debt that bankrupt sleep doth sorrow owe,   85

---

55. **brother's . . . Antipodes:** Helios was the Greek god of the sun and brother of the
    goddess of the moon; hence this phrase means to confuse noon and evening in the
    Antipodes, the other side of the world.
61. **Venus:** Roman goddess of love and beauty (known as Aphrodite in Greek)
65. **cur:** dog
71. **adder:** snake
74. **misprised:** mistaken
76. **aught:** anything

Which now in some slight measure it will pay,
If for his tender here I make some stay. *Lies down and sleeps*
OBERON [*to* PUCK]   What hast thou done? Thou hast mistaken quite
   And laid the love-juice on some true-love's sight.
   Of thy misprision must perforce ensue   90
   Some true love turned and not a false turned true.
PUCK   Then fate o'er-rules, that, one man holding troth,
   A million fail, confounding oath on oath.
OBERON   About the wood go swifter than the wind,
   And Helena of Athens look thou find.   95
   All fancy-sick she is and pale of cheer,
   With sighs of love, that costs the fresh blood dear.
   By some illusion see thou bring her here;
   I'll charm his eyes against she do appear.
PUCK   I go, I go; look how I go,   100
   Swifter than arrow from the Tartar's bow.   *Exit*
OBERON [*squeezing the juice on Demetrius' eyes*]
   Flower of this purple dye,
   Hit with Cupid's archery,
   Sink in apple of his eye.
   When his love he doth espy,   105
   Let her shine as gloriously
   As the Venus of the sky.
   When thou wak'st, if she be by,
   Beg of her for remedy.
      Enter PUCK
PUCK   Captain of our fairy band,   110
   Helena is here at hand,
   And the youth, mistook by me,
   Pleading for a lover's fee.
   Shall we their fond pageant see?
   Lord, what fools these mortals be!   115
OBERON   Stand aside: the noise they make
   Will cause Demetrius to awake.
PUCK   Then will two at once woo one—
   That must needs be sport alone,
   And those things do best please me   120
   That befall preposterously.
      Enter LYSANDER *and* HELENA
LYSANDER   Why should you think that I should woo in scorn?

---

90. misprision: mistaking
96. fancy-sick: made sick by love
101. Tartar's: Tatars, descended from Asian tribes, were famed for their archery skills.

Scorn and derision never come in tears.
Look when I vow, I weep, and vows so born,
In their nativity all truth appears.   125
How can these things in me seem scorn to you,
Bearing the badge of faith, to prove them true?
HELENA   You do advance your cunning more and more.
When truth kills truth, O devilish-holy fray!
These vows are Hermia's; will you give her o'er?   130
Weigh oath with oath, and you will nothing weigh;
Your vows to her and me, put in two scales,
Will even weigh, and both as light as tales.
LYSANDER   I had no judgment when to her I swore.
HELENA   Nor none, in my mind, now you give her o'er.   135
LYSANDER   Demetrius loves her, and he loves not you.
DEMETRIUS [*awaking*]   O Helena, goddess, nymph, perfect,
   divine!
To what, my love, shall I compare thine eyne?
Crystal is muddy! O, how ripe in show
Thy lips, those kissing cherries, tempting grow!   140
That pure congealèd white, high Taurus snow,
Fanned with the eastern wind, turns to a crow
When thou hold'st up thy hand: O, let me kiss
This princess of pure white, this seal of bliss!
HELENA   O spite! O hell! I see you all are bent   145
To set against me for your merriment.
If you were civil and knew courtesy,
You would not do me thus much injury.
Can you not hate me, as I know you do,
But you must join in souls to mock me too?   150
If you were men, as men you are in show,
You would not use a gentle lady so;
To vow, and swear, and superpraise my parts,
When I am sure you hate me with your hearts.
You both are rivals and love Hermia,   155
And now both rivals to mock Helena.
A trim exploit, a manly enterprise,
To conjure tears up in a poor maid's eyes
With your derision! None of noble sort
Would so offend a virgin, and extort   160
A poor soul's patience, all to make you sport.
LYSANDER   You are unkind, Demetrius; be not so,
For you love Hermia—this you know I know—

---

138. **eyne:** eyes
141. **Taurus:** Turkish mountains

And here, with all good will, with all my heart,
In Hermia's love I yield you up my part,   165
And yours of Helena to me bequeath,
Whom I do love and will do till my death.
HELENA   Never did mockers waste more idle breath.
DEMETRIUS   Lysander, keep thy Hermia; I will none.
    If e'er I loved her, all that love is gone.   170
    My heart to her but as guest-wise sojourned,
    And now to Helen is it home returned,
    There to remain.
LYSANDER   Helen, it is not so.
DEMETRIUS   Disparage not the faith thou dost not know,
    Lest, to thy peril, thou aby it dear.   175
    Look where thy love comes: yonder is thy dear.
        Enter HERMIA
HERMIA   Dark night, that from the eye his function takes,
    The ear more quick of apprehension makes,
    Wherein it doth impair the seeing sense,
    It pays the hearing double recompense.   180
    Thou art not by mine eye, Lysander, found;
    Mine ear, I thank it, brought me to thy sound.
    But why unkindly didst thou leave me so?
LYSANDER   Why should he stay, whom love doth press to go?
HERMIA   What love could press Lysander from my side?   185
LYSANDER   Lysander's love, that would not let him bide,
    Fair Helena, who more engilds the night
    Than all you fiery oes and eyes of light.
    [*To* HERMIA]   Why seek'st thou me? Could not this make thee
        know
    The hate I bear thee made me leave thee so?   190
HERMIA   You speak not as you think; it cannot be.
HELENA   Lo, she is one of this confederacy!
    Now I perceive they have conjoined all three
    To fashion this false sport, in spite of me.
    Injurious Hermia! Most ungrateful maid!   195
    Have you conspired, have you with these contrived
    To bait me with this foul derision?
    Is all the counsel that we two have shared,
    The sisters' vows, the hours that we have spent,
    When we have chid the hasty-footed time   200
    For parting us—O, is it all forgot?

175. **aby:** pay for
187. **engilds:** covers with gold
188. **oes and eyes:** glittering spangles and eyelets, i.e., stars
200. **chid:** chided

All school-days' friendship, childhood innocence?
We, Hermia, like two artificial gods,
Have with our needles created both one flower,
Both on one sampler, sitting on one cushion,   205
Both warbling of one song, both in one key,
As if our hands, our sides, voices and minds,
Had been incorporate. So we grow together,
Like to a double cherry, seeming parted,
But yet an union in partition: 210
Two lovely berries molded on one stem;
So, with two seeming bodies, but one heart,
Two of the first, like coats in heraldry,
Due but to one and crowned with one crest.
And will you rent our ancient love asunder,   215
To join with men in scorning your poor friend?
It is not friendly, 'tis not maidenly.
Our sex, as well as I, may chide you for it,
Though I alone do feel the injury.
HERMIA   I am amazed at your passionate words.   220
  I scorn you not; it seems that you scorn me.
HELENA   Have you not set Lysander, as in scorn,
  To follow me and praise my eyes and face,
  And made your other love, Demetrius,
  Who even but now did spurn me with his foot,   225
  To call me goddess, nymph, divine and rare,
  Precious, celestial? Wherefore speaks he this
  To her he hates? And wherefore doth Lysander
  Deny your love, so rich within his soul,
  And tender me, forsooth, affection,   230
  But by your setting on, by your consent?
  What though I be not so in grace as you,
  So hung upon with love, so fortunate,
  But miserable most, to love unloved?
  This you should pity rather than despise.   235
HERNIA   I understand not what you mean by this.
HELENA   Ay, do! Persever: counterfeit sad looks,
  Make mouths upon me when I turn my back,
  Wink each at other, hold the sweet jest up.
  This sport, well carried, shall be chronicled.   240
  If you have any pity, grace, or manners,
  You would not make me such an argument.
  But fare ye well. 'Tis partly my own fault,

---

215. **rent:** tear
237. **Persever:** persevere

Which death or absence soon shall remedy.

LYSANDER   Stay, gentle Helena: hear my excuse: 245
 My love, my life my soul, fair Helena!

HELENA   O excellent!

HERMIA [*to* LYSANDER]   Sweet, do not scorn her so.

DEMETRIUS   If she cannot entreat, I can compel.

LYSANDER   Thou canst compel no more than she entreat;
 Thy threats have no more strength than her weak prayers.   250
 Helen, I love thee, by my life, I do:
 I swear by that which I will lose for thee,
 To prove him false that says I love thee not.

DEMETRIUS   I say I love thee more than he can do.

LYSANDER   If thou say so, withdraw, and prove it too.   255

DEMETRIUS   Quick, come!

HERMIA   Lysander, whereto tends all this?

LYSANDER   Away, you Ethiope!

DEMETRIUS   No, no, sir,
 Seem to break loose, take on as you would follow,
 But yet come not. You are a tame man, go!

LYSANDER   Hang off, thou cat, thou burr! Vile thing, let loose,   260
 Or I will shake thee from me like a serpent!

HERMIA   Why are you grown so rude? What change is this?
 Sweet love—

LYSANDER   Thy love! Out, tawny Tartar, out!
 Out, loathed medicine! O hated potion, hence!

HERMIA   Do you not jest?

HELENA   Yes, sooth, and so do you.   265

LYSANDER   Demetrius, I will keep my word with thee.

DEMETRIUS   I would I had your bond, for I perceive
 A weak bond holds you. I'll not trust your word.

LYSANDER   What, should I hurt her, strike her, kill her dead?
 Although I hate her, I'll not harm her so.   270

HERMIA   What, can you do me greater harm than hate?
 Hate me! Wherefore? O me! What news, my love!
 Am not I Hermia? Are not you Lysander?
 I am as fair now as I was erewhile.
 Since night you loved me, yet since night you left me: 275
 Why, then you left me—O, the gods forbid!—
 In earnest, shall I say?

LYSANDER   Ay, by my life;
 And never did desire to see thee more.

---

263. tawny Tartar: i.e., dark-skinned Tatar belonging to Asian warrior tribes
274. erewhile: before

Therefore be out of hope, of question, of doubt;
Be certain, nothing truer—'tis no jest   280
That I do hate thee and love Helena.
HERMIA [*to* HELENA]   O me! You juggler! You canker-blossom!
    You thief of love! What, have you come by night
    And stol'n my love's heart from him?
HELENA   Fine, i'faith!
    Have you no modesty, no maiden shame,   285
    No touch of bashfulness? What, will you tear
    Impatient answers from my gentle tongue?
    Fie, fie! You counterfeit, you puppet, you!
HERMIA   "Puppet"? Why so? Ay, that way goes the game.
    Now I perceive that she hath made compare   290
    Between our statures. She hath urged her height,
    And with her personage, her tall personage,
    Her height, forsooth, she hath prevailed with him,
    And are you grown so high in his esteem
    Because I am so dwarfish and so low?   295
    How low am I, thou painted maypole? Speak!
    How low am I? I am not yet so low
    But that my nails can reach unto thine eyes.
HELENA   I pray you, though you mock me, gentlemen,
    Let her not hurt me. I was never curst;   300
    I have no gift at all in shrewishness.
    I am a right maid for my cowardice;
    Let her not strike me. You perhaps may think
    Because she is something lower than myself
    That I can match her.
HERMIA   Lower? Hark, again!   305
HELENA   Good Hermia, do not be so bitter with me.
    I evermore did love you, Hermia,
    Did ever keep your counsels, never wronged you,
    Save that, in love unto Demetrius,
    I told him of your stealth unto this wood.   310
    He followed you; for love I followed him,
    But he hath chid me hence and threatened me
    To strike me, spurn me, nay, to kill me too,
    And now, so you will let me quiet go,
    To Athens will I bear my folly back,   315
    And follow you no further. Let me go.
    You see how simple and how fond I am.

---

282. **canker-blossom:** i.e., corrupted flower
296. **maypole:** tall, decorated pole used for May Day celebrations

HERMIA   Why, get you gone. Who is't that hinders you?
HELENA   A foolish heart, that I leave here behind.
HERMIA   What, with Lysander?
HELENA   With Demetrius.   320
LYSANDER   Be not afraid. She shall not harm thee, Helena.
DEMETRIUS   No, sir, she shall not, though you take her part.
HELENA   O, when she's angry, she is keen and shrewd!
    She was a vixen when she went to school,
    And though she be but little, she is fierce.   325
HERMIA   "Little" again! Nothing but "low" and "little"?
    Why will you suffer her to flout me thus?
    Let me come to her.
LYSANDER   Get you gone, you dwarf,
    You minimus, of hindering knot-grass made,
    You bead, you acorn!
DEMETRIUS   You are too officious   330
    In her behalf that scorns your services.
    Let her alone: speak not of Helena,
    Take not her part, for, if thou dost intend
    Never so little show of love to her,
    Thou shalt aby it.
LYSANDER   Now she holds me not.   335
    Now follow, if thou darest, to try whose right,
    Of thine or mine, is most in Helena.
DEMETRIUS   Follow! Nay, I'll go with thee, cheek by jowl.
                    Exeunt LYSANDER *and* DEMETRIUS
HERMIA   You, mistress, all this coil is long of you:
    Nay, go not back.
HELENA   I will not trust you, I,   340
    Nor longer stay in your curst company.
    Your hands than mine are quicker for a fray,
    My legs are longer though, to run away.   *Exit*
HERMIA   I am amazed, and know not what to say.   *Exit*
        Enter OBERON *and* PUCK, *from behind*
OBERON   This is thy negligence. Still thou mistak'st,   345
    Or else committ'st thy knaveries wilfully.
PUCK   Believe me, king of shadows, I mistook.
    Did not you tell me I should know the man
    By the Athenian garment he had on?
    And so far blameless proves my enterprise   350

334. **aby:** pay for
339. **coil:** noisy disturbance; **long:** made longer by

That I have 'nointed an Athenian's eyes,
And so far am I glad it so did sort
As this their jangling I esteem a sport.
OBERON   Thou seest these lovers seek a place to fight:
Hie therefore, Robin, overcast the night;   355
The starry welkin cover thou anon
With drooping fog as black as Acheron,
And lead these testy rivals so astray
As one come not within another's way.
Like to Lysander sometime frame thy tongue,   360
Then stir Demetrius up with bitter wrong,
And sometime rail thou like Demetrius,
And from each other look thou lead them thus,
Till o'er their brows death-counterfeiting sleep
With leaden legs and batty wings doth creep.   365
Then crush this herb into Lysander's eye,
Whose liquor hath this virtuous property,
To take from thence all error with his might,
And make his eyeballs roll with wonted sight.
When they next wake, all this derision   370
Shall seem a dream and fruitless vision,
And back to Athens shall the lovers wend,
With league whose date till death shall never end.
Whiles I in this affair do thee employ.
I'll to my queen and beg her Indian boy,   375
And then I will her charmèd eye release
From monster's view, and all things shall be peace.
PUCK   My fairy lord, this must be done with haste,
For night's swift dragons cut the clouds full fast,
And yonder shines Aurora's harbinger,   380
At whose approach, ghosts, wandering here and there,
Troop home to churchyards. Damnèd spirits all,
That in crossways and floods have burial,
Already to their wormy beds are gone.
For fear lest day should look their shames upon,   385
They wilfully themselves exile from light
And must for aye consort with black-browed night.
OBERON   But we are spirits of another sort.

351. **'nointed**: anointed
356. **welkin**: sky
357. **Acheron**: one of five rivers of the underworld in Greek mythology
369. **wonted**: accustomed
372. **wend**: go
380. **Aurora's**: Aurora was the Roman goddess of the dawn.
387. **aye**: always

I with the morning's love have oft made sport,
And, like a forester, the groves may tread,   390
Even till the eastern gate, all fiery-red,
Opening on Neptune with fair blessèd beams,
Turns into yellow gold his salt green streams.
But, notwithstanding, haste, make no delay;
We may effect this business yet ere day.   *Exit*   395
PUCK   Up and down, up and down,
  I will lead them up and down.
  I am feared in field and town.
  Goblin, lead them up and down.
  Here comes one.   400

    Enter LYSANDER

LYSANDER   Where art thou, proud Demetrius? Speak thou now.
PUCK   Here, villain, drawn and ready! Where art thou?
LYSANDER   I will be with thee straight.
PUCK   Follow me, then,
  To plainer ground.

                         Exit LYSANDER

    Enter DEMETRIUS

DEMETRIUS   Lysander! Speak again.
  Thou runaway, thou coward, art thou fled?   405
  Speak! In some bush? Where dost thou hide thy head?
PUCK   Thou coward, art thou bragging to the stars,
  Telling the bushes that thou look'st for wars,
  And wilt not come? Come, recreant, come, thou child;
  I'll whip thee with a rod. He is defiled   410
  That draws a sword on thee.
DEMETRIUS   Yea, art thou there?
PUCK   Follow my voice. We'll try no manhood here.   *Exeunt*
    Enter LYSANDER
LYSANDER   He goes before me and still dares me on.
  When I come where he calls, then he is gone.
  The villain is much lighter-heeled than I.   415
  I followed fast, but faster he did fly,
  That fallen am I in dark uneven way,
  And here will rest me.   *Lies down*
           Come, thou gentle day!
  For if but once thou show me thy grey light,
  I'll find Demetrius and revenge this spite.   *Sleeps*   420
    Enter PUCK *and* DEMETRIUS
PUCK   Ho, ho, ho! Coward, why comest thou not?
DEMETRIUS   Abide me, if thou darest, for well I wot

422. wot: know

Thou runn'st before me, shifting every place,
And dar'st not stand, nor look me in the face.
Where art thou now?
PUCK   Come hither: I am here.   425
DEMETRIUS   Nay, then, thou mock'st me. Thou shalt buy this
    dear
If ever I thy face by daylight see.
Now, go thy way. Faintness constraineth me
To measure out my length on this cold bed.
By day's approach look to be visited.   *Lies down and sleeps*   430
        Enter HELENA
HELENA   O weary night, O long and tedious night,
    Abate thy hours! Shine comforts from the east,
    That I may back to Athens by daylight,
    From these that my poor company detest,
    And sleep, that sometimes shuts up sorrow's eye,   435
    Steal me awhile from mine own company.
                        Lies down and sleeps
PUCK   Yet but three? Come one more;
        Two of both kinds make up four.
        Here she comes, curst and sad.
        Cupid is a knavish lad,   440
        Thus to make poor females mad.
            Enter HERMIA
HERMIA   Never so weary, never so in woe,
    Bedabbled with the dew and torn with briars,
    I can no further crawl, no further go.
    My legs can keep no pace with my desires.   445
    Here will I rest me till the break of day.
    Heavens shield Lysander, if they mean a fray!
                        Lies down and sleeps
PUCK   On the ground
        Sleep sound:
        I'll apply   450
        To your eye,
        Gentle lover, remedy.
            He squeezes the juice on LYSANDER's *eyes*
        When thou wak'st,
        Thou tak'st
        True delight   455
        In the sight
        Of thy former lady's eye:
        And the country proverb known,
        That every man should take his own,
        In your waking shall be shown: 460

Jack shall have Jill;
Nought shall go ill.
The man shall have his mare again, and all shall be well.

Exit.
The lovers sleep all the Act

Act 4, Scene 1

Enter TITANIA, *Queen of Fairies, and* BOTTOM, *the* Clown,
and the Fairies PEASEBLOSSOM, COBWEB, MOTH, MUSTARD-
SEED, *and* OBERON, *King of Fairies, behind them*

TITANIA   Come, sit thee down upon this flow'ry bed,
While I thy amiable cheeks do coy,
And stick musk-roses in thy sleek smooth head,
And kiss thy fair large ears, my gentle joy.

BOTTOM   Where's Peaseblossom?   5

PEASEBLOSSOM   Ready.

BOTTOM   Scratch my head Peaseblossom. Where's Monsieur
Cobweb?

COBWEB   Ready.

BOTTOM   Monsieur Cobweb, good monsieur, get you your   10
weapons in your hand, and kill me a red-hipped humble-bee
on the top of a thistle, and, good monsieur, bring me the
honey-bag. Do not fret yourself too much in the action,
monsieur, and, good monsieur, have a care the honey-bag
break not. I would be loath to have you overflown with a   15
honey-bag, signior. Where's Monsieur Mustardseed?

MUSTARDSEED   Ready.

BOTTOM   Give me your neaf, Monsieur Mustardseed. Pray
you, leave your courtesy, good monsieur.

MUSTARDSEED   What's your will?   20

BOTTOM   Nothing, good monsieur, but to help Cavalery
Cobweb to scratch. I must to the barber's, monsieur, for
methinks I am marvellous hairy about the face, and I am
such a tender ass, if my hair do but tickle me, I must scratch.

TITANIA   What, wilt thou hear some music, my sweet love?   25

BOTTOM   I have a reasonable good ear in music. Let's have
the tongs and the bones.
Music, tongs, rural music

---

463. **mare**: i.e., woman
4.1. **Location**: another part of the forest outside Athens
2.   **coy**: stroke
21. **Cavalery**: cavaliere, or courtly gentlemen
27. **tongs and the bones**: a rustic musical instrument

TITANIA   Or say, sweet love, what thou desirest to eat.
BOTTOM   Truly, a peck of provender. I could munch your good
    dry oats. Methinks I have a great desire to a bottle of hay.   30
    Good hay, sweet hay, hath no fellow.
TITANIA   I have a venturous fairy that shall seek
    The squirrel's hoard, and fetch thee new nuts.
BOTTOM   I had rather have a handful or two of dried peas.
    But, I pray you, let none of your people stir me. I have an   35
    exposition of sleep come upon me.
TITANIA   Sleep thou, and I will wind thee in my arms.
    Fairies, begone, and be all ways away.
Exeunt Fairies

    So doth the woodbine the sweet honeysuckle
    Gently entwist; the female ivy so   40
    Enrings the barky fingers of the elm.
    O, how I love thee! How I dote on thee!
They sleep

    Enter PUCK
OBERON [*coming forward*]   Welcome, good Robin. See'st thou
    this sweet sight?
    Her dotage now I do begin to pity,
    For, meeting her of late behind the wood,   45
    Seeking sweet favors from this hateful fool,
    I did upbraid her and fall out with her,
    For she his hairy temples then had rounded
    With a coronet of fresh and fragrant flowers,
    And that same dew, which sometime on the buds   50
    Was wont to swell like round and orient pearls,
    Stood now within the pretty flowerets' eyes
    Like tears that did their own disgrace bewail.
    When I had at my pleasure taunted her,
    And she in mild terms begged my patience,   55
    I then did ask of her her changeling child,
    Which straight she gave me, and her fairy sent
    To bear him to my bower in fairy land.
    And now I have the boy, I will undo.
    This hateful imperfection of her eyes.   60
    And, gentle Puck, take this transformèd scalp
    From off the head of this Athenian swain,
    That, he awaking when the other do,
    May all to Athens back again repair,

29. **provender:** dry food such as hay
30. **bottle:** bundle
36. **exposition of:** Bottom's error for "disposition to"
49. **coronet:** small crown

And think no more of this night's accidents   65
But as the fierce vexation of a dream.
But first I will release the fairy queen.
[*Squeezing juice on her eyes*] Be as thou wast wont to be;
See as thou wast wont to see.
Dian's bud o'er Cupid's flower   70
Hath such force and blessèd power.
Now, my Titania; wake you, my sweet Queen!
TITANIA [*waking*]   My Oberon! What visions have I seen!
  Methought I was enamored of an ass.
OBERON   There lies your love.
TITANIA   How came these things to pass?   75
  O, how mine eyes do loathe his visage now!
OBERON   Silence awhile. Robin, take off this head.
  Titania, music call, and strike more dead
  Than common sleep of all these five the sense.
TITANIA   Music, ho! Music such as charmeth sleep!   80
    Music, still
PUCK [*to* BOTTOM]   Now, when thou wak'st, with thine own
  fool's eyes peep.
OBERON   Sound, music! Come, my Queen, take hands with
  me,
  And rock the ground whereon these sleepers be.
  Now thou and I are new in amity
  And will tomorrow midnight solemnly   85
  Dance in Duke Theseus' house triumphantly,
  And bless it to all fair prosperity.
  There shall the pairs of faithful lovers be
  Wedded, with Theseus, all in jollity.
PUCK   Fairy king, attend, and mark: 90
  I do hear the morning lark.
OBERON   Then, my queen, in silence sad,
  Trip we after the night's shade.
  We the globe can compass soon,
  Swifter than the wand'ring moon.   95
TITANIA   Come, my lord, and in our flight
  Tell me how it came this night
  That I sleeping here was found
  With these mortals on the ground.
                  Exeunt OBERON, TITANIA, *and* PUCK

---

70. **Dian's:** Diana was the Roman goddess of chastity (known as Artemis in Greek).
84. **amity:** friendship

Wind horns. Enter THESEUS, HIPPOLYTA, EGEUS, *and all his train*

THESEUS   Go, one of you, find out the forester,   100
For now our observation is performed,
And since we have the vaward of the day,
My love shall hear the music of my hounds.
Uncouple in the western valley: let them go.
Dispatch, I say, and find the forester.   105

Exit an Attendant

We will, fair queen, up to the mountain's top
And mark the musical confusion
Of hounds and echo in conjunction.
HIPPOLYTA   I was with Hercules and Cadmus once,
When in a wood of Crete they bayed the bear   110
With hounds of Sparta; never did I hear
Such gallant chiding, for, besides the groves,
The skies, the fountains, every region near
Seem all one mutual cry. I never heard
So musical a discord, such sweet thunder.   115
THESEUS   My hounds are bred out of the Spartan kind,
So flewed, so sanded, and their heads are hung
With ears that sweep away the morning dew,
Crook-kneed, and dew-lapped like Thessalian bulls,
Slow in pursuit, but matched in mouth like bells,   120
Each under each. A cry more tuneable
Was never halloed to, nor cheered with horn,
In Crete, in Sparta, nor in Thessaly.
Judge when you hear. But, soft! What nymphs are these?
EGEUS   My lord, this is my daughter here asleep,   125
And this, Lysander; this Demetrius is;
This Helena, old Nedar's Helena.
I wonder of their being here together.
THESEUS   No doubt they rose up early to observe
The rite of May, and hearing our intent,   130
Came here in grace our solemnity.
But speak, Egeus: is not this the day
That Hermia should give answer of her choice?
EGEUS   It is, my lord.

---

102. **vaward:** beginning
104. **Uncouple:** i.e., unleash the coupled dogs
109. **Hercules and Cadmus:** two ancient Greek heroes renowned for their prowess
116. **Spartan:** from the city of Sparta, Greece
117. **flewed:** i.e., having large chaps or jaws; **sanded:** sandy-colored
119. **Thessalian:** from Thessaly, Greece
122. **halloed:** called out
130. **rite of May:** celebration of May 1, May Day

THESEUS   Go, bid the huntsmen wake them with their horns.   135
    Horns and shout within. LYSANDER, DEMETRIUS, HELENA,
    and HERMIA *wake and start up*
  Good morrow, friends. Saint Valentine is past.
  Begin these wood-birds but to couple now?
LYSANDER   Pardon, my lord.
THESEUS   I pray you all, stand up.
  I know you two are rival enemies:
  How comes this gentle concord in the world,   140
  That hatred is so far from jealousy
  To sleep by hate, and fear no enmity?
LYSANDER   My lord, I shall reply amazedly,
  Half sleep, half waking. But as yet, I swear,
  I cannot truly say how I came here.   145
  But, as I think—for truly would I speak,
  And now do I bethink me, so it is—
  I came with Hermia hither. Our intent
  Was to be gone from Athens, where we might,
  Without the peril of the Athenian law—   150
EGEUS   Enough, enough, my lord; you have enough—
  I beg the law, the law, upon his head!
  They would have stolen away, they would, Demetrius,
  Thereby to have defeated you and me,
  You of your wife and me of my consent,   155
  Of my consent that she should be your wife.
DEMETRIUS   My lord, fair Helen told me of their stealth,
  Of this their purpose hither to this wood,
  And I in fury hither followed them,
  Fair Helena in fancy following me.   160
  But, my good lord, I wot not by what power—
  But by some power it is—my love to Hermia,
  Melted as the snow, seems to me now
  As the remembrance of an idle gaud
  Which in my childhood I did dote upon;   165
  And all the faith, the virtue of my heart,
  The object and the pleasure of mine eye,
  Is only Helena. To her, my lord,
  Was I betrothed ere I saw Hermia:
  But, like a sickness, did I loathe this food;   170
  But, as in health, come to my natural taste,
  Now I do wish it, love it, long for it,

136. **Saint Valentine:** i.e., St. Valentine's Day, February 14
137. **wood-birds:** birds of the woods
161. **wot:** know
164. **gaud:** bead or decorative item

And will for evermore be true to it.

THESEUS   Fair lovers, you are fortunately met.
Of this discourse we more will hear anon.   175
Egeus, I will overbear your will,
For in the temple by and by with us
These couples shall eternally be knit,
And, for the morning now is something worn,
Our purposed hunting shall be set aside.   180
Away with us to Athens: three and three,
We'll hold a feast in great solemnity.
Come, Hippolyta.

Exeunt THESEUS, HIPPOLYTA, EGEUS, *and train*

DEMETRIUS   These things seem small and undistinguishable,
Like far off mountains turned into clouds.   185

HERMIA   Methinks I see these things with parted eye,
When everything seems double.

HELENA   So methinks,
And I have found Demetrius like a jewel,
Mine own, and not mine own.

DEMETRIUS   Are you sure
That we are awake? It seems to me   190
That yet we sleep, we dream. Do not you think
The Duke was here, and bid us follow him?

HERMIA   Yea; and my father.

HELENA   And Hippolyta.

LYSANDER   And he did bid us follow to the temple.

DEMETRIUS   Why, then, we are awake. Let's follow him,   195
And by the way let us recount our dreams.

Exeunt all but BOTTOM

BOTTOM [*waking*]   When my cue comes, call me, and I will
answer. My next is, "Most fair Pyramus." Heigh-ho! Peter
Quince! Flute, the bellows-mender! Snout, the tinker! Starveling! God's my life, stolen hence, and left me asleep! I have had 200
a most rare vision. I have had a dream, past the wit of man to
say what dream it was. Man is but an ass if he go about to
expound this dream. Methought I was—there is no man can
tell what. Methought I was—and methought I had—but man is
but a patched fool, if he will offer to say what methought I had. 205
The eye of man hath not heard, the ear of man hath not seen,
man's hand is not able to taste, his tongue to conceive, nor his

---

205. **patched fool:** Professional fools wore clothing made up of patches.
206–208. **eye ... heart:** Bottom's errors in alluding to 1 Corinthians 2:9–10: "Eye hath
    not seen, nor ear heard, neither have entered into the heart of man, the things which
    God hath prepared for them that love him."

heart to report what my dream was. I will get Peter Quince to
write a ballad of this dream. It shall be called "Bottom's Dream,"
because it hath no bottom, and I will sing it in the latter end of   210
a play, before the Duke: peradventure, to make it the more gracious, I shall sing it at her death.   *Exit*

Act 4, Scene 2

Enter QUINCE, FLUTE, SNOUT, *and* STARVELING

QUINCE   Have you sent to Bottom's house? Is he come home
yet?

STARVELING   He cannot be heard of. Out of doubt, he is
transported.

FLUTE   If he come not, then the play is marred. It goes not   5
forward, doth it?

QUINCE   It is not possible. You have not a man in all Athens
able to discharge Pyramus but he.

FLUTE   No, he hath simply the best wit of any handicraft man
in Athens.   10

QUINCE   Yea and the best person too, and he is a very paramour for a sweet voice.

FLUTE   You must say "paragon." A paramour is, God bless us, a
thing of naught.

Enter SNUG, *the joiner*

SNUG   Masters, the Duke is coming from the temple, and   15
there is two or three lords and ladies more married. If our
sport had gone forward, we had all been made men.

FLUTE   O sweet bully Bottom! Thus hath he lost sixpence a
day during his life. He could not have 'scaped sixpence a day.
An the duke had not given him sixpence a day for playing   20
Pyramus, I'll be hanged. He would have deserved it: sixpence a day in Pyramus, or nothing.

Enter BOTTOM

BOTTOM   Where are these lads? Where are these hearts?

QUINCE   Bottom! O most courageous day! O most happy hour!

BOTTOM   Masters, I am to discourse wonders. But ask me not   25
what, for if I tell you, I am no true Athenian. I will tell you
everything, right as it fell out.

QUINCE   Let us hear, sweet Bottom.

---

211. **peradventure:** perhaps
4.2. Location: another part of the forest outside Athens
8.   **discharge:** act the role of
9.   **handicraft man:** craftsman

BOTTOM   Not a word of me. All that I will tell you is that the
duke hath dined. Get your apparel together, good strings to   30
your beards, new ribbons to your pumps. Meet presently at
the palace; every man look o'er his part, for the short and the
long is, our play is preferred. In any case, let Thisbe have
clean linen; and let not him that plays the lion pare his nails,
for they shall hang out for the lion's claws. And, most dear   35
actors, eat no onions nor garlic, for we are to utter sweet
breath, and I do not doubt but to hear them say it is a sweet
comedy. No more words. Away! Go, away!   *Exeunt*

Act 5, Scene 1

Enter THESEUS, HIPPOLYTA, PHILOSTRATE, *Lords and Attendants*
HIPPOLYTA   'Tis strange my Theseus, that these lovers speak of.
THESEUS   More strange than true. I never may believe
These antique fables, nor these fairy toys.
Lovers and madmen have such seething brains,
Such shaping fantasies, that apprehend   5
More than cool reason ever comprehends.
The lunatic, the lover and the poet
Are of imagination all compact;
One sees more devils than vast hell can hold:
That is the madman. The lover, all as frantic,   10
Sees Helen's beauty in a brow of Egypt.
The poet's eye, in fine frenzy rolling,
Doth glance from heaven to earth, from earth to heaven,
And as imagination bodies forth
The forms of things unknown, the poet's pen   15
Turns them to shapes and gives to airy nothing
A local habitation and a name.
Such tricks hath strong imagination
That if it would but apprehend some joy,
It comprehends some bringer of that joy,   20
Or in the night, imagining some fear,
How easy is a bush supposed a bear!
HIPPOLYTA   But all the story of the night told over,

30–31. **good strings to your beards:** i.e., ready your theatrical beards; **pumps:** shoes
33. **preferred:** i.e., going to be chosen
34. **linen:** i.e., undergarments
5.1. **Location:** Theseus' palace in Athens
3.   **antique:** antic, or crazy
8.   **compact:** compacted; i.e., made up of
11. **Helen:** Helen of Troy; **brow of Egypt:** i.e., a dark-skinned woman
17. **habitation:** i.e., form

And all their minds transfigured so together,
More witnesseth than fancy's images   25
And grows to something of great constancy,
But, howsoever, strange and admirable.
THESEUS   Here come the lovers, full of joy and mirth.
     Enter the Lovers, LYSANDER, DEMETRIUS, HERMIA, *and*
     HELENA
Joy, gentle friends! Joy and fresh days of love
Accompany your hearts!
LYSANDER   More than to us   30
Wait in your royal walks, your board, your bed!
THESEUS   Come now: what masques, what dances shall we
    have
To wear away this long age of three hours
Between our after-supper and bed-time?
Where is our usual manager of mirth?   35
What revels are in hand? Is there no play
To ease the anguish of a torturing hour?
Call Philostrate.
PHILOSTRATE   Here, mighty Theseus.
THESEUS   Say, what abridgement have you for this evening?
What masque? What music? How shall we beguile   40
The lazy time if not with some delight?
PHILOSTRATE   There is a brief how many sports are ripe:
Make choice of which your highness will see first.
    Giving him a paper
THESEUS [*reads*]   "The battle with the Centaurs, to be sung
By an Athenian eunuch to the harp."   45
We'll none of that; that have I told my love
In glory of my kinsman Hercules.
[*reads*]   "The riot of the tipsy Bacchanals,
Tearing the Thracian singer in their rage."
That is an old device, and it was played   50
When I from Thebes came last a conqueror.
[*reads*]   "The thrice three Muses mourning for the death
Of learning, late deceased in beggary."
That is some satire, keen and critical,

25. **fancy's:** love's
32. **masques:** courtly entertainments
39. **abridgement:** i.e., short play
42. **brief:** list
44. **Centaurs:** half-horse, half-human mythological creatures
47. **Hercules:** Greek warrior
48–49. **tipsy . . . rage:** According to Ovid, the Thracian poet Orpheus was torn to pieces
    by drunken female followers of Bacchus, the Roman god of wine.
50. **device:** i.e., play
52. **thrice three Muses:** the nine goddesses who inspire literature, science, and the arts

Not sorting with a nuptial ceremony.   55
[*reads*]   "A tedious brief scene of young Pyramus
And his love Thisbe, very tragical mirth."
Merry and tragical? Tedious and brief?
That is hot ice and wondrous strange snow.
How shall we find the concord of this discord?   60
PHILOSTRATE   A play there is, my lord, some ten words long,
  Which is as brief as I have known a play.
  But by ten words, my lord, it is too long,
  Which makes it tedious, for in all the play
  There is not one word apt, one player fitted.   65
  And "tragical," my noble lord, it is,
  For Pyramus therein doth kill himself,
  Which, when I saw rehearsed, I must confess,
  Made mine eyes water, but more merry tears
  The passion of loud laughter never shed.   70
THESEUS   What are they that do play it?
PHILOSTRATE   Hard-handed men that work in Athens here,
  Which never labored in their minds till now,
  And now have toiled their unbreathed memories
  With this same play against your nuptial.   75
THESEUS   And we will hear it.
PHILOSTRATE   No, my noble lord,
  It is not for you. I have heard it over,
  And it is nothing, nothing in the world,
  Unless you can find sport in their intents,
  Extremely stretched and conned with cruel pain,   80
  To do you service.
THESEUS   I will hear that play;
  For never anything can be amiss
  When simpleness and duty tender it.
  Go, bring them in, and take your places, ladies.

                           Exit PHILOSTRATE
HIPPOLYTA   I love not to see wretchedness o'ercharged   85
  And duty in his service perishing.
THESEUS   Why, gentle sweet, you shall see no such thing.
HIPPOLYTA   He says they can do nothing in this kind.
THESEUS   The kinder we, to give them thanks for nothing.
  Our sport shall be to take what they mistake,   90
  And what poor duty cannot do, noble respect
  Takes it in might, not merit.
  Where I have come, great clerks have purposed

---

72. **Hard-handed men:** i.e., men who work with their hands
80. **conned:** written

To greet me with premeditated welcomes,
Where I have seen them shiver and look pale,   95
Make periods in the midst of sentences,
Throttle their practiced accent in their fears
And in conclusion dumbly have broke off,
Not paying me a welcome. Trust me, sweet,
Out of this silence yet I picked a welcome,   100
And in the modesty of fearful duty
I read as much as from the rattling tongue
Of saucy and audacious eloquence.
Love, therefore, and tongue-tied simplicity
In least speak most, to my capacity.   105
   Enter PHILOSTRATE
PHILOSTRATE So please your grace, the Prologue is
  addressed.
THESEUS Let him approach.
   Flourish of trumpets. Enter QUINCE *as the Prologue*
QUINCE [*as Prologue*] If we offend, it is with our good will.
  That you should think, we come not to offend,
But with good will. To show our simple skill,   110
  That is the true beginning of our end.
Consider then we come but in despite.
  We do not come as minding to content you,
Our true intent is. All for your delight
  We are not here. That you should here repent you,   115
The actors are at hand and by their show
You shall know all that you are like to know.
THESEUS This fellow doth not stand upon points.
LYSANDER He hath rid his prologue like a rough colt; he
  knows not the stop. A good moral, my lord: it is not enough   120
  to speak, but to speak true.
HIPPOLYTA Indeed he hath played on his prologue like a child
  on a recorder—a sound, but not in government.
THESEUS His speech, was like a tangled chain, nothing
  impaired, but all disordered. Who is next?   125
   A Trumpeter before them. Enter BOTTOM *as* PYRAMUS,
   FLUTE *as* THISBE, SNOUT *as* WALL, STARVELING *as* MOON-
   SHINE, *and* SNUG *as* LION
QUINCE [*as Prologue*] Gentles, perchance you wonder at this
  show,
  But wonder on, till truth make all things plain.

---

118. **stand upon points:** i.e., use punctuation
119. **hath rid:** rode

This man is Pyramus, if you would know;
  This beauteous lady Thisbe is certain.
This man, with lime and rough-cast, doth present   130
  Wall, that vile Wall which did these lovers sunder,
And through Wall's chink, poor souls, they are content
  To whisper. At the which let no man wonder.
This man, with lanthorn, dog, and bush of thorn,
  Presenteth Moonshine; for, if you will know,   135
By moonshine did these lovers think no scorn
  To meet at Ninus' tomb, there, there to woo.
This grisly beast, which Lion hight by name,
  The trusty Thisbe, coming first by night,
Did scare away, or rather did affright,   140
And, as she fled, her mantle she did fall,
  Which Lion vile with bloody mouth did stain.
Anon comes Pyramus, sweet youth and tall,
  And finds his trusty Thisbe's mantle slain,
Whereat, with blade, with bloody blameful blade,   145
  He bravely broached is boiling bloody breast,
And Thisbe, tarrying in mulberry shade,
  His dagger drew, and died. For all the rest,
Let Lion, Moonshine, Wall, and lovers twain
At large discourse, while here they do remain.   150
     Exeunt QUINCE, BOTTOM, FLUTE, SNUG *and* STARVELING
THESEUS   I wonder if the lion be to speak.
DEMETRIUS   No wonder, my lord; one lion may, when many
    asses do.
SNOUT [*as Wall*]   In this same interlude it doth befall
  That I, one Snout by name, present a wall,
  And such a wall, as I would have you think   155
  That had in it a crannied hole or chink,
  Through which the lovers, Pyramus and Thisbe,
  Did whisper often very secretly.
  This loam, this rough-cast and this stone doth show
  That I am that same wall. The truth is so,   160
  And this the cranny is, right and sinister,
  Through which the fearful lovers are to whisper.

---

131. **sunder:** separate
134. **lanthorn:** lantern
137. **Ninus':** Ninus was the founder of Nineveh, capital of ancient Syria.
143. **Anon:** immediately
144. **mantle:** sleeveless cloak
149. **twain:** two
153. **interlude:** short comic entertainment usually shown between the acts of a play
159. **loam:** a mixture of clay and sand used for bricks and other building; **rough-cast:**
    plastering material composed of lime, water, and gravel

THESEUS   Would you desire lime and hair to speak better?
DEMETRIUS   It is the wittiest partition that ever I heard
    discourse, my lord.   165
    Enter BOTTOM *as Pyramus*
THESEUS   Pyramus draws near the wall: silence!
BOTTOM [*as Pyramus*]   O grim-looked night! O night with hue
    so black!
  O night, whichever art when day is not!
  O night, O night! Alack, alack, alack,
  I fear my Thisbe's promise is forgot!   170
  And thou, O wall, O sweet, O lovely wall,
  That stand'st between her father's ground and mine!
  Thou wall, O wall, O sweet and lovely wall,
  Show me thy chink, to blink through with mine eyne!
        SNOUT *as Wall holds up his fingers*
  Thanks, courteous wall. Jove shield thee well for this!   175
  But what see I? No Thisbe do I see.
  O wicked wall, through whom I see no bliss!
  Cursed be thy stones for thus deceiving me!
THESEUS   The wall, methinks, being sensible, should curse
    again.
PYRAMUS [*to* THESEUS]   No, in truth, sir, he should not.   180
  "Deceiving me" is Thisbe's cue: she is to enter now, and
  I am to spy her through the wall. You shall see, it will fall
  pat as I told you. Yonder she comes.
        Enter FLUTE *as Thisbe*
FLUTE [*as Thisbe*]   O wall, full often hast thou heard my moans,
    For parting my fair Pyramus and me!   185
  My cherry lips have often kissed thy stones,
    Thy stones with lime and hair knit up in thee.
BOTTOM [*as Pyramus*]   I see a voice! Now will I to the chink,
  To spy an I can hear my Thisbe's face. Thisbe?
FLUTE [*as Thisbe*]   My love thou art, my love I think.   190
BOTTOM [*as Pyramus*]   Think what thou wilt, I am thy lover's
    grace,
  And, like Limander, am I trusty still.
FLUTE [*as Thisbe*]   And I like Helen, till the Fates me kill.
BOTTOM [*as Pyramus*]   Not Shafalus to Procrus was so true.

163, 187. **lime and hair:** ingredients in a type of plasterer's cement
174. **eyne:** eye
175. **Jove:** Greek name for Jupiter, god of thunder and king of the gods
183. **pat:** ready
192. **Limander:** Bottom's error for Leander, the Greek lover of Hero
193. **Helen:** Helen of Troy, originally a Greek, was considered the world's most beautiful
    woman, and her kidnapping by the Trojans began the Trojan war with Greece;
    Fates: three mythological goddesses who controlled human destiny

FLUTE [*as Thisbe*]   As Shafalus to Procrus, I to you.   195
BOTTOM [*as Pyramus*]   O kiss me through the hole of this vile
    wall!
FLUTE [*as Thisbe*]   I kiss the wall's hole, not your lips at all.
BOTTOM [*as Pyramus*]   Wilt thou at Ninny's tomb meet me
    straightway?
FLUTE [*as Thisbe*]   'Tide life, 'tide death, I come without
    delay.   *Exeunt* PYRAMUS *and* THISBE
SNOUT [*as Wall*]   Thus have I, Wall, my part dischargèd so,   200
    And, being done, thus Wall away doth go.   *Exit*
THESEUS   Now is the mural down between the two neighbors.
DEMETRIUS   No remedy, my lord, when walls are so wilful to
    hear without warning.
HIPPOLYTA   This is the silliest stuff that ever I heard.   205
THESEUS   The best in this kind are but shadows, and the
    worst are no worse if imagination amend them.
HIPPOLYTA   It must be your imagination then, and not theirs.
THESEUS   If we imagine no worse of them than they of
    themselves, they may pass for excellent men. Here come   210
    two noble beasts in, a man and a lion.
            Enter SNUG *as Lion and* STARVELING *as Moonshine*
SNUG [*as Lion*]   You, ladies, you, whose gentle hearts do fear
    The smallest monstrous mouse that creeps on floor,
    May now perchance both quake and tremble here,
        When lion rough in wildest rage doth roar.   215
    Then know that I, one Snug the joiner, am
    A lion-fell, nor else no lion's dam,
    For, if I should as lion come in strife
    Into this place, 'twere pity on my life.
THESEUS   A very gentle beast, of a good conscience.   220
DEMETRIUS   The very best at a beast, my lord, that e'er I saw.
LYSANDER   This lion is a very fox for his valor.
THESEUS   True, and a goose for his discretion.
DEMETRIUS   Not so, my lord, for his valor cannot carry his
    discretion, and the fox carries the goose.   225
THESEUS   His discretion, I am sure, cannot carry his valor,
    for the goose carries not the fox. It is well; leave it to his
    discretion, and let us listen to the moon.
STARVELING [*as Moonshine*]   This lanthorn doth the hornèd
    moon present—

---

195. **Shafalus to Procrus:** error for Cephalus, who accidentally killed his wife Procris in
    Greek myth
202. **mural:** wall
217. **lion-fell:** fierce lion; **dam:** mother
229. **hornèd:** crescent

DEMETRIUS   He should have worn the horns on his head.   230

THESEUS   He is no crescent, and his horns are invisible
within the circumference.

STARVELING [*as Moonshine*]   This lanthorn doth the hornèd
moon present;
Myself the man i'th'moon do seem to be.

THESEUS   This is the greatest error of all the rest: the man   235
should be put into the lanthorn. How is it else the man
i'th'moon?

DEMETRIUS   He dares not come there for the candle, for, you
see, it is already in snuff.

HIPPOLYTA   I am aweary of this moon. Would he would   240
change!

THESEUS   It appears, by his small light of discretion, that he
is in the wane, but yet, in courtesy, in all reason, we must
stay the time.

LYSANDER   Proceed, Moon.   245

STARVELING [*as Moonshine, to* LYSANDER]   All that I have to
say, is, to tell you that the lanthorn is the moon, I, the man
in the moon, this thorn-bush, my thorn-bush, and this dog,
my dog.

DEMETRIUS   Why, all these should be in the lanthorn, for all   250
these are in the moon. But, silence! Here comes Thisbe.

    Enter FLUTE *as Thisbe*

FLUTE [*as Thisbe*]   This is old Ninny's tomb. Where is my
love?

SNUG [*as Lion, roaring*]   Oh—*Thisbe runs off*

DEMETRIUS   Well roared, Lion!

THESEUS   Well run, Thisbe!   255

HIPPOLYTA   Well shone, Moon! Truly, the moon shines with a
good grace.

    The Lion shakes Thisbe's mantle, and exit

THESEUS   Well moused, Lion.

DEMETRIUS   And then came Pyramus.

LYSANDER   And so the Lion vanished.   260

    Enter BOTTOM *as Pyramus*

BOTTOM [*as Pyramus*]   Sweet Moon, I thank thee for thy
sunny beams;
I thank thee, Moon, for shining now so bright;
For, by thy gracious, golden, glittering beams,
I trust to take of truest Thisby's sight.
But stay—O spite!   265
But mark, poor knight,

---

230. horns . . . head: i.e., to show he was cuckolded

What dreadful dole is here!
    Eyes, do you see?
    How can it be?
O dainty duck! O dear!   270
    Thy mantle good,
    What, stained with blood!
Approach, ye Furies fell!
    O Fates, come, come,
    Cut thread and thrum,   275
Quail, crush, conclude, and quell!

THESEUS   This passion, and the death of a dear friend, would
go near to make a man look sad.

HIPPOLYTA   Beshrew my heart, but I pity the man.

BOTTOM [as Pyramus]   O wherefore, Nature, didst thou lions   280
    frame?
    Since lion vile hath here deflowered my dear,
Which is—no, no—which was the fairest dame
    That lived, that loved, that liked, that looked with cheer.
    Come, tears, confound;
    Out, sword, and wound   285
The pap of Pyramus;
    Ay, that left pap,
    Where heart doth hop.   *Stabs himself*
Thus die I, thus, thus, thus.
    Now am I dead,   290
    Now am I fled;
My soul is in the sky.
    Tongue, lose thy light;
    Moon take thy flight: *Exit* MOONSHINE
Now die, die, die, die, die.   *Dies*   295

DEMETRIUS   No die, but an ace, for him, for he is but one.

LYSANDER   Less than an ace, man, for he is dead; he is
nothing.

THESEUS   With the help of a surgeon he might yet recover,
and yet prove an ass.   300

HIPPOLYTA   How chance Moonshine is gone before Thisbe
comes back and finds her lover?

---

267. **dole:** disorder
273. **Furies:** in Greek mythology, the female figures of vengeance
275. **thread and thrum:** i.e., good and bad together
276. **Quail:** overpower; **quell:** kill
279. **Beshrew:** curse
281. **deflowered:** disfigured, with unintended pun on "having taken the virginity of"
286. **pap:** breast
296. **die:** single dice; **ace:** one point on the die

THESEUS   She will find him by starlight. Here she comes, and
   her passion ends the play.
     Enter FLUTE *as* Thisbe
HIPPOLYTA   Methinks she should not use a long one for such   305
   a Pyramus. I hope she will be brief.
DEMETRIUS   A mote will turn the balance, which Pyramus,
   which Thisbe, is the better; he for a man, God warrant us;
   she for a woman, God bless us.
LYSANDER   She hath spied him already with those sweet eyes.   310
DEMETRIUS   And thus she means, videlicet—
FLUTE [*as Thisbe*]   Asleep, my love?
   What, dead, my dove?
  O Pyramus, arise!
    Speak, speak. Quite dumb?   315
    Dead, dead? A tomb
  Must cover thy sweet eyes.
  These lily lips,
  This cherry nose,
  These yellow cowslip cheeks,   320
    Are gone, are gone.
    Lovers, make moan:
  His eyes were green as leeks.
    O sisters three,
    Come, come to me,   325
  With hands as pale as milk;
    Lay them in gore,
    Since you have shore
  With shears his thread of silk.
    Tongue, not a word!   330
    Come, trusty sword!
  Come, blade, my breast imbrue!   *Stabs herself*
    And, farewell, friends.
    Thus Thisbe ends—
  Adieu, adieu, adieu.   *Dies*   335
THESEUS   Moonshine and Lion are left to bury the dead.
DEMETRIUS   Ay, and Wall too.
BOTTOM [*starting up*]   No, I assure you, the wall is down
   that parted their fathers. Will it please you to see the
   epilogue, or to hear a Bergomask dance between two of our   340
   company?

311. **videlicet:** that is to say
315. **dumb:** mute
320. **cowslip:** primula flower
328. **shore:** shorn
332. **imbrue:** defile; i.e., stab
340. **Bergomask:** a rustic and clownish dance originating in Bergamo, Italy

THESEUS   No epilogue, I pray you, for your play needs no
    excuse. Never excuse; for when the players are all dead, there
    needs none to be blamed. Marry, if he that writ it had played
    Pyramus and hanged himself in Thisbe's garter, it would   345
    have been a fine tragedy, and so it is, truly, and very notably
    discharged. But come, your Bergomask; let your epilogue
    alone.
        A dance
    The iron tongue of midnight hath tolled twelve:
    Lovers, to bed; 'tis almost fairy time.   350
    I fear we shall out-sleep the coming morn
    As much as we this night have overwatched.
    This palpable-gross play hath well beguiled
    The heavy gait of night. Sweet friends, to bed.
    A fortnight hold we this solemnity,   355
    In nightly revels and new jollity.   *Exeunt*
        Enter PUCK, *holding a broom*
PUCK   Now the hungry lion roars,
        And the wolf behowls the moon,
    Whilst the heavy plowman snores,
        All with weary task fordone.   360
    Now the wasted brands do glow,
        Whilst the screech-owl, screeching loud,
    Puts the wretch that lies in woe
        In remembrance of a shroud.
    Now it is the time of night   365
        That the graves, all gaping wide,
    Every one lets forth his sprite,
        In the church-way paths to glide,
    And we fairies, that do run
        By the triple Hecate's team,   370
    From the presence of the sun,
        Following darkness like a dream,
    Now are frolic; not a mouse
    Shall disturb this hallowed house.
    I am sent with broom before,   375
    To sweep the dust behind the door.
        Enter OBERON *and* TITANIA, *King and Queen of the Fairies,*
        with all their train
OBERON   Through the house give glimmering light,
        By the dead and drowsy fire.

353. **palpable-gross:** i.e., amateurish
360. **fordone:** exhausted
361. **wasted brands:** dying fires
370. **Hecate:** in mythology, the Greek goddess of witchcraft and magic

Every elf and fairy sprite
   Hop as light as bird from briar,   380
And this ditty, after me,
Sing, and dance it trippingly.
TITANIA   First, rehearse your song by rote
   To each word a warbling note.
Hand in hand, with fairy grace,   385
Will we sing, and bless this place.
    Song and dance
OBERON   Now, until the break of day,
   Through this house each fairy stray.
To the best bride-bed will we,
Which by us shall blessèd be,   390
And the issue there create
Ever shall be fortunate.
So shall all the couples three
Ever true in loving be,
And the blots of Nature's hand   395
Shall not in their issue stand.
Never mole, hare-lip, nor scar,
Nor mark prodigious, such as are
Despised in nativity,
Shall upon their children be.   400
With this field-dew consecrate,
Every fairy take his gait,
And each several chamber bless,
Through this palace, with sweet peace,
And the owner of it blest   405
Ever shall in safety rest.
Trip away; make no stay;
Meet me all by break of day.
    Exeunt OBERON, TITANIA, *and train*
PUCK   If we shadows have offended,
   Think but this, and all is mended: 410
That you have but slumbered here
While these visions did appear.
And this weak and idle theme,
No more yielding but a dream.
Gentles, do not reprehend: 415
If you pardon, we will mend.
And, as I am an honest Puck,
If we have unearnèd luck
Now to 'scape the serpent's tongue,

---

419. 'scape . . . tongue: escape the audience's hissing (hence the serpent's tongue)

We will make amends ere long,   420
Else the Puck a liar call.
So, good night unto you all.
Give me your hands, if we be friends,
And Robin shall restore amends.   *Exit*

423: Give . . . hands: i.e., applaud for me

A Note on the Text

The play was entered in the Stationers' Register on October 8, 1600, and first printed that year, probably by Richard Braddock,[1] for Thomas Fisher. Its Quarto 1 title page states, "A Midsommer nights dreame. As it hath been sundry times publickely acted, by the Right honourable, the Lord Chamberlaine his seruants. Written by William Shakespeare" (see Figure 1, p. xii). The copy used by the compositors to set the type of this edition was almost certainly Shakespeare's foul papers (or first draft) of the play, showing marginal and probably interlinear revisions that he made during or immediately after composition, most noticeably in Theseus's early speeches in Act 5, Scene 1. This text also shows the characteristic spellings and spare stage directions seen in other Shakespearean texts printed from foul papers.

This Quarto was reprinted in 1619 by William Jaggard for Thomas Pavier with a false date of 1600. Pavier also reprinted Quartos of other plays, possibly to put them together in the first collected edition, later abandoned, of Shakespeare's works. This second edition appears to derive no authority from Shakespeare or his company or the printers of Quarto 1, who would still have owned the rights to printing the play. John Heminges and Henry Condell, Shakespeare's former colleagues in the King's Men, assembled a variety of sources, including foul papers, authorial and scribal fair copies and printed Quartos annotated against theatrical manuscripts, for Isaac Jaggard and Edward Blount, who printed the 1623 First Folio edition, which began to be typeset in 1622. In the case of *A Midsummer Night's Dream*, Heminges and Condell apparently sent the printers a copy of the unauthorized Quarto 2 that had been annotated or corrected with a theatrical manuscript of the play, probably incorporating later revisions and corrections by Shakespeare. In terms of reading the text and "casting-off" their copy (i.e., estimating its length in print), the Folio compositors would have found it much easier to print their text from a printed, rather than entirely handwritten manuscript, copy.

---

1. See Robert K. Turner, Jr., "Printing Methods and Textual Problems in *A Midsummer Night's Dream Q1*," *Studies in Bibliography* 15 (1962): 33. Also see W. W. Greg, *The Shakespeare First Folio: Its Bibliographical and Textual History* (Oxford: Clarendon P, 1955), pp. 240ff.

The substantive variants between the Quarto 1 and First Folio texts are sometimes minor but show a slight streamlining on occasion of the later text, for example in the substitution of Egeus for Philostrate in Act 5, Scene 1. However, the Folio text also offers more detailed stage directions, probably reflecting the play's later staging after 1609 at the private Blackfriars playhouse, which often attracted a more sophisticated audience than at the Globe. Due to the fact that the Folio was largely printed from the unauthorized Quarto 2, which introduces numerous errors into the text, the copy-text for this Norton Critical Edition is the Quarto 1 text. However, some First Folio variants that appear to result from revision or correction are interpolated into this edition, and thus this is what textual scholars would term a "conflated edition."

The Textual Variants below record substantive but not incidental or accidental variants between Quarto 1 and the Folio text. This edition does not reproduce the heavy use of parentheses in the Folio and has not recorded the many differences in lineation between the texts. The lineation of Quarto 1 has been silently corrected when necessary. For the ease of reading, this edition does not use square brackets for expansions or corrections to stage directions or speech prefixes; instead the Textual Variants record these expansions and corrections. For further discussion of the play's textual transmission, see the Introduction.

Textual Variants

Q = Quarto 1: *A Midsommer nights dreame* (Thomas Fisher, 1600)
F = First Folio: *Mr. William Shakespeares Comedies, Histories, &*
Tragedies (Isaac Jaggard and Edward Blount, 1623)
Capell = *Comedies, Histories and Tragedies*, edited by Edward
Cappell, 10 volumes (1767–68)
Dyce = *Works*, edited by Alexander Dyce (1857)

1.1.

1.1.0 SP] *This edition; not in Q1, F*
1.1.10 New-bent] Now bent *F*
1.1.19] SD] *F; and Lysander and Helena, and Demetrius Q1*
1.1.24 Stand forth, Demetrius] SD *in Q1, F*
1.1.26 Stand forth, Lysander] SD *in Q1, F*
1.1.127 SD *Exeunt . . .* HERMIA] *F* (*Manet Lysander and*
Hermia); *not in Q1*
1.1.132 Ay me] *not in F*
1.1.139 friends] merit *F*
1.1.140 eyes] eie *F*
1.1.143 momentary] *F;* momentany *Q1*
1.1.159 remote] remou'd *F*
1.1.216 sweet] *This edition;* sweld *Q1, F*
1.1.232 vile] vilde *F*
1.1.239 so oft] often *F*

1.2.

1.2.0 SD *and* SNUG] Snug *F;* [*and* BOTTOM] Bottom *F;* [*and*
FLUTE] Flute *F; and* SNOUT] Snout *F*
1.2.62 And] If *F*

2.1.

2.1.0 SP] Robin *Q1, F, throughout the text*
2.1.3 thorough . . . thorough] through bush, through *F*
2.1.55 laugh] *This edition;* loffe *Q1, F*
2.1.61 SP] *This edition;* Queen *Q1, F, throughout the scene*
2.1.79 Aegle] Eagles *Q1, F*
2.1.144 SD TITANIA . . . *train*] *This edition; not in Q1, F*

2.1.158 the west] *F*; west *Q1*
2.1.175 round] *F*; not in *Q1*
2.1.242 SD] *This edition; not in Q1, F*
2.1.244 SD] *F; not in Q1*
2.1.246 SD] *at line 245 in Q1, F*

2.2.

2.2.0 SD TITANIA] *not in F*
2.2.9 SP] Capell; *not in Q1, F*
2.2.13 SP] Capell; *not in Q1, F*
2.2.14 our] your *F*
2.2.20 FIRST FAIRY] *Q1* (1. *Fai.*); 2. *Fairy. F*
2.2.24–30 CHORUS . . . Lullaby] Capell; *not in Q1, F*, but
    signalled by "etc" (& *c.*) at 24).
2.2.24 melody] Capell; *melody, & c. Q1, F*
2.2.31 SECOND FAIRY] *Q1* (2. *Fai.*); 1. *Fairy. F*
2.2.32 SD *Exeunt . . . sleeps*] *She sleepes. F; not in Q1*; [*They
    sleep*] *F* (*after* Enter PUCK); *not in Q1*
2.2.40 SD] *This edition; not in Q1, F*
2.2.93 SD] *F; not in Q1*
2.2.151 SD] *This edition; not in Q1, F*

3.1.

3.1.0 SD] *This edition; Enter the Clownes Q1, F*
3.1.2 marvelous] *F* (marvailous); maruailes *Q1*
3.1.26 yourselves] *F*; your selfe *Q1*
3.1.45 *Enter Pucke. F*
3.1.47 SP] *F; Cet. Q1*
3.1.51 lanthorn] *F*; lantern *Q1*
3.1.63 SD] *This edition; Robin Q1, F*
3.1.69 SP] *This edition; Pyra. Q1, F throughout the scene*
3.1.70 Odours, odours] *F*; odours, odourous *Q1*
3.1.74 SD] *Exit Pir. F*
3.1.75 SP] PUCK *F*, Quin. *Q1*; [SD] *This edition; not in Q1, F*
3.1.76 SP] *This edition; Thys. Q1, F, throughout the scene*
3.1.77, 84 SP] *This edition; Peter F*
3.1.88 SD *Enter . . . on*] *Enter Piramus with the Asse head F, at
    l. 74; not in Q1*
3.1.91 SD] *The Clownes all Exit F; not in Q1*
3.1.107 SD *Exit* SNOUT] *Exit F; not in Q1*; [SD *Enter Quince*]
    Enter Peter Quince, *F*
3.1.108 SD] *This edition; not in Q1, F*
3.1.108 ousel] *This edition; Woosell Q1, F*
3.1.112 SD] *This edition; not in Q1, F*
3.1.113 SD] *This edition; not in Q1, F*

3.1.124 On the] *not in F*

3.1.143 SD] *F*; *Pease-blossom, Cobweb, Moth, and Mustard-seed? Enter Foure Fairyes Q1*

3.1.144–48 PEASEBLOSSOM . . . go] *This edition*; *Fairies. Readie . . . goe? Q1, F, on one line*

3.1.160–63] Capell, Dyce; 1. Fai. Haile mortall, haile. / 2. Fai. Haile. / 3. Fai. Haile *Q1, F*

3.1.176] *Peas. Pease-blossome F (repeated from line 170)*

3.2.

3.2.0 SD] *Enter King of Fairies solus F*; *Enter King of Fairies, and* Robin goodfellow

3.2.3 SD] *F*; *at 3.2.0 in Q1*

3.2.40 SD] *Enter* Demetrius *and* Hermia *Q1, F*

3.2.87 SD Lies . . . sleeps] *This edition*; *Ly downe Q1, F*

3.2.88 SD] *This edition*; *not in Q1, F*

3.2.101 SD] *F*; *not in Q1*

3.2.102 SD] *This edition*; *not in Q1, F*

3.2.137 SD] *Awa. F, at end of l. 136*; *not in Q1*

3.2.173 Helen] *not in F*

3.2.175 aby] abide *F*

3.2.189 SD] *This edition*; *not in Q1, F*

3.2.220 passionate] *F*; *not in Q1*

3.2.247 SD] *This edition*; *not in Q1 or F*

3.2.282 SD] *This edition*; *not in Q1 or F*

3.2.335 aby] abide *F*

3.2.338 SD] *F*; *not in Q1*

3.2.343, 344 SD] Exeunt *Q1, at 344*; *not in F*

3.2.344 SD] Enter Oberon and Pucke *F*; *not in Q1*

3.2.395 SD] *This edition*; *not in Q1, F*

3.2.412 SD] Exit *F*; *not in Q1*; [SD] *F*; *not in Q1*

3.2.416] *F* has *shifting places* in the right margin, anticipating dialogue in l. 423

3.2.418 SD] *F*; *not in Q1*

3.2.420 SD] *This edition*; *not in F, Q1*

3.2.430 SD] *This edition*; *not in F, Q1*

3.2.436 SD] *This edition*; *Sleepe. F*; *not in Q1*

3.2.441 SD] *F*; *not in Q1, F*

3.2.447 SD] *This edition*; *not in Q1, F*

3.2.452 SD] *This edition*; *not in Q1*

3.2.463 SD] *This edition*; *They . . . Act] F* They sleep all the Act; *not in Q1*

4.1.

4.1] *Actus Quartus. F*; *not in Q1*

4.1.0 SD] *Enter Queen of Faieries, and Clowne, and Faieries,*
    and the king behinde them Q1, F

4.1.5 SP] *This edition; Clowne Q1, F, throughout scene*

4.1.27 SD *Music . . . music] F; not in Q1*

4.1.38 SD] *This edition; not in Q1, F*

4.1.42 SD] *Enter Robin goodfellow Q1; Enter Oberon and Puck F*

4.1.43 SD] *This edition; not in Q1, F*

4.1.68 SD] *This edition; not in Q1, F*

4.1.73 SD] *This edition; not in Q1, F*

4.1.79 five] Theobald; *Fine Q1, F*

4.1.80 SD] *F; not in Q1*

4.1.81 SD] *This edition; not in Q1, F*

4.1.98 found] Followed in *F* by *Sleepers Lye still*

4.1.99 SD *Exeunt . . . PUCK] Exeunt. Q1, F; SD Wind . . . train]*
    Wind horne [hornes F] / Enter Theseus and all his traine Q1, F

4.1.105 SD] *This edition; not in Q1, F*

4.1.122 halloed] *This edition; hallowd Q1; hallowed F*

4.1.135 SD] *Shoute within; they all start vp, Winde hornes. Q1;*
    Hornes and they wake. / Shout within, they all start vp. F

4.1.149 might] might be *F*

4.1.160 following] followed *F*

4.1.169 saw] *This edition; see Q1, F*

4.1.183 SD] *Exit Duke and Lords F; not in Q1*

4.1.189–190 Are . . . awake] *not in F*

4.1.196 *Exeunt all but* BOTTOM] *This edition; Exit Lovers, F; not*
    in Q1

4.1.197 SD] *This edition; not in Q1, F*

4.1.200 have] *not in F*

4.1.212 *Exit] F; not in Q1*

4.2.

4.2.] *This edition; not in Q1, F*

4.2.0 SD] *This edition; Enter Quince, Flute, Thisbie, Snout, and*
    Starveling, F; Enter Quince, Flute, Thisby and the rabble. Q1

4.2.3 SP] *Thysby, Q1, F, throughout scene*

4.2.38 SD *Exeunt] F; not in Q1*

5.1.

5.1] *Actus Quintus, F; not in Q1*

5.1.0 SD *Enter . . . Attendants] This edition; Enter Theseus,*
    Hyppolita, and Philostrate. Q1; Enter Theseus, Hippolita,
    Egeus and his Lords. F

5.1.5–8. Such . . . compact] *F; Such . . . more / Then . . .*
    lunatick / The . . . compact *Q1*

5.1.12–18 The . . . imagination] *This edition*; The . . . glance /
From . . . as / Imagination . . . things / Vnknowne . . .
shapes / And . . . habitation /And . . . imagination *Q1*;
The . . . glance / From . . . heauen / And . . . things /
Vnknowne . . . shapes / And . . . imagination *F*

5.1.28 SD] *This edition*; Enter Louers *Q1, F* (one line earlier)

5.1.38 Philostrate] *Q1*; Egeus *F*; SP PHILOSTRATE] *Q1*; Ege. *F*,
throughout the scene

5.1.43 SD] *This edition*; *not in Q1, F*

5.1.44, 48, 52, 56 SP THESEUS] *F*; *Lisander Q1*

5.1.44, 48, 52, 56 SD] *This edition*; *not in Q1, F*

5.1.84 SD] *This edition*; *not in Q1, F*

5.1.105 SD] *This edition*; *not in Q1, F*

5.1.107 SD *Flourish of trumpets . . . Prologue*] *F* (Flor. Trum. /
Enter the Prologue Quince); *Enter the Prologue. Q1*

5.1.108 SP QUINCE] *This edition*; Prologue *Q1, F*

5.1.125 SD *A . . . them*] *Tawyer with a Trumpet before them, F*;
not in Q1

5.1.125. Enter . . . MOONSHINE] *Enter* Pyramus, *and* Thisby,
and Wall, *and* Mooneshine, *and* Lyon *Q1*; *Enter* Pyramus
and Thisby, Wall, Moone-shine, *and* Lyon *F*

5.1.134 lanthorn] *F*; lanterne *Q1*

5.1.150 SD] *Exit* Lyon, Thysby, *and* Mooneshine *Q1*; *Exit all
but Wall F*, with *Exit Lyon Thisbie, and Mooneshine* at l.
150

5.1.165 SP] *Enter Pyramus. F* at l. 166; *not in Q1*

5.1.174 SD] *This edition*; *not in Q1, F*

5.1.180 SD] *This edition*; *not in Q1, F*

5.1.183 SD] *Enter Thisbie. Q1*, at l. 178 in *F*

5.1.187 in thee.] *F*; now againe

5.1.199 SD *Exeunt . . . THISBE*] *This edition*; *Not in Q1, F*

5.1.201 *Exit*] Exit Clowne *F*; *not in Q1, F*

5.1.202 SP] *This edition*; *Du. Q1, F, throughout the rest of the
scene*

5.1.202 mural down] *F* (morall downe); Moon vsed *Q1*

5.1.205 SP] *This edition*; *Dut. Q1, F*; ever] ere *F*

5.1.211 SD] *Enter* Lyon *and* Moon-shine. *Q1, F*

5.1.246 SD] *This edition*; *not in Q1, F*

5.1.252 SD] *Enter Thisby. Q1, F*

5.1.253 SD] *Lyon. Oh. The Lion roares, Thisby runs off. F*;
Lion, Oh. Q1 (at end of previous line)

5.1.257 SD] *This edition*; *not in Q1, F*

5.1.260 SD] *Enter Pyramus. Q1, F*

5.1.264 Thisby's] *F*; Thisby *Q1*

5.1.280 SD] *This edition; not in Q1, F*
5.1.288 SD] *This edition; not in Q1, F*
5.1.300 yet prove] *Q1*; prove *F*
5.1.304 SD] *Enter Thisby* on l. 303 *in F; not in Q1*
5.1.307 mote] *This edition*; moth *Q1, F*
5.1.308 he . . . us] *not in F*
5.1.308 warrant] *This edition*; warnd *Q1; not in F*
5.1.332 SD] *This edition; not in Q1, F*
5.1.335 SD] *This edition; not in Q1, F*
5.1.338 SD] *This edition; not in Q1, F*
5.1.345 hanged] hung *F*
5.1.348 SD] *This edition; not in Q1, F*
5.1.356 SD] *Enter Puck Q1, F*
5.1.358 behowls] Capell; beholds *Q1, F*
5.1.376 *Enter . . . train*] *Enter King and Queene of Fairies, with all their traine Q1*; Enter King and Queene *of* Fairies, with their traine *F*
5.1.386 SD] *This edition; The Song* / Now . . . day *F*
5.1.387 SP] *Q1, not in F*
5.1.405–6 And . . . rest] *This edition*; lines reversed in *Q1, F*
5.1.408 SD] *Exeunt Q1; not in F*
5.1.424 SD] *This edition; not in Q1, F*

SOURCES

GEOFFREY CHAUCER

From The Knight's Tale[†]

PART ONE

* * *

Whylom,° as olde stories tellen us,	*Once, formerly*
360 Ther was a duk that highte° Theseus;	*was called*
Of Athenes he was lord and governour,	
And in his tyme swich° a conquerour,	*such*
That gretter was ther noon under the sonne.	
Ful many a riche contree hadde he wonne;	
365 What with his wisdom and his chivalrye,°	*knightly prowess*
He conquered al the regne° of Femenye,[1]	*kingdom, realm*
That whylom was y-cleped° Scithia,	*called*
And weddede the quene Ipolita,°	*Hippolyta*
And broghte hire hoom with him in his contree	
370 With muchel glorie and greet solempnitee,°	*pomp, ceremony*
And eek hire yonge suster Emelye.	
And thus with victorie and with melodye	
Lete I this noble duk to Athenes ryde,	
And al his hoost, in armes, him bisyde.	
375 And certes,° if it nere° to long to here,	*certainly / were not*
I wolde have told yow fully the manere	
How wonnen was the regne of Femenye	
By Theseus, and by his chivalrye;°	*host of knights*
And of the grete bataille for the nones°	*occasion, purpose*
380 Bitwixen Athenës and Amazones;	
And how asseged° was Ipolita,	*besieged*
The faire hardy quene of Scithia;	
And of the feste that was at hir° weddinge,	*their*
And of the tempest at hir hoomcominge;	
385 But al that thing I moot° as now° forbere.	*must / at this time*
I have, God woot,° a large feeld to ere,°	*knows / harrow, plough*
And wayke° been the oxen in my plough.	*weak*
The remenant of the tale is long ynough.	
I wol nat letten° eek noon of this route;°	*hinde / company*
390 Lat every felawe telle his tale aboute,°	*in turn*
And lat see now who shall the soper winne;	

---

† From *The Canterbury Tales: Fifteen Tales and the General Prologue: A Norton Critical Edition*, 2nd ed., ed. V. A. Kolve and Glending Olson (New York: W. W. Norton, 2005), pp. 23–25, 27–30, 58–61. © 2005, 1989 by W. W. Norton & Company, Inc. Reprinted by permission of W. W. Norton & Company, Inc.
1. The country of the Amazons.

And ther° I lefte, I wol ageyn biginne.   *where*
  This duk, of whom I make mencioun,
When he was come almost unto the toun,
895 In al his wele° and in his moste pryde,   *success, happiness*
He was war,° as he caste his eye asyde,   *aware*
Where that ther kneled in the hye weye
A companye of ladies, tweye and tweye,°   *two by two*
Ech after other clad in clothes blake;
900 But swich a cry and swich a wo they make,
That in this world nis° creature livinge,   *(there) is not*
That herde swich another weymentinge;°   *lamenting*
And of this cry they nolde° nevere stenten,°   *would not / cease*
Til they the reynes of his brydel henten.°   *seized*
905   "What folk ben ye, that at myn hoomcominge
Perturben so my feste with cryinge?"
Quod Theseus. "Have ye so greet envye
Of myn honour, that° thus compleyne and crye?   *that ye*
Or who hath yow misboden° or offended?   *insulted, harmed*
910 And telleth me if it may been amended,
And why that ye ben clothed thus in blak."
  The eldeste lady of hem alle spak,   *fainted / deathly*
When she hadde swowned° with a deedly chere°   *appearance*
That it was routhe° for to seen and here.   *a pity*
915 She seyde: "Lord, to whom Fortune hath yiven°   *given*
Victorie, and as a conquerour to liven,
Noght greveth us° youre glorie and youre honour;   *We do not resent*
But we biseken° mercy and socour.°   *beseech / aid, comfort*
Have mercy on oure wo and oure distresse.
920 Som drope of pitee, thurgh thy gentillesse,
Upon us wrecched wommen lat thou falle.
For certes, lord, ther nis noon of us alle,
That she ne hath been a duchesse or a quene;
Now be we caitifs,° as it is wel sene,   *wretches*
925 Thanked be Fortune and hire false wheel,
That noon estat assureth to be weel.[2]
And certes, lord, to abyden° your presence,   *await*
Here in this temple of the goddesse Clemence°   *Mercy*
We han ben waytinge al this fourtenight;°   *fourteen nights*
930 Now help us, lord, sith° it is in thy might.   *since*

*   *   *

  The grete tour, that was so thikke and strong,
Which of the castel was the chief dongeoun

---

2. Who ensures that no estate will be (permanently) in prosperity.

(Theras the knightes weren in prisoun,
Of whiche I tolde yow and tellen shal),
060 Was evene joynant to° the gardin wal   *directly adjoining*
Ther as this Emelye hadde hir pleyinge.°   *amusement*
Bright was the sonne and cleer that morweninge,
And Palamon, this woful prisoner,
As was his wone, by leve° of his gayler,°   *permission, leave / jailer*
065 Was risen and romed in a chambre on heigh,
In which he al the noble citee seigh,°   *saw*
And eek the gardin, ful of braunches grene,
Theras this fresshe Emelye the shene°   *bright, beautiful*
Was in hire walk, and romed up and doun.
070 This sorweful prisoner, this Palamoun,
Goth in the chambre rominge to and fro,
And to himself compleyninge of his wo.
That he was born, ful ofte he seyde, "Alas!"
And so bifel, by aventure° or cas,°   *chance / accident*
075 That thurgh a window, thikke of° many a barre   *thickset with*
Of yren greet and square° as any sparre,°   *sturdy / beam*
He caste his eye upon Emelya,
And therwithal he bleynte° and cryde "A!"   *flinched*
As though he stongen were unto the herte.
080 And with that cry Arcite anon up sterte
And seyde, "Cosin myn, what eyleth° thee,   *ails*
That art so pale and deedly° on to see?°   *deathly / to look at*
Why crydestow?° Who hath thee doon offence?   *didst thou cry*
For Goddes love, tak al in pacience
085 Oure prisoun, for it may non other be;°   *may not be otherwise*
Fortune hath yeven° us this adversitee.   *given*
Som wikke aspect or disposicioun
Of Saturne, by sum constellacioun,
Hath yeven us this, although we hadde it sworn:[3]
090 So stood the hevene whan that we were born.
We moste endure it; this is the short and pleyn."
    This Palamon answerde and seyde ageyn,°   *in reply*
"Cosyn, for sothe,° of this opinioun   *in truth*
Thou hast a veyn imaginacioun.°   *foolish, mistaken idea*
095 This prison caused me nat for to crye,
But I was hurt right now thurghout myn yë°   *eye*
Into myn herte, that wol my bane° be.   *destruction*
The fairnesse of that lady that I see

---

3. Some ill-omened aspect or disposition of Saturn, in relation to the other stars, has given us this (adversity), no matter what we might have done.

	Yond° in the gardin romen to and fro	*Yonder*
1100	Is cause of al my crying and my wo.	
	I noot wher° she be womman or goddesse,	*do not know whether*
	But Venus is it soothly, as I gesse."	
	And therwithal on kneës doun he fil,°	*fell*
	And seyde: "Venus, if it be thy wil	
1105	Yow° in this gardin thus to transfigure	*Yourself*
	Bifore me, sorweful wrecched creature,	
	Out of this prisoun help that we may scapen.°	*escape*
	And if so be my destinee be shapen°	*shaped, determined*
	By eterne° word to dyen in prisoun,	*eternal*
1110	Of oure linage have som compassioun,	
	That is so lowe y-broght by tirannye."	
	And with that word Arcite gan° espye	*did*
	Wher as this lady romed to and fro;	
	And with that sighte hir beautee hurte him so,	
1115	That, if that Palamon was wounded sore,	
	Arcite is hurt as muche as he, or more.	
	And with a sigh he seyde pitously:	
	"The fresshe beautee sleeth° me sodeynly	*slays*
	Of hire that rometh in the yonder place;	
1120	And, but° I have hir mercy and hir grace,	*unless*
	That I may seen hire atte leeste weye,°	*at least*
	I nam but deed,° ther nis namore to seye."	*I am (not) but dead*
	This Palamon, whan he tho° wordes herde,	*those*
	Dispitously° he loked and answerde:	*Angrily*
1125	"Whether seistow° this in ernest or in pley?"	*sayest thou*
	"Nay," quod Arcite, "in ernest, by my fey!°	*faith*
	God help me so, me list ful yvele pleye."°	*I have no desire to jest*
	This Palamon gan knitte his browes tweye:	
	"It nere,"° quod he, "to thee no greet honour	*were not*
1130	For to be fals, ne for to be traytour	
	To me, that am thy cosin and thy brother	
	Y-sworn ful depe,[4] and ech of us til° other,	*to*
	That nevere, for to dyen in the peyne,[5]	
	Til that the deeth departe° shal us tweyne,°	*part / two*
1135	Neither of us in love to hindre other,	
	Ne in non other cas, my leve° brother;	*dear*
	But that thou sholdest trewely forthren° me	*assist*
	In every cas, as I shal forthren thee.	
	This was thyn ooth, and myn also, certeyn;	
1140	I wot right wel, thou darst° it nat withseyn.°	*darest / deny*

4. I.e., deeply sworn to you in blood brotherhood.
5. Even should it mean death by torture.

Thus artow of my counseil,° out of
    doute,°   *in on my secrets /*
                                    beyond doubt
And now thou woldest falsly been aboute°   *set about*
To love my lady, whom I love and serve,
And evere shal til that myn herte sterve.°   *die*
145 Now certes,° false Arcite, thou shalt nat so.   *surely*
I loved hire first, and tolde thee my wo
As to my counseil° and my brother sworn   *confidant*
To forthre me, as I have told biforn.
For which thou art y-bounden as a knight
150 To helpen me, if it lay in thy might,
Or elles artow fals, I dar wel seyn."
    This Arcite ful proudly spak ageyn:°   *in reply*
"Thou shalt," quod he, "be rather° fals than I;   *sooner*
But thou art fals, I telle thee outrely;°   *plainly*
155 For paramour° I loved hire first er thow.   *With passionate love*
What wiltow seyn? Thou woost° nat yet now   *knowest*
Whether she be a womman or goddesse!
Thyn is affeccioun of° holinesse,   *pertaining to*
And myn is love, as to a creature;
160 For which I tolde thee myn aventure
As to my cosin and my brother sworn.
I pose° that thou lovedest hire biforn:°   *I put the case (hypo-*
                              thetically) / first
Wostow° nat wel the olde clerkes sawe,°   *Knowest thou / saying*
That 'who shal yeve° a lovere any lawe?'   *give*
165 Love is a gretter lawe, by my pan,°   *brainpan, skull*
Than may be yeve to any erthly man.
And therefore positif lawe[6] and swich decree
Is broken al day° for love in ech degree.°   *every day / every social rank*
A man moot nedes love, maugree his heed.[7]
170 He may nat fleen° it, thogh he sholde be deed,   *flee, escape*
Al be she° mayde or widwe or elles wyf.   *Whether she be*
And eek it is nat lykly al° thy lyf   *during*
To stonden in hir grace; namore shal I;
For wel thou woost° thyselven verraily,   *knowest*
175 That thou and I be dampned° to prisoun   *condemned*
Perpetuelly; us gayneth° no raunsoun.   *we shall gain*
We stryve as dide the houndes for the boon:°   *bone*
They foughte al day, and yet hir part° was noon;   *their share*
Ther cam a kyte,° whyl that they were so wrothe,   *kite (bird)*
180 And bar awey the boon bitwixe hem bothe.
And therfore, at the kinges court, my brother,

---

6. Laws made by man rather than natural law.
7. A man must necessarily love despite his intention (not to).

Ech man for himself: ther is non other.°   *no other way*
Love if thee list,° for I love and ay° shal;   *if it pleases thee / always*
And soothly, leve° brother, this is al.   *dear*
1185 Here in this prisoun mote° we endure,°   *must / remain*
And everich° of us take his aventure."°   *each / what befalls him*

✻   ✻   ✻

PART FOUR

Greet was the feste in Athenes that day,
And eek the lusty seson of that May
2485 Made every wight to been in swich plesaunce,°   *pleasure*
That al that Monday justen° they and daunce,   *joust*
And spenden it in Venus heigh servyse.
But by the cause that° they sholde ryse   *i.e., because*
Erly, for to seen the grete fight,
2490 Unto hir reste wenten they at night.
And on the morwe, whan that day gan springe,
Of hors and harneys° noyse and clateringe   *equipment*
Ther was in hostelryes al aboute;
And to the paleys rood ther many a route°   *company*
2495 Of lordes upon stedes and palfreys.
Ther maystow seen devysing° of harneys   *fashioning, preparation*
So uncouth° and so riche, and wrought so weel°   *curious, unusual / well*
Of goldsmithrie, of browdinge,° and of steel;   *embroidery*
The sheeldes brighte, testeres,° and trappures;° *headpieces / trappings*
2500 Gold-hewen helmes, hauberkes, cote-armures;   *decorated robes /*
Lordes in paraments° on hir courseres,°   *coursers, chargers*
Knightes of retenue,° and eek squyeres   *in service*
Nailinge the speres,[8] and helmes bokelinge;   *Putting straps on /*
Gigginge of° sheeldes with layneres° lacinge—   *thongs*
2505 Ther as° need is, they weren no thing ydel;   *Wherever*
The fomy steedes on the golden brydel
Gnawinge, and faste the armurers also
With fyle and hamer prikinge° to and fro;   *riding*
Yemen° on foote and communes° many oon   *Yeomen / common people*
2510 With shorte staves, thikke as they may goon;
Pypes, trompes,° nakers,° clariounes   *trumpets / kettledrums*
That in the bataille blowen blody sounes,°   *warlike sounds*
The paleys ful of peple up and doun,
Heer three, ther ten, holding hir questioun,
2515 Divyninge of° thise Thebane knightes two.   *Speculating about*
Somme seyden thus, somme seyde it shal be so;

8. I.e., nailing the head to the shaft.

Somme helden with° him with the blake berd,   *sided with*
Somme with the balled,° somme with the thikke herd;°   *bald / haired*
Somme sayde he° loked grim, and he wolde fighte—   *that one*
520 "He hath a sparth° of twenty pound of wighte."°   *battle-ax / weight*
Thus was the halle ful of divyninge,
Longe after that the sonne gan to springe.
   The grete Theseus, that of° his sleep awaked   *out of*
With minstralcye and noyse that was maked,
525 Held yet the chambre of his paleys riche,
Til that the Thebane knightes, bothe yliche°   *equally*
Honoured, were into the paleys fet.°   *summoned*
Duk Theseus was at a window set,
Arrayed right as he were a god in trone.°   *throne*
530 The peple preesseth thiderward ful sone
Him for to seen, and doon heigh reverence,   *hear / command /*
And eek to herkne° his heste° and his sentence.°   *decision*
   An heraud on a scaffold made an "Oo!"
Til al the noyse of peple was ydo;°   *done, finished*
535 And whan he saugh the peple of noyse al stille,
Thus showed he the mighty dukes wille:
   "The lord hath of his heigh discrecioun°   *acumen*
Considered that it were destruccioun
To gentil blood to fighten in the gyse°   *manner*
540 Of mortal bataille now in this empryse.°   *undertaking*
Wherfore, to shapen° that they shal not dye,   *arrange things so*
He wol his firste purpos modifye.
No man therfore, up° peyne of los of lyf,   *upon*
No maner shot,° ne polax,° ne short knyf   *arrow, missile / battle-ax*
545 Into the listes sende,° or thider bringe;   *may send*
Ne short swerd, for to stoke° with poynt bytinge,°   *stab / piercing*
No man ne drawe ne bere it by his syde.
Ne no man shal unto his felawe° ryde   *against his opponent*
But o cours° with a sharp y-grounde spere;   *one charge*
550 Foyne,° if him list, on fote, himself to were,°   *He may parry / defend*
And he that is at meschief° shal be   *in trouble / taken,*
   take,°   *captured*
And noght slayn, but be broght unto the stake
That shal ben ordeyned° on either syde;   *set up*
But thider he shal by force, and ther abyde.[9]
555 And if so falle° the chieftayn be take   *befall, happen*
On either syde, or elles° sleen° his make,[1]   *else / slay*
No lenger shal the turneyinge laste.

9. But there he must be brought by force, and there remain.
1. I.e., the opposing leader.

God spede yow! goth forth, and ley on faste.
With long swerd and with mace fighteth youre fille.
2560 Goth now youre wey—this is the lordes wille."
        The voys of peple touchede the hevene,
So loude cryde they with mery stevene:°   voice
"God save swich a lord, that is so good,
He wilneth° no destruccioun of blood!"   desires
2565 Up goon the trompes° and the melodye,   trumpets
And to the listes rit° the companye,   rides
By ordinaunce,° thurghout the citee large,   In order
Hanged with cloth of gold and nat with sarge.°   serge
Ful lyk a lord this noble duk gan ryde,
2570 Thise two Thebans upon either syde;
And after rood the quene and Emelye,
And after that another companye
Of oon and other, after hir degree.°   according to their rank
And thus they passen thurghout the citee,
2575 And to the listes come they bytyme.°   promptly
It nas° not of the day yet fully pryme°   was / 9 A.M.
Whan set was Theseus ful riche and hye,
Ipolita the quene and Emelye,
And othere ladies in degrees° aboute.   tiers
2580 Unto the seetes preesseth al the route.°   crowd
        And westward, thurgh the gates under Marte,°   Mars
Arcite, and eek the hundred of his parte,°   on his side
With baner° reed is entred right anon;   banner
And in that selve° moment Palamon   same
2585 Is under Venus, estward in the place,
With baner whyt, and hardy chere° and face.   countenance
In al the world, to seken up and doun,
So evene° withouten variacioun,   equal
Ther nere° swiche companyes tweye.   were not
2590 For ther was noon so wys that coude seye
That any hadde of other avauntage
Of° worthinesse, ne of estaat ne age,   In
So evene were they chosen, for to gesse.°   one would guess
And in two renges° faire they hem dresse.°   rows / place themselves
2595 Whan that hir names rad° were everichoon,°   read / every one
That° in hir nombre gyle° were ther noon,   So that / deception
Tho° were the gates shet,° and cryed was loude: Then / shut
"Do now your devoir,° yonge knightes proude!"   duty
        The heraudes lefte hir priking° up and doun;   their riding
2600 Now ringen trompes loude and clarioun.
Ther is namore to seyn, but west and est

In goon the speres ful sadly° in th'arest;°   *firmly / into the spear rests*
In goth the sharpe spore° into the syde.   *spur*

✻   ✻   ✻

PLUTARCH

From Lives of the Noble Grecians and Romans[†]

From *The Life of Theseus*

Touching the voyage he made by the sea Maior, *Philochorus*, & some other holde opinion, that he went thither with *Hercules* against the AMAZONES: and that to honour his valiantnes, *Hercules* gave him ANTIOPA the AMAZONE. But the more parte of the other Historiographers, namely *Hellanicus*, *Pherecides*, and *Herodotus*, doe write, that *Theseus* went thither alone, after *Hercules* voyage, & that he tooke this AMAZONE prisoner, which is likeliest to be true. For we doe not finde theat any other who went this iorney with him, had taken any AMAZONE prisoner besides him selfe. *Bion* also the Historiographer, this notwithstanding sayeth, that he brought her away by deceit and stealth. For the AMAZONES (sayeth he) naturally louing men, dyd not flie at all when they sawe them lande in their countrye, but sente them presents, & that *Theseus* entised her to come into his shippe, who brought him a present: & so sone as she was aborde he hoysed his sayle, & so caried her away. . . .

Now heare what was the occasion of the warres of the AMAZONES, which me thinckes as not a matter of small moment, nor an enterprise of a woman. For they had not placed their campe within the very cittie of ATHENS, nor had not fought in the very place it selfe (called *Pnyce*) adjoyning to the temple of the *Muses*, if they had not first conquered or subdued all the countrye thereabouts: neither had they all comen at the first, so valiantly to assaile the cittie of ATHENS. Now, whether they came by lande from so farre a countrye, or that they passed ouer an arme of the sea, which is called *Bosphorus Cimmericus*, being frosen as *Hellanicus* sayeth: it is hardely to be credited. But that they camped within the precinct of the very cittie it selfe, the names of the places which continewe yet to this present daye doe witnesse it, & the graues also of the women which

---

† From *Lives of the Noble Grecians and Romans*, trans. Sir Thomas North (London: Thomas Vautroullier and John Wright, 1579), pp. 14–15, 3.

dyed there. But so it is, that both armies laye a great time one in the face of the other, ere they came to battell. Howbeit at the length *Theseus* hauing first made sacrifice vnto Feare the goddesse, according to the counsaill of a prophecie he had receyued, he gae them battell in the moneth of August, on the same daye, in the which the ATHENIANS doe een at this present solemnize the feat, which they all *Boedromia*. But *Clidemus* the Historiographer, desirous particularly to write all the circumstances of this encownter, sayeth that the left poynte of their battell bent towards the place which they call Amazonion: and that the right poynte marched by the side of CHRYSA, euen to the place which is called PNYCE, upon which, the ATHENIANS coming towards the temple of the *Muses*, did first geue their charge. And for proofe that this is true, the graves of the women which dyed in this first encounter, are founde yet in the great streete, which goeth towards the gate Piraica, neere vnto the chappell of the litle god *Chalcodus*. And the ATHENIANS (sayeth he) were in this place repulsed by the AMAZONES, euen to the place where the images of *Eumenides* are, that is to saye, of the furies. But on thother side also, the ATHENIANS coming towards the quarters of *Palladium*, *Ardettus*, & *Lucium*, drave backe their right poynte even to within their campe, & slewe a great number of them. Afterwards, at the ende of foure moneths, peace was taken betwene them by meanes of one of the woman called *Hyppolita*. For this Historiographer called the AMAZONE which *Theseus* married, *Hyppolita*, and not *Antiopa*. Neuertheles, some saye that she was slayne (fighting on *Theseus* side) with a darte, by another called *Molpadia*. In memorie whereof, the piller which is ioyning to the temple of the *Olympian* ground, was set vp in her honour. We are not to maruell, if the historie of things so auncient, he founde so diuersely written. For there are also that write, that Queene *Antiopa* sent those secretly which were hurte then in to the cittie of CALCIDE, where some of them recouered, & were healed: and others also dyed, which were buried neere to the place called AMAZONION. However it was, it is most certain that this warre was ended by agreement. For a place adioyning to the temple of *Theseus*, dothe beare recorde of it, being called *Orcomosium*: bicause the place was there by solemne othe concluded. And the sacrifice also dothe truly verifie it, which they haue made to the AMAZONES, before the *feast* of Theseus, long time out of minde. They of MEGARA also doe shewe a tumbe of the AMAZONES in their cittie, which I as they goe from the market place, to the place they call Rhus: where they finded an auncient tumbe cut in facion & forme of a losenge. They saye that there died other of the AMAZONES also, nere vnto the cittie of CHAERONEA, which were buried all alongest the litle broke passing by the same, which in the olde time, (in mine opinion) was called *Thermodon*, & is nowe named *Haemon*, as we haue in other places written in the life of *Demonsthenes*. And it semeth also, that they dyd not passe through THESSALIE, without fighting: for there are seene yet of their tumbes all about the cittie of SCOTVSA, hard by the rocks, which be called the doggs head. And this is that which is worthy memorie (in mine opinion) touching the warres of these AMAZONES. How the Poet telleth that the AMA-ZONES made warres with *Theseus* to reuenge the iniurie he dyd to their Queene *Antiopa*, refusing her, to marye with *Phaedra*: & as for the murder which he telleth that *Hercules* dyd, that me thinckes is altogether but deuise of Poets. It is very true, that after the death of *Antiopa*, *Theseus* maried *Phaedra*, having had before of *Antiopa* a sonne called *Hippolytus*, or as the Poet *Pindarus* writeth, *Demophon*. And for that the Historiographers doe not in any thing speake against the tragicall Poets, in that which concerneth the ill happe that chaunced to him, in the persons of this his wife & of his sonne: we must needs take it to be so, as we finde it written in the tragedies. And yet we finde many other reportes touching the mariages of *The-seus*, whose beginnings had no great good honest ground, neither fell out their endes very fortunate: & yet for all that they have made no tragedies of them, neither have they bene played in the Theaters.

From *The Comparison of Theseus with Romulus*

Theseus faults touching women and ravishements, of the twaine, had the lesse shadowe and culler of honestie. Bicause *Theseus* dyd attempt it very often: for he stale awaye *Aridane*, *Antiope*, and *Anaxo* the Troezenian. Againe being stepped in yeres, and at later age, and past marriage: he stale awaye *Helen* in her minoritie, being nothing neere to consent to marye. Then his taking of the daughters of the TROEZIANS, of the LACEDAEMONIANS, and the AMA-ZONES (neither contracted to him, nor comparable to the birthe and linadge of his owne countries where were at ATHENS and descended of the noble race and progenie of *Erichtheus*, and of *Cecrops*) dyd geue men occasion to suspect that his wommanishenes was rather to sat-isfie lust, then of any great loue. . . . The ATHENIANS contrariewise, by *Theseus* mariages, dyd get neither loue nor kynred of any one per-sonne, but rather thay procured warres, enmities, and the slaughter of their citizens, with the losse in the ende of the cittie of APHIDNES.

ANONYMOUS

From Huon of Bordeaux[†]

Chapter 21. How Gerames went with Huon and his company, and so came into the wood, whereas they found King Oberon, who conjured them to speak unto him.

When Huon had well heard Gerames how he was minded to go with him, he was thereof right joyful and thanked him of his courtesy and service and gave him a goodly horse whereon he mounted and so rode forth together, so long that they came into the wood whereas King Oberon haunted most.

Then Huon was weary of travels, and what for famine and for heat, the which he and his company had endured two days without bread or meat, so that he was so feeble that he could ride no further. And then he began piteously to weep and complained of the great wrong that King Charlemagne had done to him. And then Garyn and Gerames comforted him and had great pity of him, and they knew well by the reason of his youth, hunger oppressed him more than it did to them of greater age. Then they alighted under a great oak, to the intent to search for some fruit to eat. They let their horses go to pasture.

When they were thus alighted, the dwarf of the fairy, King Oberon, came riding by, and had on a gown so rich that it were marvel to recount the riches and fashion thereof. And it was so garnished with precious stones that the clearness of them shone like the sun. Also he had a goodly bow in his hand so rich that it could not be esteemed, and his arrows after the same sort. And they had such property that any beast in the world that he would wish for, the arrow should arrest him. Also he had about his neck a rich horn hanging by two laces of gold. The horn was so rich and fair that there was never seen one such. It was made by four ladies of the fairy in the isle of Cafalone. One of them gave to the horn such a property that whosoever heard the sound thereof, if he were in the greatest greatest famine of the world, he should be satisfied as well as though he had eaten all that he would wish for, and in likewise for drink as well as though he had drunken his fill of the best wine in all the world. The third lady, named Margale, gave to this horn yet a greater gift, and that was, whosoever heard this horn, though he were never so poor or feeble by sickness, he should have such joy

---

† From *The ancient, honorable, famous, and delightfull historie of Huon of Bordeaux, Translated out of Frenche into English by Sir J. Bourchire* [John Bourchier, Lord Berners] (London, 1601), signatures e4v–e7r.

in his heart that he should sing and dance. The forth lady, named Lempatrix, gave to this horn such a gift that whoever heard it, if he were a hundred journeys off, he should come at the pleasure of him that blew it, far or near.

Then King Oberon, who knew well and had seen the fourteen companions, he set his horn to his mouth and blew so melodious a blast that the fourteen companions, being under the tree, had so perfect a joy at their hearts that they all rose up and began to sing and dance.

"Ah, good Lord," quod Huon, "what fortune is come to us? Methinks we be in paradise. Right now I could not sustain myself for lack of meat and drink, and now I feel myself neither hungry nor thirsty. From whence may this come?"

"Sir," quod Gerames, "know for truth this is done by the dwarf of the fairy, whom ye shall soon see pass by you. But, sir, I require you in jeopardy of losing of your life that ye speak to him no word, without ye purpose to bide ever with him."

"Sir," quod Huon, "have no doubt of me, sen I know the jeopardy."

Therewith the dwarf began to cry aloud and said, "Ye fourteen men that passeth by my wood, God keep you all, and I desire you speak with me, and I conjure you thereto by God Almighty and by the Christendom that ye have received and by all that God hath made, answer me."

Chapter 22. How King Oberon was right sorrowful and sore displeased in that Huon would not speak and of the great fear that he put Huon and his company in.

When that Huon and his company heard the dwarf speak, they mounted on their horses and rode away as fast as they might without speaking of any word, and the dwarf, seeing how that they rode away and would not speak, he was sorrowful and angry. Then he set one of his fingers on his horn, out of the which issued out such wind and a tempest so horrible to hear that it bare down trees, and therewith came such a rain and hail that seemed that heaven and the earth had fought together and that the world should have ended. The beasts in the woods brayed and cried, and the fowls of the air fell down dead for fear that they were in. There was no creature but he would have been afraid of that tempest. Then suddenly appeared before them a great river that ran swifter than the birds did fly, and the water was so black and so perilous and made such a noise that it might be heard ten leagues off.

"Alas," quod Huon, "I see well now we all be all lost. We shall here be oppressed without God have pity of us. I repent me that ever I entered into this wood. I had been better a travelled a whole year than to have come hither."

"Sir," quod Gerames, "dismay you not, for all this is done by the dwarf of the fairy."

"Well," quod Huon, "I think it best to alight from our horse, for I think we shall never scape from hence, but that we shall be all oppressed."

Then Garyn and the other companions had great marvel and were in great fear. "Ah, Gerames," quod Huon, "ye showed me well that it was great peril to pass this wood. I repent me that I had not believed you."

Then they saw on the other side of the river a fair castle environed with fourteen great towers, and on every tower a clocher of fine gould by seeming, the which they long regarded . . .

Chapter 23. How King Oberon, dwarf of the Fairy, pursued so much Huon that he constrained him to speak to him at last.

When Gerames understood the company how they thought they were scaped from the dwarf, he began to smile and said, "Sirs, make none, for I believe ye shall soon see him again."

And as soon as Gerames had spoke the same words, they saw before them a bridge, the which they must pass, and they saw the dwarf on the other part. Huon saw him first and said, "I see the devil who hath done us so much trouble."

Oberon heard him and said, "Friend, thou doest me injury without cause, for I was never devil nor ill creature. I am a man as other be, but I conjure thee by the divine puissance to speak to me."

Then Gerames said, "Sirs, for God's sake let him alone, nor speak no word to him. For by his fair language he may deceive us all, as he hath done many other. It is pity that he had lived so long."

Then they rode forth a good pass, and left the dwarf alone sore displeased in that they would not speak to him. Then he took his horn and set it to his mouth and blew it. When Huon and his company heard it, they had no power to ride any further, but they began all to sing. Then Oberon the dwarf said, "Yonder company are fools and proud, that for any salutation that I can give them they disdain to answer me. But by the God that made me, or they escape me, the refuse of my words shall be dear bought."

Then he took again his horn and strake it three times on his bow and cried out aloud and said, "Ye my men, come and appear before me."

Then there came to him a four hundred men of arms and demanded of Oberon what was his pleasure and who had displeased him.

"Sirs," quod Oberon, "I shall show you, am grieved to show it. Here in this wood there passed fourteen knights who disdaineth to speak to me. But to the intent that they shall not mock me, they shall dearly

buy the refusing of their answer. Wherefore I will ye go after them
and slay them all. Let none escape."

    Then one of his knights said, "Sir, for God's sake have pity of them."

    "Certainly," quod Oberon, "mine honour saved, I cannot spare
them sen they disdain to speak to me . . ."

OVID

Pyramus and Thisbe[†]

*   *   *

"Pyramus, who was handsomest of men,
and Thisbe, of a loveliness unrivaled
in all the East, lived next to one another
in Babylon, the city that Semiramis   90
surrounded with a wall made out of brick.

    "Proximity saw to it that this couple
would get acquainted; soon, they fell in love,
and wedding torches would have flared for them
had both their parents not forbidden it,   95
although they weren't able to prevent
two captive hearts from burning equally.

    "These lovers had no go-between, yet managed
a silent conversation with the signs
and gestures they alone could understand: 100
their fire burned more hotly, being hidden.

    "In the common wall that ran between their houses,
there was a narrow cleft made by the builders
during construction and unnoticed since.
Love misses nothing! You two first descried it,   105
and made that little crack the medium
that passed your barely audible endearments.

    "Often, when they had taken up positions,
Pyramus on one side, Thisbe on the other,
and each had listened to each other's panting,   110
'O grudging wall,' they cried, 'why must you block us?
Is it too much to ask you to let lovers
embrace without impediment of stone?
Or if it is, won't you *please* let us kiss?
It's not that we're ungrateful—we admit   115

† From *Metamorphoses: A Norton Critical Edition*, trans. and ed. Charles Martin (New
York: W. W. Norton, 2010), pp. 93–96. Copyright © 2004 by Charles Martin. Reprinted
by permission of W. W. Norton & Company, Inc.

all that we both owe you, for allowing
our words to pass into attentive ears!'
    "So they (in pointless separation) spoke.
When night came on, each said goodbye and pressed
a kiss—which went no further—on the stone.   120
    "When next Aurora had put out the stars
and the Sun had burned the hoarfrost from the meadow,
they found themselves at their familiar spot,
and after much whispered lamentation,
agreed that just as soon as it was night,   125
they'd slip their guardians and leave their houses,
and once outdoors, flee from the city too.
    "And so as not to end up wandering
those open spaces by themselves, they chose
the tomb of Ninus[1] as their meeting place: 130
nearby, there was a fountain and a tall
mulberry tree, abounding with white berries;
in its dense shadows they would find concealment.
They were delighted by this plan of theirs;
daylight seemed loath to leave, but at long last,   135
the sun extinguished itself in the sea,
and from its waters came—at last—the night.
    "Discretely veiled, Thisbe unlocks her door,
lets herself out and slips into the darkness;
emboldened by love, she finds the tomb and sits   140
beneath the tree. But look! A lioness,
whose jaws are dripping from a recent kill,
approaches the fountain to assuage her thirst.
    "From far off, Thisbe sees her in the moonlight,
and with trembling steps, runs into a dark cave.   145
But in her flight, she drops her cloak and leaves it
behind her on the ground. Now, when the savage
lioness has had her fill of water
and heads back to the woods, by chance she finds
that cloak (without the girl) and pauses there   150
to mangle it in her ferocious jaws.
    "Arriving later, Pyramus discovers
tracks in the dust, as plain as day: he blanches,
and when he finds her bloodstained garment, cries,
'On this one night, two lovers come to grief!   155
For she, far more than I, deserved long life!
Mine is the guilt, poor miserable dear,

---

1. Some local color: Ninus was king of Babylon, husband of Semiramis. Presumably his
  tomb would have been prominent enough for the lovers to find in the dark.

since it was I most surely who destroyed you,
bidding you come by night to this drear place,
and me not here before you!
                   "'Come now, you lions   160
inhabiting the caves beneath this rock,
tear me to pieces and consume me quite!
But only cowards merely *beg* for death.'
  "He carries Thisbe's cloak to the tree of their pact,
and presses tears and kisses on the fabric.   165
'Drink *my* blood now,' he says, drawing his sword,
and thrusting it at once in his own guts:
a fatal blow; dying, he draws the blade
out of his burning wound, and his lifeblood
follows it, jetting high into the air,   170
as he lies on his back upon the ground.
  "It was as when a water pipe is ruptured
where the lead has rotted, and it springs a leak:
a column of water goes hissing through the hole
and parts the air with its pulsating thrusts;   175
splashed with his gore, the tree's pale fruit grow dark;
blood soaks its roots and surges up to dye
the hanging berries purple with its color.
  "But look! Where frightened still, but frightened more
that by her absence she might fail her lover,   180
Thisbe comes seeking him with eyes and soul,
all eagerness to tell him of the perils
she has escaped. But can this be the place?
That tree has a familiar shape, although
the color of its fruit leaves her uncertain.   185
  "And as she hesitates she notices
a knot of writhing limbs on the bloodstained earth;
in horror, she leaps back, as white as boxwood;
a tremor runs right through her, and she shivers
as the sea does when a breeze stirs on its surface.   190
  "In the next moment, Thisbe recognizes
her lover's body and begins to beat
her unoffending arms with small, hard fists,
tearing her hair out; she embraces him,
and the tears she sheds there mingle with his blood.   195
Kissing his cold lips, she cries, 'Pyramus,
what grave mischance has taken you from me?
Answer me, Pyramus, your darling Thisbe
is calling: hear me, raise your fallen head!'
  "And he, responding to his darling's name,   200
opens his eyes, so heavy with his death,

to close them on the image of her face.
    "And now she recognizes her own cloak
and sees his sword and its sheath of ebony:
'O poor unfortunate! You've lost your life   205
by your own hand and by your love for me!
In my hand too, there's strength to do the same,
and love that will give power to my stroke!
    "'I'll follow you until the very end;
it will be said of me I was the cause   210
as well as the companion of your ruin.
Death once had strength to keep us separate;
it cannot keep me now from joining you!
    "'And may our wretched parents, mine and yours,
be moved by this petition to allow us,   215
joined in the same last hour by unwavering love,
to lie together in a single tomb.
    "'And you, O mulberry, whose limbs now shade
one wretched corpse and soon will shelter two,
display the markings of our deaths forever   220
in the crimson of your fruit, the likeliest
memorial for two who perished here.'
    "She holds the sword tip underneath her breast
and then falls forward on the still-warm blade.
Her parents and the gods yield to her prayers;   225
for now the mulberry's ripe fruit is dark
and their blent ashes share a single urn."

REGINALD SCOT

From The Discoverie of Witchcraft[†]

Book IV, Chapter X

But to use few words herein, I hope you understand that they affirme and saie, that Incubus is a spirit; and I trust you know that a spirit hath no flesh nor bones, &c: and that he neither dooth eate nor drinke. In deede your grandams maides were woont to set aboil of milke before him and his cousine Robin good-fellow, for grinding of malt or mustard, and sweeping the house at midnight: and you have also heard that he would chafe exceedingly, if the maid or good-wife of the house, having compassion of his nakednes, laid anie clothes for him, beesides his messe of white bread and milke, which was

† From *The Discoverie of Witchcraft* (London: W. Brome, 1584), pp. 85ff.

his standing fee. For in that case he saith; What have we here? Hem-
ton hamten, here will I never more tread nor stampen.

But to proceed in this confutation. Where there is no meate eaten,
there can be no seed which thereof is ingendred: although it be
granted, that Robin could both eate and drinke, as being a-cousening
idle frier, or some such roge, that wanted nothing either belonging
to lecherie or knaverie, &c. Item, where the genitall members want,
there can be no lust of the flesh: neither dooth nature give anie
desire of generation, where there is no propagation or succession rec-
quired. And as spirits cannot be greeved with hunger, so can they
not be inflamed with lustes. And if men should hve ever, what needed
succession or heires? For that is but an ordinance of God, to supplie
the place, the number, the world, the time, and speciallie to accom-
plish his will. But the power of generation consisteth not onlie in
members, but chieflie of vitall spirits, and of the hart: which spirits
are never in such a bodie as *Incubus* hath, being but a bodie assumed,
as they themselves sale. And yet the most part of writers herein
affirme, that it is a palpable and visible bodie; though all be phan-
sies and fables that are written hereupon.

Book VII, Chapter II

But how cunninglie soever this last cited certificat be penned, or
what shew soever it carrieth of truth and plaine dealing, there maybe
found conteined therein matter enough to detect the cousening
knaverie therof. And yet diverse have been deepelie deceived thereof with, and can hardlie be removed from the credit thereof, and
without great disdaine cannot endure to heare the reproofe thereof.
And know you this by the waie, that heretofore Robin goodfellow,
and Hob gobblin were as terrible, and also as credible to the people,
as hags and witches be now: and in time to come, a witch will be as
much derided and contemned, and as plainlie perceived, as the
illusion and knaverie of Robin goodfellow. And in truth, they that
mainteine walking spirits, with their transformation, &c: have no
reason to denie Robin good-fellow, upon whom there hath gone as
manie and as credible tales, as upon witches; saving that it hath not
pleased the translators of the Bible, to call spirits by the name of
Robin goodfellow, as they have termed divinors, soothsaiers, poison-
ers, and couseners by the name of witches.

Book VII, Chapter XV

But certeinlie, some one knave in a white sheete hath cousened and
abused manie thousands that waie; speciallie when Robin good-fellow
kept such a coile in the countrie. But you shall understand, that these

bugs speciallie are spied and feared of sicke folke, children, women, and cowards, which through weaknesse of mind and bodie, are shaken with vaine dreames and continuall feare. The Scythians, being a stout and a warlike nation (as divers writers report) never see anie vaine sights or spirits. It is a common saieng; A lion feareth no bugs. But in our childhood our mothers maids have so terrified us with an ouglie divell having homes on his head, fier in his mouth, and a taile in his breech, eies like a bason, fanges like a dog, clawes like a beare, a skin like a Niger, and a voice roring like a lion, whereby we start and are afraid when we heare one crie Bough: and they have so fraied us with bull beggers, spirits, witches, urchens, elves, hags, fair-ies, satyrs, pans, faunes, sylens, kit with the cansticke, tritons, cen-taurs, dwarfes, giants, imps, calcars, conjurors, nymphes, changlings. Incubus, Robin good-fellowe, the spoorne, the mare, the man in the oke, the hell waine, the fierdrake, the puckle, Tom thombe, hob gob-blin, Tom tumbler, boneles, and such other bugs, that we are afraid of our owne shadowes: in so much as some never feare the divell, but in a darke night; and then a polled sheepe is a perillous beast, and manie times is taken for our fathers soule, speciallie in a churchyard, where a right hardie man heretofore scant durst passe by night, but his haire would stand upright. For right grave writers report, that spirits most often and speciallie take the shape of women appearing to monks, &c: and of beasts, dogs, swine, horsses, gotes, cats, haires; of fowles, as crowes, night owles, and shreeke owles; but they delight most in the likenes of snakes and dragons. Well, thanks be to God, this wretched and cowardlie infidelitie, since the preaching of the gospell, is in part forgotten: and doubtles, the rest of those illusions will in short time (by Gods grace) be detected and vanish awaie.

Book V, Chapter III

Of a man turned into an asse, and returned againe into a man by one of Bodins witches: S. Augustines opinion thereof.

It happened in the city of Salamin, in the kingdome of Cyprus (wherein is a good haven) that a ship loaden with merchandize staled there for a short space. In the meane time many of the souldiers and mariners went to shoare, to provide fresh victuals. Among which number, a certaine English man, being a sturdie yoong fellowe, went to a womans house, a little waie out of the citie, and not farre from the sea side, to see whether she had anie egs to sell. Who perceiving him to be a lustie yoong fellowe, a stranger, and farre from his count-rie (so as upon the losse of him there would be the lesse misse or inquirie) she considered with hir selfe how to destroie him; and willed him to stale there awhile, whilest she went to fetch a few egs for him. But she tarried long, so as the yoong mancalled unto hir, desiring hir to make hast: for he told hir that the tide would be spent, and by that meanes his ship would be gone, and leave him behind. Howbeit, after some detracting of time, she brought him a few egs, willing him to returne to hir, if his ship were gone when he came. The young fellowe returned towards his ship: but before he went aboord, hee would needs eate an eg or twaine to satisfie his hunger, and within short space he became dumb and out of his wits (as he afterwards said). When he would have entred into the ship, the mariners beat him backe with a cudgell, saieng; What a murren lacks the asse? Whither the divell will this asse? The asse or yoong man (I cannot tell by which name I should terme him) being many times repelled, and understanding their words that called him asse, considering that he could speake never a word, and yet could understand everie bodie; he thought that he was bewitched by the woman, at whose house he was. And therefore, when by no meanes he could get into the boate, but was driven to tarrie and see hir departure; being also beaten fiom place to place, as an asse: he remembred the witches words, and the words of his owne fellowes that called him asse, and returned to the witches house, in whose service hee remained by the space of three yeares, dooing nothing with his hands all that while, but carried such burthens as she laied on his backe; having onelie this comfort, that although he were reputed an asse among strangers and beasts, yet that both this witch, and all other witches knew him to be a man.

After three yeares were passed over, in a morning betimes he went to towne before his dame; who upon some occasion (of like to make water) staied a little behind. In the meane time being neere to a church, he heard a little saccaring bell ring to the elevation of a mor-rowe masse, and not daring to go into the church, least he should have beene beaten and driven out with cudgels, in great devotion he fell downe in the churchyard, upon the knees of his hinder legs, and did lift his forefeet over his head, as the preest doth hold the sacrament at the elevation. Which prodigious sight when certeine merchants of Genua espied, and with woonder beheld; anon com-meth the witch with a cudgell in hir hand, beating foorth the asse. And bicause (as it hath beene said) such kinds of witchcrafts are verie usuall in those parts; the merchants aforesaid made such meanes, as both the asse and the witch were attached by the judge. And she being examined and set upon the racke, confessed the whole matter, and promised, that if she might have libertie to go home, she would restore him to his old shape: and being dismissed, she did accordinglie. So as notwithstanding they apprehended hir againe,

and burned hir: and the yoong man returned into his countrie with
a joifull and merrie hart.

Upon the advantage of this storie M. Mal. Bodin, and the residue of
the witchmongers triumph; and speciallie bicause S. Augustine sub-
scribeth thereunto; or at the least to the verie like. Which I must confesse I find too common in his books, insomuch as I judge them rather
to be foisted in by some fond papist or witchmonger, than so learned a
mans dooings. The best is, that he himselfe is no eie-witnesse to any of
those his tales; but speaketh onelie by report; wherein he uttereth
these words: to wit, that It were a point of great incivilitie, &c: to dis-
credit so manie and so certeine reports. And in that respect he justifi-
eth the corporall transfigurations of Ulysses his mates, throgh the
witchcraft of Circes: and that foolish fable of Praestantius his father,
who (he saith) did eate provender and haie among other horsses, being
himselfe turned into an horsse. Yea he verifieth the starkest lie that
ever was invented, of the two alewives that used to transforme all their
ghests into horsses, and to sell them awaie at markets and faires. And
therefore I saie with Cardamis, that how much Augustin saith he hath
seen with his eies, so much I am content to beleeve. Howbeit S. Augi-
istin concludeth against Bodin. For he affirmeth these transubstantia-
tions to be but fantasticall, and that they are not according to the
veritie, but according to the appearance. And yet I cannot allow of
such appearances made by witches, or yet by divels: for I find no such
power given by God to any creature. And I would wit of S. Augustine,
where they became, whom Bodins transformed woolves devoured. But

o quam
Credula metis hofinnis,& erectae fabtilis aures!
　　Good Lord! how light of credit is
　　　　the waveriug mind of man!
　　How unto tales and lies his eares
　　　　attentive all they can?

Generall councels, and the popes canons, which so regardeth, doo
condemne and pronounce his opinions in this behalfe to be absurd;
and the residue of the witchmongers, with himselfe in the number, to
be woorsse than infidels. And these are the verie words of the canons,
which else-where I have more largelie repeated; Whosoever belee-
veth, that anie creature can be made or changed into better or
woorsse, or transformed into anie other shape, or into anie other
similitude, by anie other than by God himselfe the creator of all
things, without all doubt is an infidell, and woorsse than a pagan. And
therewithall this reason is rendered, to wit: bicause they attribute that
to a creature, which onelie belongeth to God the creator of all things.

Book XIII, Chapter XIX

That great matters may be wrought by this art, when princes esteeme and mainteine it: of divers woonderful experiments, and of strange conclusions in glasses, of the art perspective, &c.

Howbeit, these are but trifles in respect of other experiments to this effect; speciallie when great princes mainteine & give countenance to students in those magicall arts, which in these countries and in this age is rather prohibited than allowed, by reason of the abuse commonlie coupled therewith; which in truth is it that mooveth admiration and estimation of miraculous workings. As for example. If I affirme, that with certeine charmes and popish praiers I can set an horsse or an asses head upon a mans shoulders, I shall not be beleeved; or if I doo it, I shall be thought a witch. And yet if *J. Bap. Neap.* experiments be true, it is no difficult matter to make it seeme so: and the charme of a witch or papist joined with the experiment, will also make the woonder seeme to proceed thereof. The words used in such case are uncerteine, and to be recited at the pleasure of the witch or cousener. But the conclusion is this: Cut off the head of a horsse or an asse (before they be dead) otherwise the vertue or strength thereof will be the lesse effectuall, and make an earthern vessell of fit capacitie to conteine the same, and let it be filled with the oile and fat therof; cover it close, and dawbe it over with lome: let it boile over a soft fier three dales continuallie, that the flesh boiled may run into oile, so as the bare bones may be scene: beate the haire into powder, and mingle the same with the oile; and annoint the heads of the standers by, and they shall seeme to have horsses or asses heads. If beasts heads be annointed with the like oile made of a mans head, they shall seeme to have mens faces, as diverse authors soberlie affirme. If a lampe be annointed heerewith, everie thing shall seeme most monstrous. It is also written, that if that which is called *Sperma* in anie beast be burned, and anie bodies face therewithall annointed, he shall seeme to have the like face as the beast had. But if you beate arsenicke verie fine, and boile it with a little sulphur in a covered pot, and kindle it with a new candle, the standers by will seeme to be hedlesse. Aqua composita and salt being fiered in the night, and all other lights extinguished, make the standers by seeme as dead. All these things might be verie well perceived and knowne, and also practised by Jamies and Jambres. But the woonderous devises, and miraculous sights and conceipts made and conteined in glasse, doo farre exceed all other; whereto the art perspective is verie necessarie. For it sheweth the illusions of them, whose experiments be seene in diverse sorts of glasses; as in the hallowe, the plaine, the embossed, the columnarie, the pyramidate or piked, the turbinall, the bounched,

the round, the cornerd, the inversed, the eversed, the massie, the
regular, the irregular, the coloured and cleare glasses: for you may
have glasses so made, as what image or favour soever you print in
your imagination, you shall thinke you see the same therein. Others
are so framed, as therein one may see what others doo in places far
distant; others, wherby you shall see men hanging in the aire; others,
whereby you may perceive men flieng in the aire; others, wherin you
may see one comming, & another going; others, where one image
shall seeme to be one hundred, &c . . . But I thinke not but Pharaos
magicians had better experience than I for those and such like
devises. And (as Pompanacius saith) it is most true, that some for
these feats have beene accounted saints, some other witches. And
therefore I sale, that the pope maketh rich witches, saints; and bur-
neth the poore witches.

LUCIUS APULEIUS

From The Golden Ass[†]

Book III, Chapter XVII

How Apuleius thinking to be turned into a Bird,
was turned into an Asse, and how he was
led away by Theves.

After that I had well rubbed every part and member of my body, I
hovered with myne armes, and moved my selfe, looking still when I
should bee changed into a Bird as Pamphiles was, and behold neither feathers nor appearance of feathers did burgen out, but verily
my haire did turne in ruggednesse, and my tender skin waxed tough
and hard, my fingers and toes losing the number of five, changed
into hoofes, and out of myne arse grew a great taile, now my face
became monstrous, my nosthrils wide, my lips hanging downe, and
myne eares rugged with haire: neither could I see any comfort of
my transformation, for my members encreased likewise, and so without all helpe (viewing every part of my poore body) I perceived that
I was no bird, but a plaine Asse.

Then I thought to blame Fotis, but being deprived as wel of language as of humane shape, I looked upon her with my hanging lips
and watery eyes. Who as soon as shee espied me in such sort, cried
out, Alas poore wretch that I am, I am utterly cast away. The feare

---

† From *The eleuen bookes of the Golden asse containing, the metamorphosie of Lucius
Apuleius, Translated out of Latin into English by William Adlington* (London: Valentine
Simmes, 1596), signature D2v–D4r.

I was in, and my haste hath beguiled me, but especially the mistaking of the box, hath deceived me. But it forceth not much, in regard a sooner medicine may be gotten for this than for any other thing. For if thou couldst get a rose and eat it, thou shouldst be delivered from the shape of an Asse, and become my Lucius againe. And would to God I had gathered some garlands this evening past, according to my custome, then thou shouldst not continue an Asse one nights space, but in the morning I shall seek some remedy. Thus Fotis lamented in pittifull sort, but I that was now a perfect asse, and for Lucius a brute beast, did yet retaine the sence and understanding of a man. And did devise a good space with my selfe, whether it were best for me to teare this mischievous and wicked harlot with my mouth, or to kicke and kill her with my heels. But a better thought reduced me from so rash a purpose: for I feared lest by the death of Fotis I should be deprived of all remedy and help. Then shaking myne head, and dissembling myne ire, and taking my adversity in good part, I went into the stable to my owne horse, where I found another asse of Milos, somtime my host, and I did verily think that mine owne horse (if there were any natural conscience or knowledge in brute beasts) would take pitty on me, and profer me lodging for that night: but it chanced far otherwise. For see, my horse and the asse as it were consented together to work my harm, and fearing lest I should eat up their provender, would in no wise suffer me to come nigh the manger, but kicked me with their heels from their meat, which I my self gave them the night before. Then I being thus handled by them, and driven away, got me into a corner of the stable, where while I remembred their uncurtesie, and how on the morrow I should return to Lucius by the help of a Rose, when as I thought to revenge my selfe of myne owne horse, I fortuned to espy in the middle of a pillar sustaining the rafters of the stable the image of the goddesse Hippone, which was garnished and decked round about with faire and fresh roses: then in hope of present remedy, I leaped up with my fore feet as high as I could, stretching out my neck, and with my lips coveting to snatch some roses. But in an evill houre I did go about that enterprise, for behold the boy to whom I gave charge of my horse, came presently in, and finding me climbing upon the pillar, ranne fretting towards me and said, How long shall wee suffer this wild Asse, that doth not onely eat up his fellowes meat, but also would spoyl the images of the gods? Why doe I not kill this lame theefe and weake wretch. And therewithall looking about for some cudgel, hee espied where lay a fagot of wood, and chusing out a crabbed truncheon of the biggest hee could finde, did never cease beating of mee poore wretch, until such time as by great noyse and rumbling, hee heard the doores of the house burst open, and the neighbours crying in most lamentable sort, which enforced him being stricken in feare, to fly his way. And by and by a troupe of theeves entred in, and kept every part and corner of the house with weapons. And as men resorted to aid and help them which were within the doores, the theeves resisted and kept them back, for every man was armed with a sword and target in his hand, the glimpses whereof did yeeld out such light as if it had bin day. Then they brake open a great chest with double locks and bolts, wherein was layd all the treasure of Milo, and ransackt the same: which when they had done they packed it up and gave every man a portion to carry: but when they had more than they could beare away, yet were they loth to leave any behind, but came into the stable, and took us two poore asses and my horse, and laded us with greater trusses than wee were able to beare. And when we were out of the house, they followed us with great staves, and willed one of their fellows to tarry behind, and bring them tydings what was done concerning the robbery: and so they beat us forward over great hils out of the way. But I, what with my heavy burden and long journy, did nothing differ from a dead asse: wherfore I determined with myself to seek some civil remedy, and by invocation of the name of the prince of the country to be delivered from so many miseries: and on a time I passed through a great faire, I came among a multitude of Greeks, and I thought to call upon the renowned name of the Emperor and say, O Cesar, and cried out aloud O, but Cesar I could in no wise pronounce. The Theeves little regarding my crying, did lay me on and beat my wretched skinne in such sort, that after it was neither apt nor meet to make Sives or Sarces. Howbeit at last Jupiter administred to me an unhoped remedy. For when we had passed through many townes and villages, I fortuned to espy a pleasant garden, wherein beside many other flowers of delectable hiew, were new and fresh roses: and being very joyful, and desirous to catch some as I passed by, I drew neerer and neerer: and while my lips watered upon them, I thought of a better advice more profitable for me, lest if from an asse I should become a man, I might fall into the hands of the theeves, and either by suspition that I were some witch, or for feare that I should utter their theft, I should be slaine, wherefore I abstained for that time from eating of Roses, and enduring my present adversity, I did eat hay as other Asses did.

ANONYMOUS

Tragoedia Miserrima Pyrami &
Thisbes Fata Enuncians[†]

HISTORIA EX PUBLIO OUIDIO DEPROMPTA.

AUTHORE N. R.

PROLOGUS

In stately Babylon, that triumphant place
Where once Semiramis o're Assyrians raign'd
Two goodly Louers dwelt one Pyramus
By name was call'd the other Thisbe
Hee of men the fairest, whilst shee was
'Mongst all those Easterne Dames the sprusest Lasse.

But churlish Parents so their Loues did crosse
That they poore wights could only through a wall
Their amorous soules breath out, where t'was agreed
That to a shadie tree by Ninus tombe
They should repayre, & at midnight houre
Solace themselues under its pleasant bowre

But what immaturely Parents did begin
Vnhappy Fates did second. They ye Prologue
These ye Epilogue were of this short tragedy,
For Thisbe thither, beeing first approacht
A Liones shee spied which made her thence
With nimble Legs to runne for her defence.

When not long after Pyramus hee came
Vnto ye place appointed where missing Thisbe deare
Her vaile hee found sprinckled with goarie blood
Whence her devoured, thinking, hee his sword
Within his bowels sheathed him Thisbe finding so
Her soule shee woundeth with a fatall blow.

This tragick story, who will reade or heare
These sequent Lines, will it to him declare.

† "The Miserable Tragedy of Pyramus & Thisbe's Fate Reported Completely: A Story Drawn from Publius Ovidius [Ovid]," anonymously transcribed by "N.R." in the mid-seventeenth century, as reprinted in Eleanor Prescott Hammond, "A Pyramus-and-Thisbe play of Shakespeare's Time" in *The Drama: A Quarterly Review* 5.17 (February 1915): 289–300. Letters in italics signify expansions of abbreviations in the original manuscript (British Library Additional 15227, fols. 56v–61r).

ACTUS PRIMUS & VLTIMUS

SCENA Iᵃ

[*Enter* IPHIDIUS PYRAM: PATER & LABETRUS THISB: PATER.]

IPH.   I heare my deare Labetrus that my sonne
 Your daughter loues.   & that her amorous mind
 Reciprocally doth place her soule on him.

LAB.   True good Iphidius, thus did Olympio
 A freind of mine certify mee of late.
 When through ye streets wee with Lysander pass'd.

IPH.   But the erraticall motions in childrens actions
 Must to a regular forme by parents bee reduced,
 Wee are ye sunne, from whence as lesser starrs
 Their light they borrow, & must therefore looke
 That none of their designes doe any time eclipse
 Our glorious splendour.——

LAB.   Indeed this lecture Nature teacheth all
 But once affection plac'd, for to remooue
 Its hard & dangerous, this events doe shew
 Reason demonstrates this, the Carthaginian Queene
 Her inauspicious loue to great Anchises sonne
 Could not but with death disthrone——

IPH.   Yet not to try its Cowardice. Hee scarce
 Will catch ye hare who dares not giue ye chase.
 Time & diswasion will worke much, Jason left
 His Medea & Theseus his Ariadne, moreouer
 The inconstancy of women promiseth noe litle
 To our future hopes.——

LAB.   Since then you'le have it so, my deare Iphidius
 Bee you the oracle to pronounce what's fitting
 To doe in such an action, for at your sacred shrine
 My genious thoughts consult.   & what your wisdome shall
 Dictate to me, my selfe will execute.

IPH.   Keepe then your daughter from her Louers sight
 Immure her within your owne domesticke walls
 Whilst I my sonne endeavour to restraine
 From's wonted libertie, & detaine him from
 His dearest consorts company, my eyes
 Shall bee his sentinels, & my walled house,
 His prison, his feters my comaunds shall prooue
 So shall hee liue, until hee leaues to loue.

LAB.   Farewell it shall bee done.   [*Exeunt.*

SCENA II[a]

[*Enter* THISBE *sola*.]
Ah mee poore soule my Father knowes I loue,
But hence my woe hee will not let mee loue
Mee doth hee cloyster in his vncoth house
And from my tendrest obiect doth debarre
Water oftimes exasperates the fire
So Loue in mee restrain'd doth burne ye more
Ah Pyramus knewst thou thy Thisbes miserie
Pitty thou wouldst her great perplexitie.   [*Exit.*

[*Enter* PYRAMUS *solus*.]
Like as ye harmles harte with dreadfull wound
Infested, rangeth o're the spatious plaines.
So doth my hearte by Cupid wounded wander
Whilst Conter like my body standeth still.
For heere my Father hath mee close pent up,
Within his strongest walls, hee me imprisons.
What shall I doe?   I know not what to doe,
Where shall I runne, Oh runne?   I cannot goe,
Where shall I goe, Oh goe?   I cannot stirre
Bounde is poore Pyramus with a twofold band
Of Loue & duety by 2 different hands
Loue binds my soule, my Body duety binds
The chaines of Loue, will not my soule let goe
The chaines of duety will my bodie owe
Yet chaines of Loue would haue my body free
But chaines of duety will not my soule let woe.
Deformed Vulcan could faire Venus winne
Whilst I my Thisbe loose, crookbackd Endimion
Could sport in Lunaes lap & ioy in her,
Happy was Vulcan, Happy Endimion
But I, But I——   [*Exit.*

[*Enter* THISBE *sola*.]
Let woods & mountaines Eccho out my woe,
But woe is mee, nor woods nor mountaines view
Can my poore soule, nor can they heare ye sound
Of these my aerie blasts.   Thisbe loues Pyramus,
But pitteous wretch Pyramus shee can't enioy
Juno Jupiter, Helena could Paris get,
But Pyramus cannot wretched Thisbe see,
Thus like ye Turtle I with teares bemoane
Him whom my soule is forc'd to leaue alone.

[*Enter* CASINA *ancilla*.]
Your doleful sighes, your fearefull ecchoing groanes

Sounded Deare M^ris haue my eares & heart
Whence quick repayre unto this place of sorrow
With speede I made, for as ye adamant
Attracteth iron, or ye Amber, straw,
So doth your presence mine.
THISB.   I loue (Casina) but my loue is gone
    This loue breeds greife within my dismall soule
    This greife produced hath a threefold progenie
    Of sighs of teares, & of lamenting words.
    I cannot greiue, but that my heart will sigh,
    I cannot sigh, but that mine eyes will weepe,
    I cannot weepe, but that my tongue breaks foorth
    Into expressions of great passion.
    I loue, I greiue, I sigh, I weepe, I speake,
    The sound of which hath brought Casina hither.
CAS.   Loue is a passion alwaies in extreames,
    It is ye author of our life or death,
    I loue, I die, I loue, I liue, sayth hee,
    But die you shall not, you shall liue & loue,
    Our fathers old haue often sayd, that loue
    Through stone walls breaks, now now that proverb's true
    For in our wall, a rime I lately found
    In which your soule may ioy, & through which hole
    You may haue priuate Conference with your Pyramus.
    To him Ile runne, and certify I will
    Him of this new inuented proiect——
THISB.   Methinks some little influence I now feele
    Of future happines, oh how my soule reviues
    At these thy words Casina, and my spirits
    In these dry veines now caper, goe, goe, & tell,
    My Pyramus, that in thy destin'd place,
    Anon Ile meete him by ye houre of seven.

                                                    [*Exit* CASIN.

    Propitious powers fauour my designes,
    And graunt you heav'ns that this same petty rime
    To greater blisse, may ope a greater gate.
    Prosper this image Venus of thine owne,
    And make thy Cupid happy in our loues
    When that thou wert inaumoured on Mars
    Successe thou didst implore as well as I.
            [*Enter* CASINA.]
CAS.   Goe, Goe my Thisbe to thy Pyramus,
    'And with thy presence heale his wounded heart
    Thy person hee attends in that same place
    Where last I left him, & where thou must goe,

There vent your loues your soules oh comfort there,
With pleasing murmure, pleasing words out send,
'And each his sweetest breath to other lend.

[*Exeunt.*

SCENA III^{tis}

[*Enter* PYRAMUS & THISBE, *speaking through ye cranye of a wall.*]

PYR.   Were I great Ninus ye Assyrians king
    Or heere did Orpheus tune his sweetest harpe
    Were ye whole world, a table for my diet,
    Or did mee Tagus golden sands environ,
    These were but shadowes to that mightie ioy
    Which in thee Thisbe now my soule conceiues.

THISB.   Were I Semiramis ye Assyrian Queene,
    Were I the obiect of Apollos loue,
    Did I drinke Nectar & Ambrosia,
    They were but as ye litle, least pins head,
    Vnto a mountaine great, or as this globe of earth
    Vnto the highest shining Spheare in heaven,
    Compared with that happines, which in the
    My soule receiues, & as ye tender dew
    Before ye Sunne, so at thy presence great
    They melt, & vanish would.

PYR.   My heart sweet soule is like a ship at sea
    Which long hath tattered beene with blustring blasts
    Of furious Aeolus, who hath oft gainst rockes
    Of drearie feare, & sad despayre it dasht
    But now at last some happie gale of wind
    Hath brought it safe unto ye harbouring hauen,
    But land I cannot, I can not but see
    My Thisbe deare, Coetera, fata negant.

THISB.   My soule sweet heart is like ye shee palme tree,
    Which angry winds haue often torne & rent.
    Its strength decayed hath, its naturall force
    Is spent & gone, till now at last conioyn'd
    To thee its mate it doth recouer & liue.

PYR.   Noe ioyning Thisbe by embraces sweet
    Doe yet attend our blessed wished hopes,
    O Envious stones why doe you hinder thus
    Two wretched louers, what were it for you
    To suffer now these bodies for to ioyne.
    Or were that happiness too much to graunt
    Let but our lips each others to salute.

Ingratefull soules wee are not.   what wee haue
From you wee confesse giuen, but did you more
Affoord, more thankes you should receiue.

THISB.   Oh that with Salmacis I were conioyn'd
Vnto thy louely corpse, as once shee was
To her Hermaphrodite, & that wee both were one.
But since that blisse this place to us denyes
Another shall it graunt, by silent night
Let's striue to breake foorth from our keepers hands
And them deceiue, as once ye piping boy
Did Junoes Argus, & his hundred eyes.

PYR.   I am content, but least our devious steps
Should wander too much in ye spatious feilds,
Let Ninus tombe, ye place appointed bee
Of our intended meeting.   there a tree
With scattered boughs stands ready to receiue
Our louely soules.   there let our persons meete,
There let us both each other kindly greete.

                                          [*Exeunt.*

SCENA IV^{ta}

[*Enter* LABETRUS & IPHIDIUS.]

LAB.   Your worthy councel S^r I haue obseru'd
My daughter's mew'd up in her father's house,
But there with Niobe shee spends ye time
In fearefull sighs, in tragick dolefull straines,
Pyram*u*s, Pyram*u*s, her voice alwaies sounds
As Hercules did Hylas, Hylas faire.

IPH.   As doth thy Thisbe, so my Pyramus
Hee weeps & moanes, his fortune hee laments,
But time I hope will heale his wounds of loue
And from his cheekes wipe of all brinie teares
Our naturalists obserue it as an axiome,
That violent motions least perpetuall are.

          [*Enter* STRATON *servus.*]

STRAT.   Mr Labetrus, Thisbe is escap'd
The doores are shut, but her wee cannot find.

LAB.   This my Iphidius is ye end of all,
This, this, I fear'd, this, this is come to passe
Goe range thou Babels streets, & narrowly
Search out my daughter, lest her ranging mind
Her feete shall also cause to runne & shee
Away from mee may steale——   [*Exit* STRATON.

          [*Enter* CLITIPHO *servus.*]

CLITIPHO.   Mr Iphidius, Pyramus is gone,
   But whether none knowes, neither know they when.
IPH.   Both gone & flowne?   haue both escap'd our hands.
   Tis strange, vnles some stupid negligence,
   The keepers hath ore-taken, or that fates
   With vs full angry, our designes to crosse
   Haue sworne & vow'd, & now gone who knowes
   What may befall them, in their dismall flight?
   But may I find my Sonne, with stricter eye,
   I will obserue him least hee from mee fly.

                                        [*Exeunt.*

                        SCENA Vᵗᵃ

      [*Enter* THISBE *sola.*]
   Descended now hath golden Phoebus bright
   The westerne climates, where his glorious rayes,
   That Hemisphaere enlighten, Dame Diana now
   The sable world salutes, whilst lesser starrs
   By brightsome splendor, shine on darksome earth,
   When now I Thisbe wayte by Ninus tombe
   Of fairest Pyramus ye kind approach
   Heere doe I hope to meete my tender loue
   Whose loue did promise, for to meete mee heere.
   Come, Come my deare, why stayest thou so long
   Doe Parents hinder, or to golden loue
   Hast put on leaden feete, but ah my heart
   Fayles at yon dreadfull, horrid fearefull sight,
      [*Shee sees ye Liones.*]
   Loe loe a raging Liones from ye woods
   With full careere makes hither nimble speed
   Oh Thisbe runne, or else thy flesh sheele rend
   Fly with ye wind, or else thy purple blood
   Sheele sprinckle on insatiate earth, but loe
   A Denne I see which shall my corpse receiue,
   Vntil ye danger is o'repast and I
   May issue foorth, free from all feare to die.   [*Exit in antrum.*
      [*Enter* PYRAMUS *solus.*]
   Reioyce o Pyramus in thy future hopes,
   And ioy thou Thisbe in thy dearest loue.
   My drowsy keepers haue I now deceiu'd
   And now I'me iourneying to ye appointed place
   Whare mee should meete ye image of [my] soule
   But sure these ominous steps portend not good.
      [*Hee seeth ye Lions footsteps.*]

What fierce wild beast, hath heere its footsteps left
Where should my Thisbe tread.   these o my deare
Are not ye reliques of thy princely feete,
But ah whats this?
> [*Hee takes up* THISBES *vayle which shee had left behind
> her & ye Lyon had besmeared wt blood.*]

Now perish Pyramus & let ne're thine eyes
Open to see another sunshine day.
This, this one night two louers shall destroy
And end that loue, which nought but death can end
Oh that my soule would languish, and my blood
Forsake my tenderest heart, perish you beyng
To conquering death let life now yeeld ye feild.
Thou wert unworthy Thisbe of this end
And worthy wert to liue a longer life.
Thy soule was spotles, mine was full of guilt
Twas I that sent thee to this fearefull place
And now feareles man will follow thee.
But ah, my death, will not to thee giue life,
Oh that it would, that mightie kindnes then
Which once Orestes shew'd to Pylades,
Should now in mee reviue, but since th'art dead
This only can I doe to dye with thee.
Ah savage beast why didst thou kill my loue,
Could noe prey satisfie thee but her life.
Come then you rabid Lions & take mine.
These wicked bowels teare with cruell teeth.
Sed timidi est optare necem.   ah pitteous vayle
Deied with ye tincture of my Thisbes blood,
Thee let me kisse, because thy mistris deare
I cannot now salute, now Fatall knife,
Beceiue my blood, & let thou out my life.
> [*Hee kils him selfe.*]
> [*Enter* THISBE.]

The Liones is gone, ye coast is cleare.
Come foorth now Thisbe to thy Pyramus.
Is this ye tree under whose spreading bowre
My Loue & I should meete, but what spectacle
> [*Shee sees* PYRAM.]

Presents it selfe to my amazed sight
A man lyes slaine.   his members beate ye earth
Oh how my blood mee fayles, oh how I feare
Lest yon dead man my Pyra*mus* should prooue
> [*Shee views ye corpse.*]

Oh its my Pyramus.   hee hee is slaine

Rend wretched armes now my disheveld hayre
Gush foorth mine eyes, fountains of mournefull teares,
That I with christall waters may thy blood
Mixe o my deare, oh let these hands embrace
Thy now inanimate body, let these lips
Salute thy tender cold, & pale-swolne cheeks.
What cruel fate Pyramus thee tooke from mee?
Answere o Pyramus, thee thy Thisbe calls.
     [*Hee opens his eyes upon her, & shuts them.*]
Ah, never shut those now thine opened eyes.
Wilt thou but see thy Thisbe & then die?
Thy Loue to me retcht out that fatall hand,
That fatall hand drew out this mortall sword
This mortall sword, sent that immortall soule,
Out of this murthered body, & so shall
My loue, this hand, that sword now doe to mee.
Thee will I follow in this tragick scene.
And in thyne end Ile thy companion bee.
O you that were ye wretched Parents of us twaine
Graunt, that whom truest loue, whom latest houre
Did ioyne together, may not bee disioyn'd
By a disunion in a severall tombe.
And thou O tree that with thy shadie boughs
This wretched corpse dost couer, shew that once
Two louers under thee did end their liues,
And let thy fruit, bee coloured with our blood.
Now bloodie sword bee sheathed in my brest
And send my soule into eternall rest.   [*Shee dies.*

CRITICISM

FRANCIS MERES
From Palladis Tamia[†]

As *Plautus* and *Seneca* are accounted the best for Comedy and Tragedy among the Latines: so *Shakespeare* among the English is ye
most excellent in both kinds for the stage. For Comedy, witnes his
Gentlemen of Verona, his *Errors*, his *Loue labors lost*, his *Loue labours
wonne*, his *Midsummers night dreame*, & his *Merchant of Venice*; For
Tragedy, his *Richard the 2*, *Richard the 3*, *Henry the 4*, *King Iohn*,
Titus Andronicus, and his *Romeo* and *Iuliet*.

SAMUEL PEPYS
From The Diary of Samuel Pepys[‡]

[September] 29th (Michaelmas day). * * * I sent for some dinner and
there dined, Mrs. Margaret Pen being by, to whom I had spoke to go
along with us to a play this afternoon, and then to the King's Theatre, where we saw "Midsummer's Night's Dream," which I had never
seen before, nor shall ever again, for it is the most insipid ridiculous
play that ever I saw in my life. I saw, I confess, some good dancing
and some handsome women, which was all my pleasure. * * *

NICHOLAS ROWE
From Some Account of the Life, etc. of
Mr. William Shakespear[*]

His plays are properly to be distinguish'd only into Comedies and
Tragedies. Those which are called Histories, and even some of his
Comedies, are really Tragedies, with a run or mixture of Comedy
amongst 'em. That way of Trage-Comedy was the common Mistake
of that Age, and is indeed become so agreeable to the English Tast,
that tho' the severer Critiques among us cannot bear it, yet the

---

[†] From *Palladis Tamia* (London, printed by P. Short for Cuthbert Burby, 1598), p. 282.
[‡] From diary entry for September 29, 1662, reprinted in *Diary and Correspondence of
Samuel Pepys*, vol. II, ed. Richard Lord Braybrooke and Rev. Mynors Bright (New York:
Dodd, Mead & Company, 1884), p. 343.
[*] From "Some Account of the Life, etc. of Mr. William Shakespear" in *The Works of
Mr. William Shakespear in Six Volumes*, vol. 1 (London: Jacob Tonson, 1709), pp. xvii,
xxxii.

generality of our Audiences seem to be better pleas'd with it than with an exact Tragedy. *The Merry Wives of Windsor, The Comedy of Errors*, and *The Taming of the Shrew* are all pure Comedy; the rest, however they are call'd, have something of both Kinds. 'Tis not very easie to determine which way of Writing he was most Excellent in. There is certainly a great deal of Entertainment in his Comical Humours; and tho' they did not then strike at all Ranks of People, as the Satyr of the present Age has taken the Liberty to do, yet there is a pleasing and a well-distinguish'd Variety in those Characters which he thought fit to meddle with. * * *

But certainly the greatness of this author's Genius do's nowhere so much appear, as where he gives his Imagination an entire Loose, and raises his Fancy to a flight above mankind and the Limits of the visible World. Such are his Attempts in *The Tempest, Midsummer-Night's Dream, Macbeth* and *Hamlet*.

ALEXANDER POPE

From Preface to *The Works of Shakespear*[†]

If ever any Author deserved the name of an Original, it was Shakespear. Homer himself drew not his art so immediately from the fountains of Nature, it proceeded thro' Ægyptian strainers and channels, and came to him not without some tincture of the learning, or some cast of the models, of those before him. The Poetry of Shakespear was Inspiration indeed: he is not so much an Imitator, as an Instrument, of Nature; and 'tis not so just to say that he speaks from her, as that she speaks thro' him. His Characters are so much Nature herself, that 'tis a sort of injury to call them by so distant a name as Copies of her. Those of other Poets have a constant resemblance, which shews that they receiv'd them from one another, and were but multipliers of the same image: each picture like a mock-rainbow is but the reflexion of a reflexion. But every single character in Shakespear is as much an Individual, as those in Life itself; it is as impossible to find any two alike; and such as from their relation or affinity in any respect appear most to be twins, will upon comparison be found remarkably distinct. To this life and variety of Character, we must add the wonderful preservation of it; which is such throughout his Plays, that had all the Speeches been printed without the very names of the Persons, I believe one might have apply'd them with certainty to every speaker. * * *

† From Preface, *The Works of Shakespear: In Eight Volumes*, vol. 1, ed. A. Pope and W. Warburton (London: J. and P. Knapton, et al., 1747), pp. xxx, xxxii, xxxix.

It must be allowed that Stage-Poetry of all other, is more particularly levell'd to please the Populace, and its success more immediately depending upon the Common Suffrage. One cannot therefore wonder, if Shakespear, having at his first appearance no other aim in his writings than to procure a subsistence, directed his endeavours solely to hit the taste and humour that then prevailed. The Audience was generally composed of the meaner sort of people; and therefore the Images of Life were to be drawn from those of their own rank: accordingly we find, that not our Author's only but almost all the old Comedies have their Scene among Tradesmen and Mechanicks: And even their Historical Plays strictly follow the common Old Stories or Vulgar Traditions of that kind of people. * * *

It is not certain that any one of his Plays was published by himself. During the time of his employment in the Theatre, several of his pieces were printed separately in Quarto. What makes me think that most of these were not publish'd by him, is the excessive carelessness of the press: every page is so scandalously false spelled, and almost all the learned or unusual words so intolerably mangled, that it's plain there either was no Corrector to the press at all, or one totally illiterate. If any were supervised by himself, I should fancy the two parts of *Henry the 4th*, and *Midsummer-Night's Dream* might have been so: because I find no other printed with any exactness; and (contrary to the rest) there is very little variation in all the subsequent editions of them.

SAMUEL JOHNSON

From Preface to Shakespeare[†]

Shakespeare is above all writers, at least above all modern writers, the poet of nature; the poet that holds up to his readers a faithful mirrour of manners and of life. His characters are not modified by the customs of particular places, unpractised by the rest of the world; by the peculiarities of studies or professions, which can operate but upon small numbers; or by the accidents of transient fashions or temporary opinions: they are the genuine progeny of common humanity, such as the world will always supply, and observation will always find. His persons act and speak by the influence of those general passions and principles by which all minds are agitated, and the whole system of life is continued in motion. In the writings of

---

† From *Preface to Shakespeare* in *The Plays of William Shakespeare in Eight Volumes*, vol. 1 (London: J. and R. Tonson, 1765), A3r, A7v–A8r.

other poets a character is too often an individual; in those of *Shake-speare* it is commonly a species. * * *

Shakespeare engaged in dramatick poetry with the world open before him; the rules of the ancients were yet known to few; the publick judgment was unformed; he had no example of such fame as might force him upon imitation, nor criticks of such authority as might restrain his extravagance. He therefore indulged his natural disposition, and his disposition, as Rhymer has remarked, led him to comedy. In tragedy he often writes with great appearance of toil and study, what is written at last with little felicity; but in his comick scenes, he seems to produce without labour, what no labour can improve. In tragedy he is always struggling after some occasion to be comick, but in comedy he seems to repose, or to luxuriate, as in a mode of thinking congenial to his nature. In his tragick scenes there is always something wanting, but his comedy often surpasses expectation or desire. His comedy pleases by the thoughts and the language, and his tragedy for the greater part by incident and action. His tragedy seems to be skill, his comedy to be instinct.

The force of his comick scenes has suffered little diminution from the changes made by a century and a half, in manners or in words. As his personages act upon principles arising from genuine passion, very little modified by particular forms, their pleasures and vexations are communicable to all times and to all places; they are natural, and therefore durable; the adventitious peculiarities of personal habits, are only superficial dies, bright and pleasing for a little while, yet soon fading to a dim tinct, without any remains of former lustre; but the discriminations of true passion are the colours of nature; they pervade the whole mass, and can only perish with the body that exhibits them.

From Notes on *A Midsummer Night's Dream,* Act 1, Scene 2[†]

In this Scene *Shakespeare* takes advantage of his knowledge of the theatre to ridicule the prejudices and competitions. *Bottom*, who is generally acknowledged the principal Actor, declares his inclination to be for a tyrant, for a part of fury, tumult, and noise, such as every young man pants to perform when he first steps upon the Stage. The same *Bottom*, who seems bred in a tiring-room, has another histrionical passion. He is for engrossing every part and would exclude his inferiors from all possibility of distinction. He is therefore desirous to play *Pyramus*, *Thisbe* and the *Lyon* at the same time.

[†] From "Notes on *A Midsummer Night's Dream*, Act 1, Scene 2," in *The Plays of William Shakespeare in Eight Volumes*, ed. Johnson, 1:100.

WILLIAM HAZLITT

From Characters of Shakespeare's Plays[†]

The Midsummer Night's Dream

Bottom the Weaver is a character that has not had justice done him. He is the most romantic of mechanics. And what a list of companions he has—Quince the Carpenter, Snug the Joiner, Flute the Bellows-mender, Snout the Tinker, Starveling the Tailor; and then again, what a group of fairy attendants, Puck, Peaseblossom, Cobweb, Moth, and Mustard-seed! It has been observed that Shakespeare's characters are constructed upon deep physiological principles; and there is something in this play which looks very like it. Bottom the Weaver, who takes the lead of

> "This crew of patches, rude mechanicals,
> That work for bread upon Athenian stalls,"

follows a sedentary trade, and he is accordingly represented as conceited, serious, and fantastical. He is ready to undertake anything and everything, as if it was as much a matter of course as the motion of his loom and shuttle. He is for playing the tyrant, the lover, the lady, the lion. "He will roar that it shall do any man's heart good to hear him"; and this being objected to as improper, he still has a resource in his good opinion of himself, and "will roar you an 'twere any nightingale." Snug the Joiner is the moral man of the piece, who proceeds by measurement and discretion in all things. You see him with his rule and compasses in his hand. "Have you the lion's part written? Pray you, if it be, give it me, for I am slow of study."—"You may do it extempore," says Quince, "for it is nothing but roaring." Starveling the Tailor keeps the peace, and objects to the lion and the drawn sword. "I believe we must leave the killing out when all's done." Starveling, however, does not start the objections himself, but seconds them when made by others, as if he had not spirit to express his fears without encouragement. It is too much to suppose all this intentional; but it very luckily falls out so. Nature includes all that is implied in the most subtle analytical distinctions; and the same distinctions will be found in Shakespeare. Bottom, who is not only chief actor, but stage-manager for the occasion, has a device to obviate the danger of frightening the ladies: "Write me a prologue, and let the prologue seem to say, we will do no harm with our swords, and that Pyramus is not killed indeed; and for better assurance, tell

† From *Characters of Shakespeare's Plays* (London: Taylor and Hessey, 1818), pp. 126–34.

them that I, Pyramus, am not Pyramus, but Bottom the Weaver; this will put them out of fear." Bottom seems to have understood the subject of dramatic illusion at least as well as any modern essayist. If our holiday mechanic rules the roost among his fellows, he is no less at home in his new character of an ass, "with amiable cheeks, and fair large ears." He instinctively acquires a most learned taste, and grows fastidious in the choice of dried peas and bottled hay. He is quite familiar with his new attendants, and assigns them their parts with all due gravity. "Monsieur Cobweb, good Monsieur, get your weapon in your hand, and kill me a red-hipt humble-bee on the top of a thistle, and, good Monsieur, bring me the honey-bag." What an exact knowledge is here shown of natural history!

Puck, or Robin Goodfellow, is the leader of the fairy band. He is the Ariel of the MIDSUMMER'S NIGHT DREAM; and yet as unlike as can be to the Ariel in THE TEMPEST. No other poet could have made two such different characters out of the same fanciful materials and situations. Ariel is a minister of retribution, who is touched with a sense of pity at the woes he inflicts. Puck is a madcap sprite, full of wantonness and mischief, who laughs at those whom he misleads—"Lord, what fools these mortals be!" Ariel cleaves the air, and executes his mission with the zeal of a winged messenger; Puck is borne along on his fairy errand like the light and glittering gossamer before the breeze. He is, indeed, a most Epicurean little gentleman, dealing in quaint devices and faring in dainty delights. Prospero and his world of spirits are a set of moralists; but with Oberon and his fairies we are launched at once into the empire of the butterflies. How beautifully is this race of beings contrasted with the men and women actors in the scene, by a single epithet which Titania gives to the latter, "the human mortals"! It is astonishing that Shakespeare should be considered, not only by foreigners, but by many of our own critics, as a gloomy and heavy writer, who painted nothing but "gorgons and hydras, and chimeras dire." His subtlety exceeds that of all other dramatic writers, insomuch that a celebrated person of the present day said that he regarded him rather as a metaphysician than a poet. His delicacy and sportive gaiety are infinite. In the MIDSUMMER'S NIGHT DREAM alone, we should imagine, there is more sweetness and beauty of description than in the whole range of French poetry put together. What we mean is this, that we will produce out of that single play ten passages, to which we do not think any ten passages in the works of the French poets can be opposed, displaying equal fancy and imagery. Shall we mention the remonstrance of Helena to Hermia, or Titania's description of her fairy train, or her disputes with Oberon about the Indian boy, or Puck's account of himself and his employments, or the Fairy Queen's exhortation to the elves to pay due attendance upon her favourite, Bottom; or Hippolita's description of a chace, or Theseus's answer? The two last are as heroical and spirited as the others are full of luscious tenderness. The reading of this play is like wandering in a grove by moonlight: the descriptions breathe a sweetness like odours thrown from beds of flowers.

Titania's exhortation to the fairies to wait upon Bottom, which is remarkable for a certain cloying sweetness in the repetition of the rhymes, is as follows:

> "Be kind and courteous to this gentleman.
> Hop in his walks, and gambol in his eyes,
> Feed him with apricocks and dewberries,
> With purple grapes, green figs and mulberries;
> The honey-bags steal from the humble bees,
> And for night tapers crop their waxen thighs,
> And light them at the fiery glow-worm's eyes,
> To have my love to bed, and to arise:
> And pluck the wings from painted butterflies,
> To fan the moon-beams from his sleeping eyes;
> Nod to him, elves, and do him courtesies."

The sounds of the lute and of the trumpet are not more distinct than the poetry of the foregoing passage, and of the conversation between Theseus and Hippolita:

> "THESEUS.   Go, one of you, find out the forester,
>   For now our observation is perform'd;
>   And since we have the vaward of the day,
>   My love shall hear the music of my hounds.
>   Uncouple in the western valley, go,
>   Dispatch, I say, and find the forester.
>   We will, fair Queen, up to the mountain's top,
>   And mark the musical confusion
>   Of hounds and echo in conjunction.
> HIPPOLITA.   I was with Hercules and Cadmus once,
>   When in a wood of Crete they bay'd the bear
>   With hounds of Sparta; never did I hear
>   Such gallant chiding. For besides the groves,
>   The skies, the fountains, every region near
>   Seem'd all one mutual cry. I never heard
>   So musical a discord, such sweet thunder.
> THESEUS.   My hounds are bred out of the Spartan kind,
>   So flew'd, so sanded, and their heads are hung
>   With ears that sweep away the morning dew;
>   Crook-knee'd and dew-lap'd, like Thessalian bulls,
>   Slow in pursuit, but matched in mouth like bells,
>   Each under each. A cry more tuneable
>   Was never halloo'd to, nor cheer'd with horn,

In Crete, in Sparta, nor in Thessaly:
Judge when you hear."—

Even Titian never made a hunting-piece of a gusto so fresh and lusty,
and so near the first ages of the world as this.

It had been suggested to us, that the MIDSUMMER'S NIGHT
DREAM would do admirably to get up as a Christmas after-piece;
and our prompter proposed that Mr. Kean should play the part of
Bottom, as worthy of his great talents. He might, in the discharge
of his duty, offer to play the lady like any of our actresses that he
pleased, the lover or the tyrant like any of our actors that he pleased,
and the lion like "the most fearful wild-fowl living." The carpenter,
the tailor, and joiner, it was thought, would hit the galleries. The
young ladies in love would interest the side-boxes; and Robin Goodfellow and his companions excite a lively fellow-feeling in the
children from school. There would be two courts, an empire within
an empire, the Athenian and the Fairy King and Queen, with their
attendants, and with all their finery. What an opportunity for pro-
cessions, for the sound of trumpets and glittering of spears! What a
fluttering of urchins' painted wings; what a delightful profusion of
gauze clouds and airy spirits floating on them!

Alas, the experiment has been tried, and has failed; not through
the fault of Mr. Kean, who did not play the part of Bottom, nor of
Mr. Liston, who did, and who played it well, but from the nature of
things. THE MIDSUMMER NIGHT'S DREAM, when acted, is
converted from a delightful fiction into a dull pantomime. All that
is finest in the play is lost in the representation. The spectacle was
grand; but the spirit was evaporated, the genius was fled.—Poetry
and the stage do not agree well together. The attempt to reconcile
them in this instance fails not only of effect, but of decorum. The
IDEAL can have no place upon the stage, which is a picture without perspective; everything there is in the foreground. That which
was merely an airy shape, a dream, a passing thought, immediately
becomes an unmanageable reality. Where all is left to the imagination (as is the case in reading) every circumstance, near or remote,
has an equal chance of being kept in mind, and tells according to
the mixed impression of all that has been suggested.

But the imagination cannot sufficiently qualify the actual impressions of the senses. Any offence given to the eye is not to be got rid
of by explanation. Thus Bottom's head in the play is a fantastic illusion, produced by magic spells: on the stage, it is an ass's head, and
nothing more; certainly a very strange costume for a gentleman to
appear in. Fancy cannot be embodied any more than a simile can
be painted; and it is as idle to attempt it as to personate *Wall* or
Moonshine. Fairies are not incredible, but fairies six feet high are

so. Monsters are not shocking, if they are seen at a proper distance. When ghosts appear at midday, when apparitions stalk along Cheapside, then may the MIDSUMMER'S NIGHT DREAM be represented without injury at Covent Garden or at Drury Lane. The boards of a theatre and the regions of fancy are not the same thing.

SAMUEL TAYLOR COLERIDGE

From a Marginal Note[†]

I will go tell him of fair Hermia's flight, &c. [1.1.246]

I am convinced that Shakspeare availed himself of the title of this play in his own mind, and worked upon it as a dream throughout, but especially, and, perhaps, unpleasingly, in this broad determination of ungrateful treachery in Helena, so undisguisedly avowed to herself, and this, too, after the witty cool philosophizing that precedes. The act itself is natural, and the resolve so to act is, I fear, likewise too true a picture of the lax hold which principles have on a woman's heart, when opposed to, or even separated from, passion and inclination. For women are less hypocrites to their own minds than men are, because in general they feel less proportionate abhorrence of moral evil in and for itself, and more of its outward consequences, as detection, and loss of character than men,—their natures being almost wholly extroitive. Still, however just in itself, the representation of this is not poetical; we shrink from it, and cannot harmonize it with the ideal.

ALGERNON SWINBURNE

From Shakespeare[‡]

'A Midsummer Night's Dream' is outside as well as above all possible imaginative criticism. It is probably or rather surely the most beautiful work of man. No human hand can ever have bequeathed us anything properly or rationally comparable with this. Beauty pure and simple as the spring's 'when hawthorn buds appear' informs every verse with life as lovely and as happy as the life of flowers when

† From Coleridge's notes in an edition of Shakespeare by Lewis Theobald (8 vols., 1773); reprinted in *Coleridge's Essays & Lectures on Shakespeare & Some Other Old Poets & Dramatists*, ed. Ernest Rhys (London: J. M. Dent & Sons; New York: E. P. Dutton & Co., 1907), pp. 76–77.
‡ From *Shakespeare* (London: Henry Frowde, 1909), pp. 33–34.

'every flower enjoys the air it breathes'. The lyric part is hardly and only lovelier than the rest because the lyric is of its very nature the sweetest and most perfect form of poetry. The fresh and matchless fragrance of Shakespeare's inborn and ever living and ever present loving kindness imbues with something of April life the very interludes of farce. Were this the one surviving work of Shakespeare, his place would still be high in the first order of poets: but all words fall short of our thanksgiving when we remember that the same hand which gave us this gift gave us likewise 'Othello' and 'King Lear'.

JOHN DOVER WILSON

From The Copy for
A Midsummer-Night's Dream, 1600[†]

The Manuscript

* * * We shall, at any rate, not hesitate to assume in what follows that the 'copy' for *A Midsummer-Night's Dream*, 1600, was actually Shakespeare's autograph manuscript, and we are in hopes that, when we have said our say, the reader will think the assumption a justifiable one.

(1) *A PAGE OF SHAKESPEARIAN COPY.*

In earlier volumes of this edition we have frequently drawn attention to the value of irregular verse-lining as a clue to the history of dramatic texts. A very beautiful illustration of the kind occurs at the beginning of Act 5 of the present play. The passage is here printed just as it appears in the Quarto, except that the disarranged verse has been italicised and slanting strokes inserted to show where the lines should rightly end.

5.1.1–84.

Enter Theseus, Hyppolita, and Philostrate.
HIP.   'Tis strange, my Theseus, that these louers speake of.
THE.   More straunge then true. I neuer may beleeue
These antique fables, nor these Fairy toyes.

†   From "The Copy for *A Midsummer-Night's Dream*, 1600" in *The Works of Shakespeare: A Midsummer-Night's Dream*, ed. Sir Arthur Quiller-Couch and John Dover Wilson (Cambridge: Cambridge UP, 1924), pp. 80–86. Copyright © 1924 Cambridge University Press. Reprinted with the permission of Cambridge University Press.

Louers, and mad men haue such seething braines,
Such shaping phantasies, that apprehend/more,   5
Then coole reason euer comprehends./The lunatick,
The louer, and the Poet/are of imagination all compact./
One sees more diuels, then vast hell can holde:
That is the mad man. The louer, all as frantick,   10
Sees Helens beauty in a brow of Ægypt.
The Poets eye, in a fine frenzy, rolling,/doth glance
From heauen to earth, from earth to heauen,/And as
Imagination bodies forth/the formes of things
Vnknowne: the Poets penne/turnes them to shapes,   15
And giues to ayery nothing,/a local/ habitation,
*And a name./*Such trickes hath strong imagination,
That if it would but apprehend some ioy,
It comprehends some bringer of that ioy.   20
Or in the night, imagining some feare,
How easie is a bush suppos'd a Beare?
 HYP. But, all the story of the night told ouer,
And all their minds transfigur'd so together,
More witnesseth than fancies images,   25
And growes to something of great constancy:
But howsoeuer, strange and admirable.
   Enter Louers; Lysander, Demetrius, Hermia and Helena.
 THE. Here come the louers, full of ioy and mirth.
Ioy, gentle friends, ioy and fresh daies
Of loue/accompany your hearts.
 LYF. More then to us,/waite in your royall walkes, your
 boorde, your bedde.   30
 THE. Come now: what maskes, what daunces shall wee
To weare away this long age of three hours,/betweene
Or[1] *after supper, & bed-time?/Where is our usuall manager*
Of mirth?/What Reuels are in hand? Is there no play,/   35
To ease the anguish of a torturing hower?/Call Philostrate.
 Philostrate. Here mighty Theseus.
 THE. Say, what abridgement haue you for this euening?
What maske, what musicke? How shall we beguile   40
The lazy tyme, if not with some delight?
 Philost. There is a briefe, how many sports are ripe.
Make choyce, of which your Highnesse will see first.
 THE. The battell with the Centaures to be sung,
By an Athenian Eunuche, to the Harpe?   45
Weele none of that. That haue I tolde my loue,
In glory of my kinsman Hercules.

1. I.e. 'Our'.

The ryot of the tipsie Bachanals,
Tearing the Thracian singer, in their rage?
That is an olde deuise: and it was plaid,   50
When I from Thebes came last a conqueror.
The thrise three Muses, mourning for the death
Of learning, late deceast, in beggery?
That is some Satire keene and criticall,
Not sorting with a nuptiall ceremony.   55
A tedious briefe Scene of young Pyramus
And his loue Thisby; very tragicall mirth?
Merry, and tragicall? Tedious, and briefe?/That is hot Ise,
And wodrous[2] strange snow./How shall we find the cõcord
Of this discord?   60
     PHILOST.   A play there is, my Lord, some ten words long;
Which is as briefe, as I haue knowne a play:
But, by ten words, my Lord it is too long:
Which makes it tedious. For in all the Play,
There is not one word apt, one player fitted.   65
And tragicall, my noble Lord, it is./For Pyramus,
Therein, doth kill himselfe./Which when I saw
Rehearst, I must confesse,/made mine eyes water:
But more merry teares/the passion of loud laughter
Neuer shed./   70
     THESE.   What are they, that doe play it?
     PHIL.   Hard handed men, that worke in Athens here,
Which neuer labour'd in their minds till now:
And now haue toyled their vnbreathed memories,
With this same Play, against your nuptiall.   75
     THE.   And wee will heare it.
     PHIL.   No, my noble Lord,/*it is not for you. I have heard*
It ouer,/and it is nothing, nothing in the world;/
Vnlesse you can find sport in their entents,
Extreamely stretcht, and cond with cruell paine,   80
To do you seruice.
     THE.   I will heare that play./*For neuer any thing*
Can be amisse,/when simplenesse and duety tender it./
Goe bring them in, and take your places, Ladies.

     How came the compositor to divide the verse incorrectly in these
eighty-four lines? And why should he go wrong in fits, so to speak;
running smoothly enough 'in the even road of blank verse' for parts
of the way, but on eight separate occasions suddenly swerving aside
for a line or two? Submit the passage to a very simple operation; read

2. I.e. 'wõdrous'.

it through, omitting the lines italicised in our transcript; and the responsibility for the eccentric verse-lining is seen to belong not to the compositor but in some way or other to Shakespeare himself. For what is left after the twenty-nine lines in italics have been dissected out are fifty-five lines of regularly divided verse, which are complete in themselves both in sense and metre, and must clearly, at some stage in the history of the text, have stood by themselves and run continuously.[3] Nevertheless, though the eight patches of disarranged verse are unnecessary to the bare sense, they contain all the beauty, all the life, all the memorable things of the passage. They are in our view mature Shakespearian verse, and their masterly diction and vigorous sweep, which pays no attention to line-termination but runs on until the idea which impels it is exhausted, introduce a note of intellectual energy that makes the whole glow with poetic genius. The remaining fifty-five lines, on the other hand, are simple, metrically regular, antithetical, end-stopped and just a little monotonous—in a word early Shakespearian verse. Indeed, the last two lines of Theseus' first speech are so poor that they have even been regarded as an interpolation by some critics.

And the dramatic contrast between the roman and the italic lines is quite as remarkable as the poetic. The lovers enter, and Theseus announces them (to the audience) in a single line—and there an end, as far as the version in roman print goes. It is the three lines following in italic that bring the stage-business to life by the simple device of giving Theseus and Lysander a genial exchange of greetings, so that we can see the latter bowing and smiling. Or consider the character of Philostrate. Save for one line (5. 1. 106), the passage quoted contains everything that he speaks in the play—a matter of some twenty-two lines. Seven of these, five belonging to one speech and two to another, are irregularly arranged, and it is noteworthy that all seven relate to some rehearsal of Quince's play at which Philostrate professes to have been present. Now there are two things to be said about this rehearsal: (i) that according to the commentators, who know Shakespeare's plays so much more exactly than he ever bothered to know them himself, no such rehearsal can have taken place, seeing that the one and only possible rehearsal was performed in the wood, with Puck as the sole 'auditor';[4] and (ii) that the account Philostrate gives us of this impossible rehearsal and of his merriment thereat—merriment which seems about to break forth afresh in his suppressed chuckle, 'nothing, nothing in the

---

3. It is of course possible that some of the original draft was deleted when the additions were made; e.g. the fact that ll. 19–20 seem to echo ll. 5–6 (note 'apprehend . . . comprehend') has suggested to Dr W. W. Greg that the latter took the place of cancelled matter containing the same idea less admirably expressed.

4. v. Furness, *Variorum*, p. xxxiv.

world'—provides us with the only human touch in his portrait. The rehearsal, in short, was needed to endow Philostrate with laughter, tears, and life; that 'historically speaking' it can never have taken place mattered neither to Shakespeare nor to his audience. Further—a fascinating point—the italicised portions of Theseus' opening speech are concerned with 'the poet'; in the correctly arranged blank verse Theseus laughs, somewhat woodenly, at the 'seething brains' of lovers and madmen, but says nothing about poets at all. In a word, 'the poet' was an afterthought, inserted, like that sally about players which Theseus utters later on in the scene (ll. 210–11), with the object of quizzing the player-poet's own craft. Finally, it is delightful to discover that the gracious words—

> For never anything can be amiss,
> When simpleness and duty tender it—

come down to us with all the emphasis of a deliberate insertion.

By this time the direction in which the facts are taking us will be clear. The fifty-five regularly arranged lines which stand by themselves were composed early—probably, if we are to judge from their style, very early in Shakespeare's dramatic career: the eight patches of irregularly arranged verse were added later, and being written on the margin of the MS, in such space as could be found, they presented a problem in line-arrangement which the compositor was quite unable to solve. Furthermore, seeing that fifty-five lines represent about the quantity of blank verse which Shakespeare probably wrote to a page of foolscap,[5] it is possible—we think, even likely—that we are here dealing with the revision of a single page of Shakespearian MS. We can, of course, only guess at the length of the interval between this revision and Shakespeare's first handling of the page; but that it was a matter of years rather than of hours or days is, we believe, suggested not merely by the comparative maturity of style in the later material, but also by the addition of 'the poet' in ll. 5–8, 12–17. As a young man Shakespeare would, we may suppose, take the muse too seriously to fling a jest at her, while only a poet who rode easy in his seat and had triumphs behind him would be likely to kick up his heels so frankly as Shakespeare does in the glorious quip beginning 'The poet's eye, in a fine frenzy rolling.'

* * *

5. v. *Shakespeare's Hand in the play of 'Sir Thomas More,'* p. 116. It seems clear that Shakespeare was writing about 54 lines to a page in the MS of *2 Hen. IV*. Possibly he was more economical of paper at the date of the first draft of *M.N.D.* If so then the hypothetical page may have comprised ll. 1–88.

G. WILSON KNIGHT

From The Shakespearean Tempest[†]

* * *

In *A Midsummer Night's Dream* all the best of Shakespeare's earlier poetry is woven into so comprehensive and exquisite a design that it is hard not to feel that this play alone is worth all the other romances. We have observed plays where 'ill-dispersing' tempests are associated or contrasted with magic lands of fun, reunion, and final happiness. The happier elements of these plays are most perfectly embodied in Feste, song and comedy entwined, and perhaps this is why *Twelfth Night* appears so exquisite a flowering of humour and romance. Tempests and merchants, gold, jewels, and music are recurrent. But, whether love's setting be Arden, Ephesus, Belmont, or Illyria, we know that it is in reality a land of purely fanciful delight, a fairyland of successful, tempest-vanquishing romance. 'Illyria' is, indeed, more truly 'Elysium'. Yet such must be clearly related to those other images where, in the Histories and Early Tragedies, amid more realistic and tragic stress, the poet makes fleeting suggestion of the soul's desire set beyond rough seas of disaster and disorder, fairy riches on far-off Indian strands of the soul. Here we are actually introduced to this Indian fairyland; or, rather, the fairies have come from their Indian home to the 'wood near Athens' which is our scene. In this play fairyland interpenetrates the world of human action. And that world is varied, ranging from the rough simplicity of the clowns, through the solid common sense and kind worldly wisdom of Theseus, to the frenzied fantasies of the lovers: which in their turn shade into fairyland itself. The play thus encloses remarkably a whole scale of intuitions. Nor in any other early romance is the interplay of imagery more exquisitely varied. The night is a-glimmer with moon and star, yet it is dark and fearsome; there are gentle birds and gruesome beasts. There is a gnomish, fearsome, Macbeth-like quality about the atmosphere, just touching nightmare: yet these fairies are the actualization of Shakespeare's Indian dream. The total result resembles those dreams, of substance unhappy to the memorizing intellect, which yet, on waking, we find ourselves strangely regretting, loath to part from that magic even when it leaves nothing to the memory but incidents which should be painful. Such are the fairies here. They are neither good nor bad. They are wayward spirits which cause trouble to men, yet also woo human love and favour: as when

† From *The Shakespearean Tempest* (Oxford: Oxford UP, 1932), pp. 141–46, 166–67.

Oberon and Titania quarrel for their Indian boy or wrangle in jealousy of Theseus or Hippolyta. The whole vision sums and expresses, as does no other work, the magic and the mystery of sleep, the dewy sweetness of a midsummer dream, dawn-memoried with sparkling grass and wreathing mists; a morning slope falling from a glade where late the moonbeams glimmered their fairy light on shadowed mossy boles and fearsome dells, and the vast woodland silence.

The action depends largely on Oberon's quarrel with Titania. Dissension has entered fairyland itself, due to these spirits' desire for human love, just as later human beings are caused trouble by their contact with the fairies:

> Why art thou here,
> Come from the farthest steppe of India?
> But that, forsooth, the bouncing Amazon,
> Your buskin'd mistress and your warrior love,
> To Theseus must be wedded, and you come
> To give their bed joy and prosperity.　　(ii. i. 68)

Oberon parries Titania's speech with reciprocal jealousy. Now this dissension makes 'tempests' in nature, untuning the melodic procession of the seasons:

> TITANIA.　These are the forgeries of jealousy:
> And never, since the middle summer's spring,
> Met we on hill, in dale, forest, or mead,
> By paved fountain, or by rushy brook,
> Or in the beached margent of the sea,
> To dance our ringlets to the whistling wind,
> But with thy brawls thou hast disturb'd our sport.
> Therefore the winds, piping to us in vain,
> As in revenge, have suck'd up from the sea
> Contagious fogs; which, falling in the land,
> Have every pelting river made so proud
> That they have overborne their continents:
> The ox hath therefore stretch'd his yoke in vain,
> The ploughman lost his sweat; and the green corn
> Hath rotted ere his youth attain'd a beard;
> The fold stands empty in the drowned field,
> And crows are fatted with the murrion flock;
> The nine-men's morris is fill'd up with mud;
> And the quaint mazes in the wanton green
> For lack of tread are undistinguishable:
> The human mortals want their winter here;
> No night is now with hymn or carol blest:
> Therefore the moon, the governess of floods,
> Pale in her anger, washes all the air,

That rheumatic diseases do abound:
And thorough this distemperature we see
The seasons alter: hoary-headed frosts
Fall in the fresh lap of the crimson rose,
And on old Hiems' thin and icy crown
An odorous chaplet of sweet summer buds
Is, as in mockery, set: the spring, the summer,
The childing autumn, angry winter, change
Their wonted liveries: and the 'mazed world,
By their increase, now knows not which is which:
And this same progeny of evil comes
From our debate, from our dissension;
We are their parents and original.   (II. i. 81–117)

Unruly floods, disorder in the seasons, storm and mud and all natural confusion result from this dissension in fairyland. And this tempest is at the heart of the play, sending ripples outward through the plot, vitalizing the whole middle action. Hence our dissensions and mistakes, our comedy; in fact, our drama: most of the action is related to the Oberon-Titania quarrel.

Fairyland is set against mortality. Close to her tempest speech Titania has a lovely passage on the fairies' Indian home:

TITANIA.   Set your heart at rest:
   The fairy land buys not the child of me.
   His mother was a votaress of my order:
   And, in the spiced Indian air, by night,
   Full often hath she gossip'd by my side,
   And sat with me on Neptune's yellow sands,
   Marking the embarked traders on the flood,
   When we have laugh'd to see the sails conceive
   And grow big-bellied with the wanton wind;
   Which she, with pretty and with swimming gait
   Following,—her womb then rich with my young squire,—
   Would imitate, and sail upon the land,
   To fetch me trifles, and return again,
   As from a voyage, rich with merchandise. . . .
                                            (II. i. 121)

Notice the 'spiced air' and also the 'yellow sands', reminding us of Venus's promise to dance, like a nymph, on the sands, 'and yet no footing seen'; and also the ship and 'merchandise' imagery; and the thought of Titania and her Indian 'votaress' amused at 'the traders on the flood'. India, we must remember, is fairyland itself; and the Indian votaress all but an immortal. Therefore, as we watch Titania and her loved friend laughing at the 'traders on the flood', imitating their 'voyage' on the waters of life, we see fairyland laughing at storm-tossed mortality.

We must not forget the universal suggestion with which voyages are impregnated in Shakespeare. This is, indeed, an exquisite prologue to the middle action, where Puck befools poor mortals:

> Shall we their fond pageant see?
> Lord, what fools these mortals be!
> (III. ii. 114)

Titania's merchandise speech beautifully reflects this essential spirit, as a prologue to our middle scenes.

For humanity here indeed suffers some cruelly comic distresses. In the first scene we find tragic tempests:

> LYSANDER.   How now, my love! why is your cheek so pale?
>   How chance the roses there do fade so fast?
> HERMIA.   Belike for want of rain, which I could well
>   Beteem them from the tempest of my eyes.   (I. i. 128)

In this play passionate love gives vent to 'showers of oaths' (I. i. 245), and Bottom by the power of his acting will 'move storms' (I. ii. 29). Now in the midnight wood the troubles of Hermia and Helena are increased. These scenes are dark; dark with distress of lovers, dark with the shadowed and gnomish fearsomeness that reigns through a woodland night. Lysander and Hermia have lost their way in the forest (II ii. 36); Hermia is 'faint' with wandering (II. ii. 35). Helena follows Demetrius, imploring pity, receiving curses from the love-tormented and distracted youth. She is 'out of breath' with her fond chase (II. ii. 88). Then she finds Lysander, sleeping:

> But who is here? Lysander! on the ground!
> Dead? or asleep? I see no blood, no wound.
> Lysander, if you live, good sir, awake.
> (II. ii. 100)

'Dead', 'blood': this play is full of fears, and such satanic suggestions are frequent. Again,

> If thou hast slain Lysander in his sleep,
> Being o'er shoes in blood, plunge in the deep,
> And kill me too.   (III. ii. 47)

This recalls *Macbeth*. Again,

> It cannot be but thou hast murder'd him;
> So should a murderer look, so dead, so grim.
> (III. ii. 56)

The play continually suggests a nightmare terror. It is dark and fearsome. The nights here are 'grim-look'd' (v. i. 171). And yet this atmosphere of gloom and dread is the playground for the purest comedy. Romance and fun interthread our tragedies here. So, too, a pale light falls from moon and star into the darkened glades, carving the trees into deeper darkness, black voiceless giants; yet silvering the mossy slopes; lighting the grass with misty sparkles of flame; setting green fire to the glimmering eyes of prowling beasts; dissolving Oberon and Puck invisible in their magic beams.

*　*　*

Three persons here have especial autonomy, existing, as it were, in their own right: Theseus, Oberon, and Bottom. Each is sovereign in his sphere, king over his companions, and demands our respect. Nor can we, who watch, say with confidence that one is more real than the others. And the remarks I am to make on Theseus and the fairies must not be taken to mean that those fairies are purely unreal. Rash fancies may be dangerous, inexpedient to man: it does not follow that they are untrue. Now at the start we have a discord, among men and fairies, and in each world the discord may be said to derive from the other. The Athenian lovers and Egeus find their imaginations and desires conflicting with actualities; that is, their fairy dreams of happiness will not materialize. And in the wood Oberon and Titania quarrel, and their dissension is due wholly to their contact with humanity—rivalry for the Indian boy, jealousy respectively of Theseus and Hippolyta. Oberon accuses Titania of leading Theseus 'through the glimmering night' and making him break faith with Perigenia, Aegle, Ariadne, and Antiopa—is she then a personification, from a mortal's view, of the unrestful fancy and love-longing which torments mankind? And Titania also accuses Oberon of disguising himself as Corin and piping love to 'amorous Phillida' (II. i. 61–80). Oberon cures Titania of her violent love for the boy by making her love the ass-headed Bottom: after that, she suffers a revulsion from excessive mortal desire. Dissension thus enters fairyland through the fairies' love of mortals; there is dissension at Athens through mortals aspiring to the fairyland of their love. The lovers then violently pursue their love into the magic wood, and find themselves in confusion. Thus the action shows us first the clash, then the reharmonizing of fairyland and human life. So the original tempest gives place finally to music, revelry, and feast.

*　*　*

C. L. BARBER

From Shakespeare's Festive Comedy[†]

Magic Imagination: The Ironic Wit

In promoting the mastery of passion by expression, dramatic art can provide a civilized equivalent for exorcism. The exorcism represented as magically accomplished at the conclusion of the comedy is accomplished, in another sense, by the whole dramatic action, as it keeps moving through release to clarification. By embodying in the fairies the mind's proclivity to court its own omnipotence, Shakespeare draws this tendency, this "spirit," out into the open. They have the meaning they do only because we see them in the midst of the metamorphic region we have just considered—removed from this particular wood, most of their significance evaporates, as for example in *Nymphidia* and other pretty floral miniatures. One might summarize their role by saying that they represent the power of imagination. But to say what they *are* is to short-circuit the life of them and the humor. They present themselves moment by moment as actual persons; the humor keeps *recognizing* that the person is a personification, that the magic is imagination.

The sceptical side of the play has been badly neglected because romantic taste, which first made it popular, wanted to believe in fairies. Romantic criticism usually praised *A Midsummer Night's Dream* on the assumption that its spell should be complete, and that the absolute persuasiveness of the poetry should be taken as the measure of its success. This expectation of unreserved illusion finds a characteristic expression in Hazlitt:

> All that is finest in the play is lost in the representation. The spectacle is grand; but the spirit was evaporated, the genius was fled. Poetry and the stage do not agree well together. . . . Where all is left to the imagination (as is the case in reading) every circumstance, near or remote, has an equal chance of being kept in mind and tells according to the mixed impression of all that has been suggested. But the imagination cannot sufficiently qualify the actual impressions of the senses. Any offense given to the eye is not to be got rid of by explanation. Thus Bottom's head in the play is a fantastic illusion, produced by magic spells; on the stage it is an ass's head, and nothing more; certainly a very strange costume for a gentleman to

† From *Shakespeare's Festive Comedy: A Study of Dramatic Form and Its Relation to Social Custom* (Princeton: Princeton UP, 2011), pp. 159–68. Reprinted by permission of the publisher.

appear in. Fancy cannot be embodied any more than a simile can be painted; and it is as idle to attempt it as to personate *Wall* or *Moonshine*. Fairies are not incredible, but Fairies six feet high are so.[1]

Hazlitt's objections were no doubt partly justified by the elaborate methods of nineteenth-century production. A superfluity of "actual impressions of the senses" came into conflict with the poetry by attempting to reduplicate it. But Hazlitt looks for a complete illusion of a kind which Shakespeare's theater did not provide and Shakespeare's play was not designed to exploit; failing to find it on the stage, he retires to his study, where he is free of the discrepancy between imagination and sense which he finds troublesome. The result is the nineteenth-century's characteristic misreading, which regards "the play" as a series of real supernatural events, with a real ass's head and real fairies, and, by excluding all awareness that "the play" is a play, misses its most important humor.

The extravagant subject matter actually led the dramatist to rely more heavily than elsewhere on a flexible attitude toward representation. The circumstances of the original production made this all the more inevitable: Puck stood in a hall familiar to the audience. We have noticed how in holiday shows, it was customary to make game with the difference between art and life by witty transitions back and forth between them. The aim was not to make the auditors "forget they are in a theater," but to extend reality into fiction. The general Renaissance tendency frankly to accept and relish the artificiality of art, and the vogue of formal rhetoric and "conceited" love poetry, also made for sophistication about the artistic process. The sonneteers mock their mythological machinery, only to insist the more on the reality of what it represents:

> It is most true, what we call Cupid's dart,
> An image is, which for ourselves we carve.

Yet it is

> True and most true, that I must Stella love.[2]

Shakespeare's auditors had not been conditioned by a century and a half of effort to achieve sincerity by denying art. Coleridge has a remark about the advantages that Shakespeare enjoyed as a dramatist which is particularly illuminating in connection with this feeling for art in *A Midsummer Night's Dream*. He observes that "the

---

1. *Characters of Shakespeare's Plays* (1817) in *The Complete Works*, ed. P. P. Howe (London, 1930), IV, 247–248; quoted in *Variorum*, pp. 299–300.
2. Sir Philip Sidney, *Astrophel and Stella*, No. V, in *Arcadia, 1593, and Astrophel and Stella*, ed. Albert Feuillerat (Cambridge, 1922), p. 244.

circumstances of acting were altogether different from ours; it was much more of recitation," with the result that "the idea of the poet was always present."[3] The nearly bare stage worked as Proust observed that the bare walls of an art gallery work, to isolate "the essential thing, the act of mind."

It is "the act of mind" and "the idea of the poet" which are brought into focus when, at the beginning of the relaxed fifth act, Theseus comments on what the lovers have reported of their night in the woods. I shall quote the passage in full, despite its familiarity, to consider the complex attitude it conveys:

> The lunatic, the lover, and the poet
> Are of imagination all compact.
> One sees more devils than vast hell can hold:
> That is the madman. The lover, all as frantic,
> Sees Helen's beauty in a brow of Egypt.
> The poet's eye, in a fine frenzy rolling,
> Doth glance from heaven to earth, from earth to heaven;
> And as imagination bodies forth
> The forms of things unknown, the poet's pen
> Turns them to shapes, and gives to airy nothing
> A local habitation and a name.
> Such tricks hath strong imagination
> That, if it would but apprehend some joy,
> It comprehends some bringer of that joy;
> Or in the night, imagining some fear,
> How easy is a bush suppos'd a bear!
>
> (V.i.7–22)

The description of the power of poetic creation is so beautiful that these lines are generally taken out of context and instanced simply as glorification of the poet. But the praise of the poet is qualified in conformity with the tone Theseus adopts towards the lover and the madman. In his comment there is wonder, wonderfully expressed, at the power of the mind to create from airy nothing; but also recognition that the creation may be founded, after all, merely on airy nothing. Neither awareness cancels out the other. A sense of the plausible life and energy of fancy goes with the knowledge that often its productions are more strange than true.

Scepticism is explicitly crystallized out in the *détente* of Theseus' speech; but scepticism is in solution throughout the play. There is a delicate humor about the unreality of the fairies even while they are walking about in a local habitation with proper names. The usual

3. Coleridge, *Select Poetry and Prose*, ed. Stephen Potter (London, 1933), p. 342.

production, even now, rides rough-shod over this humor by trying to act the fairies in a "vivid" way that will compel belief—with much fluttery expressiveness that has led many to conclude that the fairies are naïve and silly. Quite the contrary—the fairy business is exceedingly sophisticated. The literal and figurative aspects of what is presented are both deliberately kept open to view. The effect is well described by Hermia's remark when she looks back at her dream:

> Methinks I see these things with parted eye,
> When everything seems double.
> (IV.i.192–193)

As we watch the dream, the doubleness is made explicit to keep us aware that strong imagination is at work:

> And I serve the Fairy Queen,
> To dew her orbs upon the green.
> The cowslips tall her pensioners be;
> In their gold coats spots you see.
> Those be rubies, fairy favours;
> In those freckles live their savours.
> (II.i.8–13)

These conceits, half botany, half personification, are explicit about remaking nature's economy after the pattern of man's: "spots you see. / Those be rubies . . ." The same conscious double vision appears when Puck introduces himself:

> sometime lurk I in a gossip's bowl
> In very likeness of a roasted crab . . .
> The wisest aunt, telling the saddest tale,
> Sometime for three-foot stool mistaketh me;
> (II.i.47–52)

The plain implication of the lines, though Puck speaks them, is that Puck does not really exist—that he is a figment of naïve imagination, projected to motivate the little accidents of household life.

This scepticism goes with social remoteness from the folk whose superstitions the poet is here enjoying. Puck's description has the aloof detachment of genre painting, where the grotesqueries of the subject are seen across lines of class difference. As a matter of fact there is much less popular lore in these fairies than is generally assumed in talking about them. The fairies do, it is true, show all the main characteristics of fairies in popular belief: they appear in the forest, at midnight, and leave at sunrise; they take children, dance in ringlets. But as I have remarked already, their whole quality is drastically different from that of the fairies "of the villagery," creatures who, as Dr. Minor White Latham has shown, were dangerous to meddle with, large enough to harm, often malicious, sometimes the consorts of witches.[4] One can speak of Shakespeare's having changed the fairies of popular superstition, as Miss Latham does. Or one can look at what he did in relation to the traditions of holiday and pageantry and see his creatures as pageant nymphs and holiday celebrants, colored by touches from popular superstition, but shaped primarily by a very different provenance. Most of the detailed popular lore concerns Puck, not properly a fairy at all; even he is several parts Cupid and several parts mischievous stage page (a cousin of Moth in *Love's Labour's Lost* and no doubt played by the same small, agile boy). And Puck is only *using* the credulity of the folk as a jester, to amuse a king.

Titania and Oberon and their trains are very different creatures from the *gemütlich* fairies of middle-class folklore enthusiasm in the nineteenth century. The spectrum of Shakespeare's imagination includes some of the warm domestic tones which the later century cherished. But the whole attitude of self-abnegating humility before the mystery of folk imagination is wrong for interpreting this play. His fairies are creatures of pastoral, varied by adapting folk superstitions so as to make a new sort of arcadia. Though they are not shepherds, they lead a life similarly occupied with the pleasures of song and dance and, for king and queen, the vexations and pleasures of love. They have not the pastoral "labours" of tending flocks, but equivalent duties are suggested in the tending of nature's fragile beauties, killing "cankers in the musk-rose buds." They have a freedom like that of shepherds in arcadias, but raised to a higher

4. *The Elizabethan Fairies, The Fairies of Folklore and the Fairies of Shakespeare* (New York, 1930), Ch. V and passim. Professor Latham's excellent study points out in detail how Shakespeare, in keeping such features of popular superstition as, say, the taking of changelings, entirely alters the emphasis, so as to make the fairies either harmless or benign, as Titania is benign in rearing up the child of her dead vot'ress "for her sake." Dr. Latham develops and documents the distinction, recognized to a degree by some commentators from the time of Sir Walter Scott, between the fairies of popular belief and those of *Dream*. In particular she emphasizes that, in addition to being malicious, the fairies of common English belief were large enough to be menacing (Ch. II and passim). This difference in size fits with everything else—though it is not borne out by quite all of the evidence, especially if one considers, as Dr. Louis Wright has suggested to me in conversation, that Warwick is close enough to Wales to have possibly been influenced by Welsh traditions. (We have no direct knowledge, one way or the other, about Warwickshire lore in the Elizabethan period.)

Although Dr. Latham summarizes the appearances of fairies in entertainment pageantry, she does not consider the influence of this tradition, nor of the May game, in shaping what Shakespeare made of his fairies—or more accurately, in shaping what Shakespeare made of his play and so of the fairies in it. But her book made a decisive, cogent contribution to a subject that is often treated with coy vagueness. She surveys in Ch. VI the traditions current before Shakespeare about Robin Goodfellow, pointing out that he had not been a native of fairyland until Shakespeare made him so, but "occupied the unique position of the national practical joker" (p. 223).

power: they are free not only of the limitations of place and purse but of space and time.

The settled content of regular pastoral is possible because it is a "low" content, forgoing wealth and position; Shakespeare's fairies too can have their fine freedom because their sphere is limited. At times their tiny size limits them, though this is less important than is generally suggested by summary descriptions of "Shakespeare's fairy race." The poet plays the game of diminution delightfully, but never with Titania and Oberon, only with their attendants, and not all the time with them. It seems quite possible that Peaseblossom, Cobweb, Moth, and Mustardseed were originally played by children of the family—their parts seem designed to be foolproof for little children: "Ready.—And I.—And I.—And I." Diminutiveness is *the* characteristic of the Queen Mab Mercutio describes in *Romeo and Juliet*, and, as Dr. Latham has shown, it quickly became the hallmark of the progeny of literary fairies that followed;[5] but it is only occasionally at issue in *A Midsummer Night's Dream*. More fundamental is their limited time. Oberon can boast that, by contrast with horrors who must "willfully themselves exile from light,"

> we are spirits of another sort.
> I with the Morning's love have oft made sport;
> And, like a forester, the groves may tread
> Even till the eastern gate, all fiery red,
> Opening on Neptune, with fair blessed beams
> Turns into yellow gold his salt green streams.
> (III.ii.388–393)

But for all his pride, full daylight is beyond him: "But notwithstanding, haste; . . . We must effect this business yet ere day." The enjoyment of any sort of pastoral depends on an implicit recognition that it presents a hypothetical case as if it were actual. Puck's lines about the way the fairies run

> From the presence of the sun,
> Following darkness like a dream,
> (V.i.392–393)

summarizes the relation between their special time and their limited sort of existence.

5. Dr. Latham (*Fairies*, pp. 194–216) traces the way fairies derived from Shakespeare were perpetuated by Drayton and William Browne and others by elaborating conceits about their small size and their relationship to flowers. She develops the point that other writers had suggested earlier, that Shakespeare's influence soon altered popular conceptions of the fairies—and in the process of making them benign and tiny, made them purely literary creatures, without a hold on belief.

This explicit summary comes at the close, when the whole machinery is being distanced to end with "If we shadows have offended. . . ." But the consciousness and humor which I am concerned to underline are present throughout the presentation of the fairies. It has been easy for production and criticism to ignore, just because usually amusement is not precipitated out in laughter but remains in solution with wonder and delight. In the scene of the quarrel between Titania and Oberon, the fragility of the conceits corresponds finely to the half-reality of their world and specialness of their values. The factitiousness of the causes Titania lays out for the weather is gently mocked by the repeated *therefore*'s: "Therefore the winds . . . Therefore the moon . . . The ox hath therefore. . . ." Her account makes it explicit that she and Oberon are tutelary gods of fertility, but with an implicit recognition like Sidney's about Cupid's dart—"an image . . . which for ourselves we carve." And her emphasis makes the wheat blight a disaster felt most keenly not for men who go hungry but for the green wheat itself, because it never achieves manhood:

> and the green corn
> Hath rotted ere his youth attain'd a beard.
> (II.i.94–95)

Her concern for the holiday aspect of nature is presented in lines which are poised between sympathy and amusement:

> The human mortals want their winter cheer;
> No night is now with hymn or carol blest . . .
> The seasons alter. Hoary-headed frosts
> Fall in the fresh lap of the crimson rose;
> And on old Hiems' thin and icy crown
> An odorous chaplet of sweet summer buds
> Is, as in mockery, set.
> (II.i.101–102, 107–111)

Part of the delight of this poetry is that we can enjoy without agitation imaginative action of the highest order. It is like gazing in a crystal: what you see is clear and vivid, but on the other side of the glass. Almost unnoticed, the lines have a positive effect through the amorous suggestion implicit in the imagery, even while letting it be manifest that those concerned are only personifications of flowers and a pageant figure wearing the livery of the wrong season. Titania can speak of "the human mortals" as very far off indeed; the phrase crystallizes what has been achieved in imaginative distance and freedom. But Titania is as far off from us as we are from her.

The effect of wit which in such passages goes along with great imaginative power is abetted by the absence of any compelling interest in passion or plot. Producers utterly ruin the scene when they have the fairy couple mouth their lines at each other as expressively as possible. Titania, after all, leaves before that point is reached: "Fairies, away! / We shall chide downright if I longer stay" (II.i.144–145). At moments of dramatic intensity, the most violent distortion can go unnoticed; what the poet is doing is ignored in responding to what his people are doing. But here a great part of the point is that we *should* notice the distortion, the action of the poet, the wit. Plot tension launches flights of witty poetry which use it up, so to speak, just as the tensions in broad comedy are discharged in laughter. Rhetorical schematizations, or patterns of rhyme, are often used in *A Midsummer Night's Dream* to mark off the units of such verse. But blank verse paragraphs are also constructed so as to form autonomous bravura passages which reach a climax and come to rest while actor and audience catch their breath. Oberon's description of the mermaid, and his tribute to Elizabeth (II.i.148–164), are two such flights, each a rhythmical unit, the first punctuated by Puck's "I remember," the second by Oberon's change of tone at "Yet mark'd I where the bolt of Cupid fell." The formal and emotional isolation of the two passages is calculated to make the audience respond with wonder to the effortless reach of imagination which brings the stars madly shooting from their spheres. In a tribute to Elizabeth, the prominence of "the idea of the poet" in the poetry obviously was all to the good. By Oberon's remark to Puck, "that very time I saw, but thou couldst not," courtly Shakespeare contrived to place the mythology he was creating about Elizabeth on a level appropriately more sublime and occult than that about the mermaid.

* * *

JAN KOTT

From Titania and the Ass's Head[†]

* * *

A feature peculiar to Shakespeare is the suddenness of love. There is mutual fascination and infatuation from the very first glance, the

† From *Shakespeare Our Contemporary*, trans. Bolesław Taborski (New York and London: W. W. Norton, 1974), pp. 218–23, 225–29, 233–36. Copyright © 1964 by Panstwowe Wydawnictwo Naukowe and Doubleday, an imprint of Penguin Random House LLC. Used by permission of Doubleday, an imprint of the Knopf Doubleday Publishing Group, a division of Penguin Random House LLC. All rights reserved. Any third party use of this material, outside of this publication, is prohibited.

first touch of hands. Love falls down like a hawk; the world has
ceased to exist; the lovers see only each other. Love in Shakespeare
fills the entire being with rapture and desire. All that is left in the
Dream of these amorous passions is the suddenness of desire:

LYSANDER
I had no judgment when to her I swore.
HELENA
Nor none, in my mind, now you give her o'er.
LYSANDER
Demetrius loves her; and he loves not you.
DEMETRIUS (*awakes*)
O Helen, goddess, nymph, perfect, divine!
To what, my love, shall I compare thine eyne?
Crystal is muddy.

(III, 2)

The *Dream* is the most erotic of Shakespeare's plays. In no other
tragedy, or comedy, of his, except *Troilus and Cressida*, is the eroticism expressed so brutally. Theatrical tradition is particularly intol-
erable in the case of the *Dream*, as much in its classicist version,
with tunic-clad lovers and marble stairs in the background, as in its
other, operatic variation, with flowing transparent muslin and rope-
dancers. For a long time theatres have been content to present the
Dream as a Brothers Grimm fable, completely obliterating the pun-
gency of the dialogue and the brutality of the situations.

LYSANDER
Hang off, thou cat, thou burr! Vile thing, let loose,
Or I will shake thee from me like a serpent!
HERMIA
Why are you grown so rude? What change is this,
Sweet love?
LYSANDER
Thy love? Out, tawny Tartar, out!
Out, loathed med'cine! O hated potion, hence!

(III, 2)

Commentators have long since noticed that the lovers in this love
quartet are scarcely distinguishable from one another. The girls differ only in height and in the colour of their hair. Perhaps only Hermia has one or two individual traits, which let one trace in her an
earlier version of Rosaline in *Love's Labour's Lost*, and the later Rosa-
lind in *As You Like It*. The young men differ only in names. All four
lack the distinctness and uniqueness of so many other, even earlier
Shakespearean characters.

The lovers are exchangeable. Perhaps that was his purpose? The entire action of this hot night, everything that has happened at this drunken party, is based on the complete exchangeability of love partners. I always have the impression that Shakespeare leaves nothing to chance. Puck wanders round the garden at night and encounters couples who exchange partners with each other. It is Puck who makes the observation:

> This is the woman; but not this the man.
> (III, 2)

Helena loves Demetrius, Demetrius loves Hermia, Hermia loves Lysander. Helena runs after Demetrius, Demetrius runs after Hermia. Later Lysander runs after Helena. This mechanical reversal of the objects of desire, and the interchangeability of lovers is not just the basis of the plot. The reduction of characters to love partners seems to me to be the most peculiar characteristic of this cruel dream; and perhaps its most modern quality. The partner is now nameless and faceless. He or she just happens to be the nearest. As in some plays by Genet, there are no unambiguous characters, there are only situations. Everything has become ambivalent.

> HERMIA
> . . . Wherefore? O me! what news, my love?
> Am not I Hermia? Are not you Lysander?
> I am as fair now as I was erewhile.
> (III, 2)

Hermia is wrong. For in truth there is no Hermia, just as there is no Lysander. Or rather there are two different Hermias and two different Lysanders. The Hermia who sleeps with Lysander and the Hermia with whom Lysander does not want to sleep. The Lysander who sleeps with Hermia and the Lysander who is running away from Hermia.

* * *

> Give me that boy, and I will go with thee.
> (II, 1)

Shakespeare does not show the boy whom Titania to spite Oberon has stolen from the Indian king. But he mentions the boy several times and stresses the point. For the plot the boy is quite unnecessary. One could easily invent a hundred other reasons for the conflict between the royal couple. Apparently the introduction of the boy was essential to Shakespeare for other, non-dramatic purposes.

It is not only the Eastern page boy who is disturbing. The behaviour of all the characters, not only the commoners but also the royal and princely personages, is promiscuous:

> . . . the bouncing Amazon,
> Your buskin'd mistress and your warrior love, . . .
> (II, 1)

The Greek queen of the Amazons has only recently been the mistress of the king of the fairies, while Theseus has just ended his liaison with Titania. These facts have no bearing on the plot, nothing results from them. They even blur a little the virtuous and somewhat pathetic image of the betrothed couple drawn in Acts I and V. But these details undoubtedly represent allusions to contemporary persons and events.

I do not think it is possible to decipher all the allusions in the *Dream*. Nor is it essential. I do not suppose it matters a great deal either whether we discover for whose marriage Shakespeare hastily completed and adapted his *Midsummer Night's Dream*. It is only necessary for the actor, designer, and director to be aware of the fact that the *Dream* was a contemporary play about love. Both "contemporary" and "love" are significant words here. The *Dream* is also a most truthful, brutal, and violent play. Coming after *Romeo and Juliet*, as it did, the *Dream* was, as it were, a *nouvelle vague* in the theatre of the time.

*   *   *

On the soft grass, the entwined couples are still asleep:

> Good morrow, friends. Saint Valentine is past.
> Begin these woodbirds but to couple now?
> (IV, 1)

Hermia is the first to rise, though she had gone to sleep last. For her it was the craziest night. Twice she changed lovers. She is tired and can hardly stand on her feet.

> Never so weary, never so in woe;
> Bedabbled with the dew, and torn with briers;
> I can no further crawl, no further go; . . .
> (III, 2)

She is ashamed. She does not quite realize yet that day has come. She is still partly overwhelmed by night. She has drunk too much.

Methinks I see these things with parted eye,
When everything seems double.

(IV, 1)

The entire scene of the lovers' awakening in the morning abounds
in that brutal and bitter poetry that every stylized theatre production is bound to annihilate and destroy.

* * *

It is this passing through animality that seems to us the midsummer night's dream, or at least it is this aspect of the *Dream* that is
the most modern and revealing. This is the main theme joining
together all three separate plots running parallel in the play. Titania and Bottom will pass through animal eroticism in a quite literal, even visual sense. But even the quartet of lovers enter the dark
sphere of animal love-making:

HELENA
. . . I am your spaniel; and, Demetrius,
The more you beat me, I will fawn on you.
Use me but as your spaniel—spurn me, strike me, . . .

(II, 1)

And again:

What worser place can I beg in your love . . .
Than to be used as you use your dog?

(II, 1)

Pointers, kept on short leashes, eager to chase or fawning upon
their masters, appear frequently in Flemish tapestries representing
hunting scenes. They were a favourite adornment on the walls of
royal and princely palaces. But here a girl calls herself a dog fawning
on her master. The metaphors are brutal, almost masochistic.

It is worth having a closer look at the "bestiary" evoked by Shakespeare in the *Dream*. As a result of the romantic tradition, unfortunately preserved in the theatre through Mendelssohn's music, the
forest in the *Dream* still seems to be another version of Arcadia. But
in the actual fact, it is rather a forest inhabited by devils and lamias,
in which witches and sorceresses can easily find everything required
for their practices.

You spotted snakes with double tongue,
Thorny hedgehogs, be not seen;
Newts and blindworms, do no wrong,
Come not near our Fairy Queen.

(II, 2)

Titania lies down to sleep on a meadow among wild thyme, ox-lips, musk-roses, violets, and eglantine, but the lullaby sung by the fairies in her train seems somewhat frightening. After the creatures just quoted they go on to mention long-legged poisonous spiders, black beetles, worms, and snails. The lullaby does not forecast pleasant dreams.

The bestiary of the *Dream* is not a haphazard one. Dried skin of a viper, pulverized spiders, bats' gristles appear in every medieval or Renaissance prescription book as drugs to cure impotence and women's afflictions of one kind or another. All these are slimy, hairy, sticky creatures, unpleasant to touch and often arousing violent aversion. It is the sort of aversion that is described by psychoanalytic textbooks as a sexual neurosis. Snakes, snails, bats, and spiders also form a favourite bestiary of Freud's theory of dreams. Oberon orders Puck to make the lovers sleep that kind of sleep when he says:

> . . . lead them thus
> Till o'er their brows death-counterfeiting sleep
> With leaden legs and batty wings doth creep.
>
> (III, 2)

Titania's fairies are called: Peaseblossom, Cobweb, Moth, Mustardseed. In the theatre Titania's retinue is almost invariably represented as winged goblins, jumping and soaring in the air, or as a little ballet of German dwarfs. This sort of visual interpretation is so strongly suggestive that even commentators on the text find it difficult to free themselves from it. However, one has only to think on the very selection of these names to realize that they belong to the same love pharmacy of the witches.

I imagine Titania's court as consisting of old men and women, toothless and shaking, their mouths wet with saliva, who sniggering procure a monster for their mistress.

> The next thing then she, waking, looks upon
> (Be it on lion, bear, or wolf, or bull,
> On meddling monkey or on busy ape)
> She shall pursue it with the soul of love.
>
> (II, 1)

Oberon openly announces that as a punishment Titania will sleep with a beast. Again the selection of these animals is most characteristic, particularly in the next series of Oberon's threats:

> Be it ounce or cat or bear,
> Pard, or boar with bristled hair . . .
>
> (II, 2)

All these animals represent abundant sexual potency, and some of them play an important part in sexual demonology. Bottom is eventually transformed into an ass. But in this nightmarish summer night, the ass does not symbolize stupidity. From antiquity up to the Renaissance the ass was credited with the strongest sexual potency and among all quadrupeds was supposed to have the longest and hardest phallus.

* * *

> Thou art as wise as thou art beautiful.
> (III, 1)

The scenes between Titania and Bottom transformed into an ass are often played for laughs in the theatre. But I think that if one can see humour in this scene, it is the English kind of humour, "*humeur noire*", cruel and scatological, as it often is in Swift.

The slender, tender, and lyrical Titania longs for animal love. Puck and Oberon call the transformed Bottom a monster. The frail and sweet Titania drags the monster to bed, almost by force. This is the lover she wanted and dreamed of; only she never wanted to admit it, even to herself. The sleep frees her from inhibitions. The monstrous ass is being raped by the poetic Titania, while she still keeps on chattering about flowers:

> TITANIA
> The moon, methinks, looks with a wat'ry eye;
> And when she weeps, weeps every little flower,
> Lamenting some enforced chastity.
> Tie up my love's tongue, bring him silently.
> (III, 1)

Of all the characters in the play Titania enters to the fullest extent the dark sphere of sex where there is no more beauty and ugliness; there is only infatuation and liberation. In the coda of the first scene of the *Dream* Helena had already forecast:

> Things base and vile, holding no quantity,
> Love can transpose to form and dignity.
> (I, 1)

The love scenes between Titania and the ass must seem at the same time real and unreal, fascinating and repulsive. They are to rouse rapture and disgust, terror and abhorence. They should seem at once strange and fearful.

Come, sit thee down upon this flow'ry bed,
While I thy amiable cheeks do coy,
And stick musk-roses in thy sleek smooth head,
And kiss thy fair large ears, my gentle joy.
                                                    (IV, 1)

Chagall has depicted Titania caressing the ass. In his picture the
ass is sad, white, and affectionate. To my mind, Shakespeare's Titania, caressing the monster with the head of an ass, ought to be closer
to the fearful visions of Bosch and to the grotesque of the surreal-
ists. I think, too, that modern theatre, which has passed through
the poetics of surrealism, of the absurd, and through Genet's brutal
poetry, can depict this scene truly for the first time. * * *

                            *   *   *

The night is drawing to a close and the dawn is breaking. The lovers have already passed through the dark sphere of animal love. Puck
will sing an ironic song at the end of Act III. It is at the same time
a coda and a "song" to summarize the night's experiences.

Jack shall have Jill;
Naught shall go ill;
The man shall have his mare again, and all shall be well.
                                                    (III, 2)

Titania wakes up and sees a boor with an ass's head by her side.
She slept with him that night. But now it is daylight. She does not
remember ever having desired him. She remembers nothing. She
does not want to remember anything.

                          TITANIA
My Oberon, what visions have I seen!
Methought I was enamour'd of an ass.
                          OBERON
There lies your love.
                          TITANIA
                    How came these things to pass?
O, how mine eyes do loathe his visage now!
                                                    (IV, 1)

All are ashamed in the morning: Demetrius and Hermia, Lysander
and Helena. Even Bottom. Even he does not want to admit his dream:

Methought I was—there is no man can tell what.
Methought I was, and methought I had—But man is but a
patch'd fool if he will offer to say what methought I had.
                                                    (IV, 1)

In the violent contrast between the erotic madness liberated by the night and the censorship of day which orders everything to be forgotten, Shakespeare seems most ahead of his time. The notion that "life's a dream" has, in this context, nothing of baroque mysticism. Night is the key to day!

> . . . We are such stuff
> As dreams are made on; . . .
> (*The Tempest*, IV, 1)

Not only is Ariel an abstract Puck with a sad and thoughtful face; the philosophical theme of the *Dream* will be repeated in *The Tempest,* doubtless a more mature play. But the answers given by Shakespeare in *A Midsummer Night's Dream* seem more unambiguous, perhaps one can even say, more materialistic, less bitter.

> The lunatic, the lover, and the poet
> Are of imagination all compact.
> (V, 1)

The madness lasted throughout the June night. The lovers are ashamed of that night and do not want to talk about it, just as one does not want to talk of bad dreams. But that night liberated them from themselves. They were their real selves in their dreams.

> . . . And sleep, that sometimes shuts up sorrow's eye,
> Steal me awhile from mine own company.
> (III, 2)

The forest in Shakespeare always represents Nature. The escape to the Forest of Arden is an escape from the cruel world in which the way to the crown leads through murder, brother robs brother of his inheritance, and a father asks for his daughter's death if she chooses a husband against his will. But it is not only the forest that happens to be Nature. Our instincts are also Nature. And they are as mad as the world.

> Lovers and madmen have such seething brains. . . .
> (V, 1)

The theme of love will return once more in the old tragedy of Pyramus and Thisby, performed at the end of the *Dream* by Master Quince's troupe. The lovers are divided by a wall, cannot touch each other, and only see each other through a crack. They will never be joined together. A hungry lion comes to the rendezvous place, and Thisby flees in panic. Pyramus finds her blood-stained mantle and

stabs himself. Thisby returns, finds Pyramus's body, and stabs herself with the same dagger. The world is cruel for true lovers.

The world is mad, and love is mad. In this universal madness of
Nature and History, brief are the moments of happiness:

> . . . swift as a shadow, short as any dream,
> Brief as the lightning in the collied night. . . .
>
> (I, 1)

LYNDA E. BOOSE

From The Father and the Bride in Shakespeare[†]

The aristocratic family of Shakespeare's England was, according to
social historian Lawrence Stone, "patrilinear, primogenitural, and
patriarchal." Parent-child relations were in general remote and formal, singularly lacking in affective bonds and governed solely by a
paternal authoritarianism through which the "husband and father
lorded it over his wife and children with the quasi-authority of a des-
pot" (*Crisis* 271). Stone characterizes the society of the sixteenth
and early seventeenth centuries as one in which "a majority of individuals . . . found it very difficult to establish close emotional ties
to any other person" (*Family* 99)[1] and views the nuclear family as a
burdensome social unit, valued only for its ability to provide the
means of patrilineal descent. Second and third sons counted for
little and daughters for even less. A younger son could, it is true, be
kept around as a "walking sperm bank in case the elder son died
childless," but daughters "were often unwanted and might be regarded
as no more than a tiresome drain on the economic resources of the
family" (Stone, *Family* 88, 112).[2]

---

† From *PMLA* 97.3 (1982): 325–27, 341–44. Reprinted by permission of the copyright
 owner, the Modern Language Association of America.
1. Stone accounts for the drama and poetry of the sixteenth and early seventeenth centuries by modifying his "rather pessimistic view of a society with little love and generally
 low affect" to allow for "romantic love and sexual intrigue . . . in one very restricted
 social group . . . that is the households of princes and great nobles" (*Family* 103–04).
 This qualification does not extend to his view of parent-child relationships.
2. Stone also points out that the high infant-mortality rate, "which made it folly to
 invest too much emotional capital in such ephemeral beings," was as much responsi-
 ble for this lack of affective family ties as were any economic motives (*Family* 105).
 For Stone, paternal authority—not affection—was the almost exclusive source of the
 family's coherence. Furthermore, the domestic patriarchy of the sixteenth century
 was not merely a replica of family structures inherited from the past but a social pattern consciously exploited and reinforced by the state to emphasize the injunctions of
 obedience and authority; nor was it replaced until absolute monarchy was over-
 thrown (see *Family* 151–218). Meanwhile, because of the prevalent child-rearing
 practices, the maternal impact was relatively insignificant, hence not nearly so
 important to the psychological process of maturation; in Stone's estimate, our familiar "maternal, child-oriented, affectionate and permissive mode" of child rearing did

Various Elizabethan documents, official and unofficial, that comment on family relations support Stone's hypothesis of the absence of affect.[3] Yet were we to turn from Stone's conclusions to those we might draw from Shakespeare's plays, the disparity of implication—especially if we assume that the plays to some extent mirror the life around them—must strike us as significant. Shakespeare's dramas consistently explore affective family dynamics with an intensity that justifies the growing inference among Shakespearean scholars that the plays may be primarily "about" family relations and only secondarily about the macrocosm of the body politic.[4] Not the absence of affect but the possessive overabundance of it is the force that both

---

not emerge till about 1800 (*Family* 405). During the Elizabethan era, the upper-class practice of transferring a newborn infant immediately to a village wet nurse, who nurtured the child for two years, substantially muted any maternal influence on child development and no doubt created an inestimable psychological distance between mother and child. Stone cites the strained and formal relationship between Juliet and Lady Capulet as vivid testimony of the absence of affective mother-child bonds that results from such an arrangement (106); in the Capulet household, it is even left up to the nurse, not the mother, to remember Juliet's birthday. Yet Stone does not measure the relationship between Juliet and her father against his hypothesis of the absence of affect. Old Capulet is indeed the authoritarian dictator of Stone's model, but he is also a "careful father" who dearly loves his child. Instead of being eager to have her off his hands, Capulet is notably reluctant to give up the daughter he calls "the hopeful lady of my earth" (1.2.15; all Shakespeare quotations are from the Evans ed.); his bull-headed determination to marry her to Paris following Tybalt's death is born, paradoxically enough, from the deeply rooted affection that Stone's hypothesis excludes.

3. As Christopher Hill suggests in his review of Stone's *Family*, much of the evidence used could well imply its opposite: "The vigour of the preachers' propaganda on behalf . . . of breaking children's wills, suggests that such attitudes were by no means so universally accepted as they would have wished" (461). Hill and others have criticized Stone for asserting that love and affection were negligible social phenomena before 1700 and for presuming throughout "that values percolate downwards from the upper to the lower classes" (Hill 462). Because of the scope and importance of Stone's subject, his book has been widely reviewed. As David Berkowitz comments, "the possibility of endless symposia on Stone's vision and performance looms as a fashionable activity for the next half-dozen years" (396). Hill's review and the reviews by Keith Thomas and John Demos seem particularly well balanced.

4. One could chart the new emphasis on the family by reviewing the Shakespeare topics at recent MLA conventions. The 1979 convention featured Marriage and the Family in Shakespeare, Shirley Nelson Garner chairing, as its Shakespeare Division topic and also included a related special session, The Love between Shakespeare's Fathers and Daughters, Paul A. Jorgensen chairing. Before becoming the division topic, the subject had been examined in special sessions for three consecutive years: 1976, Marianne Novy chairing; 1977, John Bean and Coppélia Kahn chairing; and 1978, Carol Thomas Neely chairing. Special sessions continued in 1980 and 1981, with Shirley Nelson Garner and Madelon S. Gohlke as chairs. A parallel phenomenon has meanwhile been taking place in sixteenth-, seventeenth-, and eighteenth-century historical scholarship, which Hill explains by saying that ". . . the family as an institution rather suddenly became fashionable, perhaps as a by-product of the women's liberation movement" (450).

Most of the work on fathers and daughters in Shakespeare has been done, as might be expected, on the romances. See the essays by Cyrus Hoy, D. W. Harding, and Charles Frey. Of particular interest is the Schwartz and Kahn collection, which was published after I had written this paper but which includes several essays that express views related to my own. See esp. David Sundelson's "So Rare a Wonder'd Father: Prospero's *Tempest*," C. L. Barber's "The Family in Shakespeare's Development: Tragedy and Sacredness," and Coppélia Kahn's "The Providential Tempest and the Shakespearean Family."

defines and threatens the family in Shakespeare. When we measure Stone's assertions against the Shakespeare canon, the plays must seem startlingly ahistorical in focusing on what would seem to have been the least valued relationship of all: that between father and daughter.

While father and son appear slightly more often in the canon, figuring in twenty-three plays, father and daughter appear in twenty-one dramas and in one narrative poem. As different as these father-daughter plays are, they have one thing in common: almost without exception the relationships they depict depend on significant underlying substructures of ritual. Shakespeare apparently created his dramatic mirrors not solely from the economic and social realities that historians infer as having dictated family behavior but from archetypal models, psychological in import and ritual in expression. And the particular ritual model on which Shakespeare most frequently drew for the father-daughter relationship was the marriage ceremony.[5]

In an influential study of the sequential order or "relative positions within ceremonial wholes," Arnold van Gennep isolated three phases in ritual enactment that always recur in the same underlying arrangement and that form, in concert, "the pattern of the rites of passage": separation, transition, and reincorporation.[6] The church marriage service—as familiar to a modern audience as it was to Shakespeare's—contains all three phases. When considered by itself, it is basically a separation rite preceding the transitional phase of consummation and culminating in the incorporation of a new family unit. In Hegelian terms, the ceremonial activities associated

---

5. Margaret Loftus Ranald has done substantial work on the legal background of marriage in Shakespeare plays. I have found no marriages (or funerals) staged literally in the plays of Shakespeare or of his contemporaries. Although, for instance, the marriage of Kate and Petruchio would seem to offer a rich opportunity for an indecorously comic scene appropriate for *The Taming of the Shrew*, the action occurs offstage and we only hear of it secondhand. Nor do we witness the Olivia-Sebastian marriage in *Twelfth Night*. Even the fragment of the botched ceremony in *Much Ado* does not follow the liturgy with any precision but presents a dramatized version of it. This omission—apparently consistent in Elizabethan and Jacobean drama—may have resulted from the 1559 Act of Uniformity of Common Prayer and Divine Service in the Church, which stipulates sanctions against "any persone or persones whatsoever . . . [who] shall in anye Entreludes Playes Songes, Rymes or by other open Woordes, declare or speake anye thing in the derogation depraving or despising of the same Booke, or of any thing therein conteyned" (1 Elizabeth I, c. 2, in *Statutes* 4:355–58). Given the rising tempo of the Puritan attack on the theaters at this time, we may reasonably infer that the omission of liturgy reflects the dramatists' conscientious wish to avoid conflict. Richmond Noble's study corroborates this assumption (82). Of the services to which Shakespeare does refer, Noble notes that the allusions to "distinctive features, words, and phrases of Holy Matrimony are extremely numerous" (83).

6. Van Gennep built his study on the work of Hartland, Frazer, Ciszewski, Hertz, Crowley, and others who had noted resemblances among the components of various disparate rites. His tripartite diachronic structure provides the basis for Victor W. Turner's discussions in the essay "Liminality and Communitas" (*Ritual Process* 94–203).

with marriage move from thesis through antithesis to synthesis; the anarchic release of fertility is positioned between two phases of relative stasis. The ritual enables society to allow for a limited transgression of its otherwise universal taboo against human eroticism. Its middle movement is the dangerous phase of transition and transgression; its conclusion, the controlled reincorporation into the stability of family. But before the licensed transgression can take place—the transgression that generates the stability and continuity of society itself—the ritual must separate the sanctified celebrants from the sterile forces of social interdiction. The marriage ritual is thus a pattern of and for the community that surrounds it, as well as a rite of passage of and for the individuals who enact it. It serves as an especially effective substructure for the father-daughter relation because within its pattern lies the paradigm of all the conflicts that define this bond at its liminal moment of severance. The ceremony ritualizes two particularly significant events: a daughter and a son are being incorporated into a new family unit, an act that explicitly breaks down the boundaries of two previously existing families; yet, at the same time, the bonds being dissolved, particularly those between father and daughter, are being memorialized and thus, paradoxically, reasserted. In early comedies like *The Taming of the Shrew*, Shakespeare followed the Roman design of using the father of the young male lover as the *senex iratus*, a blocking figure to be circumvented. The mature comedies, tragedies, and romances reconstruct the problems of family bonds, filial obedience, and paternal possessiveness around the father and daughter, the relation put into focus by the marriage ceremony. When marriage activities are viewed from the perspective of their ritual implications, the bride and groom are not joined until the transitional phase of the wedding-night consummation; before that, a marriage may be annulled. What the church service is actually all about is the separation of the daughter from the interdicting father.

The wedding ceremony of Western tradition has always recognized the preeminence of the father-daughter bond. Until the thirteenth century, when the church at last managed to gain control of marriage law, marriage was considered primarily a private contract between two families concerning property exchange. The validity and legality of matrimony rested on the *consensus nuptialis* and the property contract, a situation that set up a potential for conflict by posing the mutual consent of the two children, who owed absolute obedience to their parents, against the desires of their families, who must agree beforehand to the contract governing property exchange. However true it was that the couple's willing consent was necessary for valid matrimony and however vociferously the official conduct books urged parents to consider the compatibility of the match, fathers like Cymbeline, Egeus, and Baptista feel perfectly free to disregard these requirements. Although lack of parental consent did not affect the validity of a marriage and, after 1604, affected the legality only when a minor was involved,[7] the family control over the dowry was a powerful psychological as well as economic weapon. Fathers like Capulet, Lear, and Brabantio depend on threats of disinheritance to coerce their children. When their daughters nonetheless wed without the paternal blessing, the marriages are adversely affected not because any legal statutes have been breached but because the ritual base of marriage has been circumvented and the psychological separation of daughter from father thus rendered incomplete. For in Shakespeare's time—as in our own—the ceremony acknowledged the special bond between father and daughter and the need for the power of ritual to release the daughter from its hold.

As specified in the 1559 *Book of Common Prayer*, the marriage ritual enjoins that the father (or, in his absence, the legal guardian)[8] deliver his daughter to the altar, stand by her in mute testimony that there are no impediments to her marriage, and then witness her pledge henceforth to forsake all others and "obey and serve, love honor and keep" the man who stands at her other side. To the priest's

7. The church canons of 1604 seem to have confused the situation further by continuing to recognize the validity of the nuptial pledge but forbidding persons under twenty-one to marry without parental consent; this ruling would make the marriage of minors illegal but nonetheless binding for life and hence valid (Stone, *Family* 32). Until the passage of Lord Hardwicke's Marriage Act in 1753, confusion was rife over what constituted a legal marriage and what a valid one. In addition to bringing coherence to the marriage laws, this act was designed to protect increasingly threatened parental interests by denying the validity as well as the legality of a religious ceremony performed without certain conditions, including parental consent for parties under twenty-one (Stone, *Family* 35–36).

   The concern for parental approval has always focused on, and in fact ritualized, the consent of the bride's father. In 1858, the Reverend Charles Wheatly, a noted authority on church law, attributed the father's giving away his daughter as signifying the care that must be taken of the female sex, "who are always supposed to be under the tuition of a father or guardian, whose consent is necessary to make their acts valid" (496). For supportive authority Wheatly looks back to Richard Hooker, whose phrasing is substantially harsher. Hooker felt that the retention of the custom "hath still this vse that it putteth we men in mind of a dutie whereunto the verie imbecillitie of their [women's] nature and sex doth binde them, namely to be alwaies directed, guided and ordered by others . . ." (215).

   Even though the validity of a marriage was not vested in parental consent, "the Protestants, including the Anglicans, considered the consent of the parents to be as essential to the marriage as the consent of the bride and bridegroom" (Flandrin 131). Paradoxically, "both Church and State claimed to be supporting, at one and the same time, freedom of marriage and the authority of parents" (Flandrin 132). The ambiguity arose because the child was obliged, under pain of mortal sin, to obey the parent. Technically, the child was free to choose a marriage partner, but since the church never took steps against the prerogatives of the father, the notion of choice was problematic.

8. Given the high parent mortality rate, a number of brides necessarily went to the altar on the arms of their legal guardians Peter Laslett notes that in Manchester between 1553–1657 over half of the girls marrying for the first time were fatherless (103), but some historians have criticized his reliance on parish registers as the principal demographic barometer.

question, "Who giveth this woman to be married unto this man?"—
a question that dates in English tradition back to the York manual
(*Book of Common Prayer* 290–99; 408, n.)—the father must silently
respond by physically relinquishing his daughter, only to watch the
priest place her right hand into the possession of another man. Following this expressly physical symbolic transfer, the father's role in
his daughter's life is ended; custom dictates that he now leave the
stage, resign his active part in the rite, and become a mere observer.
After he has withdrawn, the couple plight their troths, and the groom
receives the ring, again from the priest. Taking the bride's hand into
his, the groom places the ring on her finger with the words, "With
this ring I thee wed, with my body I thee worship, and with all my
worldly goods I thee endow," thus solemnizing the transfer in its
legal, physical, and material aspects.[9]

Before us we have a tableau paradigmatic of the problematic
father-daughter relation: decked in the symbols of virginity, the bride
stands at the altar between her father and husband, pulled as it were
between the two important male figures in her life. To resolve the
implied dilemma, the force of the priest and the community presides
over and compels the transfer of an untouched daughter into
the physical possession of a male whom the ceremony authorizes
both as the invested successor to the father's authority and as the

9. The groom's pledge suggests the wedding ring's dual sexual and material symbolism.
Historically, the ring symbolizes the dowry payment that the woman will receive from
her husband by the entitlement of marriage; it apparently superseded the custom of
placing tokens of espousal on the prayer book (see *Book of Common Prayer* 408). It also
signifies the physical consummation, a point frequently exploited in Renaissance
drama and also implied by the rubrics in the older Roman Catholic manuals, which
direct the placing of the ring. The Martène manual specifies that the bride is to wear it
on the left hand to signify "a difference between the estate and the episcopal order, by
whom the ring is publicly worn on the right hand as a symbol of full and entire chastity" (Legg 207). *The Rathen Manual*, which follows the Use of Sarum, contains a
rather charming piece of folklore widely believed through the eighteenth century. It,
too, allusively suggests the sexual significance of the ring: "For in the fourth finger
there is a certain vein proceeding to the heart and by the chime of silver there is represented the internal affection which ought always to be fresh between them" (35–36;
see also Wheatly 503). Even after the priest took over the ceremonial role of transferring the bride's hand from her father's to her husband's, he did not also become the
intermediary in transferring the ring from the groom's keeping to the bride's finger.
Such an incorporation of duties might seem logical were it not that this part of the ritual simultaneously imitates and licenses the sexual act.
   The English reformers retained both the symbol of the ring and the groom's accompanying pledge to "worship" his wife's body, a retention that generated considerable
attack from the more radical reformers. The controversy over this wording occupies the
major portion of Hooker's defense of the Anglican marriage rite (see also Stone, *Family*
522, on the attempts in 1641 and 1661 to alter the wording of the vow from "worship"
to "honor"). Hooker justifies the husband's "worship" as a means of transferring to the
wife the "dignitie" incipient in her husband's legitimizing of the children he now allows
her to bear. She furthermore receives, by this annexation of his worship, a right to
participate in his material possessions. The movement of the vow, from sexual to material pledge, thus sequences a formal rite of passage, a pattern alluded to in Hooker's
phrase, "the former branch hauing granted the principal!, the latter graunteth that
which is annexed thereunto" (216).

sanctified transgressor of prohibitions that the father has been compelled to observe.[1] By making the father transfer his intact daughter to the priest in testimony that he knows of no impediments to her lawful union, the service not only reaffirms the taboo against incest but implicitly levels the full weight of that taboo on the relationship between father and daughter. The groom's family does not enter into the archetypal dynamics going on at this altar except through the priest's reference to marriage as the cause why a man "shall leave father and mother and shall be joined unto his wife." The mother of the bride is a wholly excluded figure—as indeed she is throughout almost the entire Shakespeare canon. Only the father must act out, must dramatize his loss before the audience of the community. Within the ritual circumscription, the father is compelled to give his daughter to a rival male; and as Georges Bataille comments:

> The gift itself is a renunciation. . . . Marriage is a matter less for the partners than for the man who gives the woman away, the man whether father or brother who might have freely enjoyed the woman, daughter or sister, yet who bestows her on someone else. This gift is perhaps a substitute for the sexual act; for the exuberance of giving has a significance akin to that of the act itself; it is also a spending of resources.[2]   (218)

---

1. The ceremonial transfer of the father's authority to the husband is acknowledged by the Reverend John Shepherd in his historical commentary accompanying the 1853 *Family Prayer Book*: ". . . the ceremony shows the father's consent; and that the authority, which he before possessed, he now resigns to the husband" (Brownell 465). By implication, however, the ceremony resolves the incestuous attraction between father and daughter by ritualizing his "gift" of her hand, a signification unlikely to be discussed in the commentary of church historians. When first the congregation and next the couple are asked to name any impediments to the marriage, there are, Wheatly says, three specific impediments the church is charging all knowledgeable parties to declare: a preceding marriage or contract, consanguinity or affinity, and want of consent (483). The final act of Ben Jonson's *Epicoene* enumerates all the possible legal impediments that might be subsumed under these three.

   The bride's father, by virtue of his special prominence in the ritual, functions as a select witness whose presence attests to the validity of the contract. The Friar in *Much Ado* asks Hero and Claudio whether they "know any inward impediment why you should not be cojoin'd" (4.1.12–13). Leonato dares to respond for Claudio, "I dare make his answer, none," because, as father of the bride, he presumes to have full knowledge that no impediment exists. When he learns of Hero's supposed taint, the rage he vents over the loss of his own honor is more comprehensible when we understand his special position in the ceremony as a sworn witness to the transfer of an intact daughter.

2. The sections on the celebration of "Festiuall daies" and times of fast that precede Hooker's defense of the English "Celebration of Matrimonie" are especially helpful in understanding Elizabethan ritual, for in these sections Hooker expands his defense of the Anglican rites into an explanation of, and rationale for, the whole notion of ritual. Having first isolated three sequential elements necessary for festival—praise, bounty, and rest—he goes on to justify "bountie" in terms remarkably compatible with the theories of both Bataille and Lévi-Strauss on the essential "spending-gift" nature of marriage. To Hooker, the "bountie" essential to celebration represents the expression of a "charitable largenesse of somewhat more then common bountie. . . . Plentifull and liberall expense is required in them that abounde, partly as a signe of their owne ioy in the goodnesse of

By playing out his role in the wedding ceremony, the father implic-itly gives the blessing that licenses the daughter's deliverance from family bonds that might otherwise become a kind of bondage. Hence in *A Midsummer Night's Dream*, a play centered on marriage, the intransigent father Egeus, supported by the king-father figure Theseus, poses a threat that must be converted to a blessing to ensure the comic solution. In *Love's Labor's Lost*, the sudden death of the Princess' father, who is likewise the king-father figure for all the French ladies, prevents the necessary blessing, thus cutting sharply across the movement toward comic resolution and postponing the happy ending. In plots constructed around a daughter without a father, the absent father frequently assumes special dramatic prominence. This absence felt almost as a presence may well contribute to the general unease and unresolved tensions emanating from the three "problem plays," for Helena, Isabella, and Cressida are all daughters severed from their fathers.

✳   ✳   ✳

WORKS CITED

Barber, C. L. *Shakespeare's Festive Comedy*. Princeton: Princeton Univ. Press, 1959.

Bataille, Georges. *Death and Sensuality: A Study of Eroticism and the Taboo*. 1962; rpt. New York: Arno, 1977.

God towards them" (292, 293). Bounty is important to all festival rites, but within the marriage rite this "spending" quality incorporates the specific idea of sexual orgasm as the ultimate and precious expenditure given the bride by her husband, a notion alluded to in Bataille and one that functioned as a standard Elizabethan metaphor apparent in phrases like "Th' expense of spirit" (sonnet 129) or Othello's comment to Desdemona, "The purchase made, the fruits are to ensue; / That profit's yet to come 'tween me and you" (2.3.9–10). The wedding ceremony ritualizes this notion of bounty as the gift of life by having the father give the groom the family treasure, which the father cannot "use" but can only bequeath or hoard. The groom, who ritually places coins or a gold ring on the prayer book as a token "bride price," then fully "purchases" the father's treasure through his own physical expenditure, an act that guarantees the father's "interest" through future generations. This money-sex image complex is pervasive and important in many of Shake-speare's plays. The pattern and its relation to festival are especially evident in Juliet's ecstatic and impatient speech urging night to come and bring her husband:

> O, I have bought the mansion of a love,
> But not possess'd it, and though I am sold,
> Not yet enjoy'd. So tedious is this day
> As is the night before some festival.
> (3.2.26–29).

In another context, this pattern enables us fully to understand Shylock's miserly refusal to give or spend and the implications of his simultaneous loss of daughter and hoarded fortune. His confusion of daughter and ducats is foreshadowed when he recounts the story of Jacob and equates the increase of the flock through the "work of generation" to the increase of money through retentive "use." To Antonio's question, "Or is your gold and silver ewes and rams?" Shylock responds, "I cannot tell, I make it breed as fast" (*MV* 1.3.95–96).

Berkowitz, David. *Renaissance Quarterly* 32(1979): 396–403.

The Book of Common Prayer, 1559. Ed. John E. Booty. Charlottesville: Univ. of Virginia Press, 1967.

Boose, Lynda E. "Othello's Handkerchief: 'The Recognizance and Pledge of Love.'" *English Literary Renaissance* 5(1975): 360–74.

Brownell, Thomas Church, ed. *The Family Prayer Book; or,* The Book of Common Prayer *according to the Use of the Protestant Episcopal Church.* New York: Stanford and Swords, 1853.

The Church and the Law of Nullity of Marriage. Report of a commission appointed by the archbishops of Canterbury and York in 1949. London: Society for Promoting Christian Knowledge, 1955.

Demos, John. *New York Times Book Review,* 25 Dec. 1977, 1.

Dundes, Alan. "'To Love My Father All': A Psychoanalytic Study of the Folktale Source of *King Lear.*" *Southern Folklore Quarterly* 40(1976): 353–66.

Eliade, Mircea. *The Sacred and the Profane.* Trans. Willard R. Trask. New York: Harcourt, 1959.

Evans, G. Blakemore, ed. *The Riverside Shakespeare.* Boston: Houghton, 1974.

Flandrin, Jean-Louis. *Families in Former Times: Kinship, Household and Sexuality.* Trans. Richard Southern. Cambridge: Cambridge Univ. Press, 1979.

Frey, Charles. "'O sacred, shadowy, cold, and constant queen': Shakespeare's Imperiled and Chastening Daughters of Romance." *South Atlantic Bulletin* 43(1978): 125–40.

The Geneva Bible. 1560; facsim. rpt. Madison: Univ. of Wisconsin Press, 1961.

Harding, D. W. "Father and Daughter in Shakespeare's Last Plays." *TLS,* 30 Nov. 1979, 59–61.

Hill, Christopher, "Sex, Marriage and the Family in England." *Economic History Review,* 2nd ser., 31(1978): 450–63.

Hooker, Richard. *Of the Lawes of Ecclesiasticall Politie.* 1594; facsim. rpt. Amsterdam: Theatrum Orbis Terrarum, 1971.

Howard, George Elliott. *A History of Matrimonial Institutions.* London: T. Fisher Unwin, 1904.

Hoy, Cyrus. "Fathers and Daughters in Shakespeare's Romances." In *Shakespeare's Romances Reconsidered.* Ed. Carol McGinnis Kay and Henry E. Jacobs. Lincoln: Univ. of Nebraska Press, 1978, 77–90.

Kelly, Henry Ansgar. *The Matrimonial Trials of Henry VIII.* Stanford, Calif.: Stanford Univ. Press, 1976.

Laslett, Peter. *The World We Have Lost.* 2nd ed. 1965; rpt. London: Methuen, 1971.

LeClercq, R. V. "Crashaw's Epithalamium: Pattern and Vision." *Literary Monographs* 6. Madison: Univ. of Wisconsin Press, 1975, 73–108.

Legg, J. Wickham. *Ecclesiological Essays*. London: De La More Press, 1905.

Lévi-Strauss, Claude. *The Elementary Structures of Kinship*. Trans. James Harle Bell. Ed. John Richard von Sturmer and Rodney Needham. Paris, 1949; rpt. Boston: Beacon, 1969.

McCown, Gary M. "'Runnawayes Eyes' and Juliet's Epithalamion." *Shakespeare Quarterly* 27(1976): 150–70.

Noble, Richmond. *Shakespeare's Use of the Bible and* The Book of Common Prayer. London: Society for the Promotion of Biblical Knowledge, 1935.

Partridge, Eric. *Shakespeare's Bawdy*. 1948; rpt. New York: Dutton, 1969.

Rabkin, Norman. *Shakespeare and the Problem of Meaning*. Chicago: Univ. of Chicago Press, 1981.

Ranald, Margaret Loftus. "'As Marriage Binds, and Blood Breaks': English Marriage and Shakespeare." *Shakespeare Quarterly* 30(1979): 68–81.

The Rathen Manual. Ed. Duncan MacGregor. Aberdeen: Aberdeen Ecclesiological Society, 1905.

Schoenbaum, S. *William Shakespeare: A Compact Documentary Life*. Oxford: Oxford Univ. Press, 1975.

Schwartz, Murray M., and Coppélia Kahn, eds. *Representing Shakespeare: New Psychoanalytic Essays*. Baltimore: Johns Hopkins Univ. Press, 1980.

The Statutes of the Realm. London: Record Commissions, 1820–28; facsim. ed. 1968.

Stone, Lawrence. *The Crisis of the Aristocracy: 1558–1660*. Abridged ed. London: Oxford Univ. Press, 1971.

———. *The Family, Sex and Marriage in England: 1500–1800*. New York: Harper, 1977.

Thomas, Keith. *TLS*, 21 Oct. 1977, 1226.

Tufte, Virginia. *The Poetry of Marriage*. Los Angeles: Tinnon-Brown, 1970.

Turner, Victor W. *The Ritual Process: Structure and Anti-Structure*. Chicago: Aldine, 1969.

Van Gennep, Arnold. *The Rites of Passage*. Trans. Monika B. Vizedom and Gabrielle L. Caffee. 1908; rpt. London: Routledge and Kegan Paul, 1960.

Wheatly, Charles. *A Rational Illustration of* The Book of Common Prayer *according to the Use of the Church of England*. Cambridge: Cambridge Univ. Press, 1858.

MARGO HENDRICKS

From "Obscured by dreams": Race, Empire, and Shakespeare's A Midsummer Night's Dream†

* * *

At the beginning of Act 2, Puck informs one of the queen's fairies (and the audience) that Titania has a "lovely boy," allegedly the "stol'n" son of an "Indian king," whom Oberon desires to be a "Knight of his train, to trace the forests wild" (2.1.25). On a textual level Puck has little reason to establish the boy's identity beyond distinguishing him as a source of tension between the fairy queen and king; as I suggested earlier, the play's dramatic structure would not have been violated had this information been omitted or had Shakespeare identified the child as an English boy. Similarly, if the fairies are to be seen as English, there is no obvious reason for Shakespeare to specify India as Oberon's most recent place of resort. Titania demands,

> Why art thou here,
> Come from the farthest step of India,—
> But that, forsooth, the bouncing Amazon,
> Your buskined mistress and your warrior love,
> To Theseus must be wedded. . . .
>
> (2.1.68–72)

Though Titania answers her own question—"Why art thou here"—her words do not entirely explain Shakespeare's invocation of India.

Oberon is, of course, explicitly connected with India in the literary tradition from which Shakespeare draws. However, this explanation does not help us to address the query—why an Indian boy? * * * Perhaps another way to get at an answer is to examine Shakespeare's characterization in terms of his use of the lexicon engendered by early modern English mercantile activity in India. In this way we can make intelligible India's function as the center of linguistic and ideological exchanges between Athens and fairyland. Like Athens, India is an actual geographic place, and, like fairyland, it is still figured as a place of the imagination. This simultaneity permits the articulation of a racial fantasy in A Midsummer Night's Dream where Amazons and fairies signify an alien yet domestic paradox in an otherwise stable, homogeneous world.

† From Shakespeare Quarterly 47.1 (1996): 51–56. © 1996 Folger Shakespeare Library. Reprinted with permission of Johns Hopkins University Press.

When Titania offers Oberon the reason for her resistance to his wishes, in a poignant (and poetic) vision of female and mercantile fecundity, this vision is, in effect, a mapping of this reality:

> His mother was a votress of my order,
> And in the spicèd Indian air by night
> Full often hath she gossiped by my side . . .
> Marking th'embarkèd traders on the flood,
> When we have laughed to see the sails conceive
> And grow big-bellied with the wanton wind;
> Which she, with pretty and with swimming gait
> Following (her womb then rich with my young squire),
> Would imitate, and sail upon the land
> To fetch me trifles, and return again
> As from a voyage, rich with merchandise.
> But she, being mortal, of that boy did die,
> And for her sake do I rear up her boy;
> And for her sake I will not part with him.
>
> (2.1.123–37)

Titania's words in this scene vividly reproduce the idealized imagery in the writings of travelers to India. The votaress embodies what India could (and would) represent to Europe as, like the merchant ships, she returns "from a voyage, rich with merchandise," to bring Titania the exotic "trifles" of an unfamiliar world.[1]

Her speech "rich" with the language of English mercantilism, Titania evokes not only the exotic presence of the Indian woman's native land but also the power of the "traders" to invade and domesticate India and, aided by the "wanton wind," return to Europe "rich with merchandise." In Shakespeare's "poetic geography," India becomes the commodified space of a racialized feminine eroticism that (to judge by the written accounts of such men as Vertomannus and van Linschoten) paradoxically excited and threatened the masculinity of European travelers. This racial subtext, which complicates the "shaping fantasy" of *A Midsummer Night's Dream*, is not obvious when Titania and Oberon first appear onstage. Their initial exchange is accusatory and fraught with erotic tension that masks their far greater conflict.

In response to Titania calling Hippolyta his "buskined mistress and warrior love," Oberon retorts: "How canst thou thus, for shame,

---

1. In an unpublished essay, Joan Pong Linton has noted that, within the early modern English lexicon, *trifles* was generally used to describe the type of exchanges between Native Americans and English sailors. For a different analysis of relations of exchange between the English and Native Americans, see Pong Linton, "*Jack of Newbery* and Drake in California: Domestic and Colonial Narratives of English Cloth and Manhood," *ELH* 59 (1992): 23–51.

Titania, / Glance at my credit with Hippolyta, / Knowing I know thy
love to Theseus?" (2.1.74–76). Oberon then lists the women Theseus
has seduced and abandoned, apparently with Titania's aid.[2] Titania
casually dismisses Oberon's accusation: "these are the forgeries of
jealousy" (l. 81). The audience soon discovers what is really at the
core of Titania's and Oberon's estrangement: she has refused to give
him the child of her votaress, the "little changeling boy." As the text
presents it, Titania's interest in the boy is sentimental, linked to her
relationship with his mother and the promise the fairy queen made.
Oberon's interest, on the other hand, is textually much more ambiguous. In fact, if both he and Puck are to be taken at their word,
Oberon's interest in the Indian boy is primarily one of dominion:
possession is linked to Oberon's political authority.

From the beginning both Oberon and Puck make clear that
Oberon desires to have the boy as a "henchman" or "Knight of his
train." Furthermore, Oberon's desire for the boy seems very much
connected to desire for dominion over Titania. Hence I am inclined
to view Oberon's quest for the boy less as the embodiment of fatherly
love or pride than as the manifestation of a perceived prerogative to
claim possession—to have "all . . . tied to" him. The paternal interest that many critics argue lies at the heart of Oberon's desire is not
evident in his words.[3] One finds in his exercise of paternalism the
very ideology that made it "the smart thing for titled and propertied
families in England to have a black slave or two among the household
servants."[4] Like the growing number of non-European (particularly
African) children who were imported into England to serve as badges
of status for England's aristocracy, the "changeling boy" is desired
as an exotic emblem of Oberon's worldly authority. Oberon's desire
to claim the Indian boy as his servant should not be trivialized; in
another century or so Asian Indians would become the household
fashion.

2. One wonders whether this accusation might also imply that Titania is the real object of
   Theseus's love, that it is for love of her that he left the other women.
3. In this I diverge from Louis A. Montrose, who reads this conflict in terms of the psychology of the nuclear family, where Oberon's efforts are seen as an "attempt to take
   the boy from an infantilizing mother and to make a man of him" ("A Midsummer Night's
   Dream and the Shaping Fantasies of Elizabethan Culture: Gender, Power, Form" in
   Rewriting the Renaissance: The Discourses of Sexual Difference in Early Modern
   Europe, Margaret W. Ferguson, Maureen Quilligan, and Nancy J. Vickers, eds. [Chi-
   cago and London: U of Chicago P, 1986], 65–87, esp. 74). Allan Dunn also sees the play
   in terms of this psychology, though he reads this familial conflict from the changeling's
   point of view, in his "The Indian Boy's Dream Wherein Every Mother's Son Rehearses
   His Part: Shakespeare's A Midsummer Night's Dream," Shakespeare Studies 20 (1988):
   15–32. It seems to me that both monarchs operate within a feudal ideology about social
   responsibilities and status. Thus the Indian boy elicits from the monarchs very different interpretations of their social roles.
4. Peter Fryer, Staying Power: The History of Black People in Britain (London and Sydney:
   Pluto Press, 1984), 9. See also Folarin Shyllon, Black People in Britain 1555–1833,
   published for The Institute of Race Relations (London: Oxford UP, 1977); and James
   Walvin, The Black Presence in Britain (London: Orbach and Chambers, 1971).

But why the insistence on possession of the Indian boy? Dramatically, both Oberon's and Titania's obduracy is crucial to the plot structure but not dependent on the changeling's being Indian. The answer is to be found in Shakespeare's rewriting of the figure of Oberon and in the larger problem that *A Midsummer Night's Dream* explores in some detail: gender relations. And, as we shall see, a changeling is not always a mere changeling.

The idea of change (or transformation) is central to the dramatic plot and to the specific resolution of the dissension between Oberon and Titania. In order to dissolve the stalemate, Oberon must produce willingness in Titania to "amend" their "debate"; that is, he must persuade her to change her mind about giving up the Indian boy. The flower, "love-in-idleness," itself a product of change, enables Oberon to achieve his desire—the changeling child. The curious thing about this situation, and one worth exploring, is why Oberon feels it necessary to provide Nick Bottom as a substitute for the Indian boy.[5] Luce Irigaray suggests that men "make commerce *of* [women] . . . , but they do not enter into any exchanges *with* them," largely because "the economy of exchange—of desire—is man's business."[6] Because there is no other male of equal rank and power with whom Oberon can negotiate an exchange, and because the object he desires is not a wife but a page, he is forced to rewrite the rules governing this "economy of exchange" so that a direct transaction with Titania can take place. Importantly, the objects of exchange must be equivalents, and thus Oberon must provide a changeling for a changeling.

When Nick Bottom reappears from the brake, his head transformed into that of an ass, Snout declares, "O Bottom, thou art changed. What do I see on thee?" (3.1.96). Peter Quince considers Bottom "monstrous" and later declares that Bottom has been "translated" (ll. 86, 98). Puck's alteration of Bottom enacts a familiar literary emblem.[7] Bottom, intriguingly, is "translated" into neither centaur nor satyr; it is not his body that is altered but his head: "An ass's nole I fixed on his head" (3.2.17). The alien(ness) Bottom represents is a mixture of the familiar and the foreign; with the exception of his head, Nick Bottom remains distinctly human. What is striking about Puck's trick and Oberon's exploitation of it is not only

---

5. The substitution of Nick Bottom as the object of Titania's affections, his regression to an infantile state, and the sexual significance of this new relationship have long received critical attention. For an insightful examination of sexuality, bodily functions, and shame in *A Midsummer Night's Dream*, see Gail Kern Paster, *The Body Embarrassed: Drama and the Disciplines of Shame in Early Modern England* (Ithaca, NY, and London: Cornell UP, 1993), esp. 125–43.
6. Luce Irigaray, "Women on the Market" in *This Sex Which is Not One*, trans. Catherine Porter (Ithaca, NY, and London: Cornell UP, 1985), 172 and 177.
7. For a discussion of Apuleius's *The Golden Ass* and Ovid's *Metamorphoses* as sources for Shakespeare's representation of Bottom, see Foakes, ed., 9–10.

that it violates the sociocultural endogamy—the commerce that upholds patriarchal traffic in women—but that, in the substitution of the "translated" Nick Bottom for the Indian boy as the other male in the triangular relationship of desire, it irrevocably redefines both sexual and racial parameters in fairyland.

While the boy changeling may be viewed as the object of maternal affection, the adult changeling clearly invokes a different response in the fairy queen. In Titania's bower, Bottom, though subject to the fairy queen, clearly is not perceived as a mere child. On the contrary, as Titania's behavior indicates, Bottom becomes a substitute for Oberon as well. By employing Bottom as the erotic trap that permits him to "steal the boy," Oberon finds himself ensnared by the "hateful imperfection" of monstrous humanity that he has engendered: "For, meeting her of late behind the wood / Seeking sweet favours for this hateful fool, / I did upbraid her and fall out with her" (4.1.60, 45–47). For Oberon, who is initially pleased with Puck's prank, the "sweet sight" (l. 43) of Titania embracing a "translated" Bottom in her bower eventually loses its charm. Once central to Titania's erotic desires, Oberon finds himself displaced twice: first by a changeling and then, in Bottom, by a monstrous "changeling" to boot. And while Oberon may now possess the Indian boy, it appears that the new changeling has become for the fairy king more than the "fierce vexation of a dream" (l. 66).

Change, rather than dreams, is the defining trope of *A Midsummer Night's Dream*. Whether in the changed story of the lovers Apollo and Daphne or in the "little western flower," in Lysander's drug-induced change or in Hippolyta's weariness with the moon—"Would he would change!" (5.1.238)—change generates not something unintelligible and fundamentally alien but something that, because of its composition, is (paradoxically) differently the same. In effect, what is constituted is the hybrid. Even so, Hippolyta's moon, Hermia's Lysander, and the "little western flower" remain intelligible to all as moon, man, and flower despite their transformation. The change that Bottom and the Indian boy literally and symbolically register, on the other hand, is of a more particularized form—it is an ethnic (or racial) change that involves the forcible removal of a person from one culture to another and, in the case of Bottom, a change that produces a phenotypical transformation as well. And, not surprisingly, the ease with which change is accommodated, even accepted, produces general anxiety within fairyland.

At the center of this trope of change is a concept linked to the Spanish term *mestizaje*, or mixedness. The *Diccionario de Uso del Español* defines *mestizaje* as the "*cruzamiento de razas*" (crossbreeding of races) or the "*conjunto de mestizos*" (group of mestizos) and relates it to the verb *mestizar*, defined as "*adulterar la puerza de una raza por el cruce con otras*" (adulterating the purity of one race by mixing with others).[8] Both Bottom and the changeling child exemplify this hybrid state: in Bottom we see the *cruzamiento* of two species—human and equine (literally, the *mulatto*)—and in the Indian boy the possibility of human and fairy mixedness (the *mestizo*).

It is, of course, critically problematic to label Bottom and the Indian boy in the terms of a racial lexicon that is not employed in Shakespeare's play. Yet I believe such a move is both theoretically and heuristically appropriate given Shakespeare's own framing of fairyland as a borderland between India and Athens. In this space, through his "translation" and incorporation into fairyland, Bottom becomes the figurative and literal instantiation of that newly engendered lexical hybrid, the *mulatto*. Similarly, while the Indian boy's enigmatic textual history must forever occlude the "facts" of his genesis (is Puck right when he declares the boy's father to be an Indian king, or is this merely one more of the mischievous sprite's fabrications?), Titania's narrative of the Indian boy's origins and her own behavior are so symptomatic of the accounts of Indian women by the travelers van Linschoten and Vertomannus that it is worthwhile linking these representations to the emerging linguistic taxonomy of cultural difference. Shakespeare's use of India calls attention to this parallel discourse; and if we look closely at its lexical and taxonomic matrices, we can shed light on the way race works in *A Midsummer Night's Dream*. . . . The conflicting terrain of fairyland, with its easy violation of borders—both speciegraphical and geographical—adumbrates an ontological engagement with the linguistic complexities of *mestizaje*.

PETER BROOK

A Cook and a Concept: Dreaming the *Dream*[†]

Once a computer was asked, 'What is the truth?' It took a very long time before the reply came, 'I will tell you a story . . .'

Today, this is the only way I can answer the question I've been asked so often: 'Why don't you write about *A Midsummer Night's Dream*? You must have so much to say!'

So—I'll tell you a story.

When I was eighteen or nineteen, my one ambition was to make a film. By chance, I met the most eminent producer of the day, Sir Alexander Korda, a Hungarian of humble origins who had emigrated

8. María Moliner, *Diccionario de Uso del Español*, 2 vols. (Madrid: Editorial Gredos, 1967), 2:402.
† From *The Quality of Mercy: Reflections on Shakespeare* (London: Nick Hern Books, 2013), pp. 75–85. Reprinted by permission of the publisher.

to make his fortune first in France, then in Britain, where he rose to power, was ennobled by the King and married a beautiful star, Merle Oberon, who for my father was 'the perfect woman'.

I had just been on a trip to Seville during Holy Week, was thrilled by the multitude of mysterious impressions and imagined a story set in this extraordinary background.

'Sir Alexander,' I began, 'I have an idea for a film—'

He cut me off with an unforgettable phrase that contained in a few words the period in which it was uttered, the British class system and the snobbery of a newly enlisted member of the upper classes. With a light dismissal of the hand he said: 'Even a cook can have an idea.'

This was virtually the end of the meeting. 'Come back when you have developed your "idea" enough to have a real story to offer me.'

It took many years to free his phrase from its period and context and to hear the deep truth it contained.

This brings me directly to *A Midsummer Night's Dream*. It had never occurred to me to think of directing the *Dream*. I had seen many charming productions with pretty scenery and enthusiastic girls pretending to be fairies. Yet, when I was invited to do the play in Stratford, I discovered to my surprise that my answer was 'Yes'. Somewhere in me there was an intuition that I had ignored.

Then, the first visit to Europe of the Peking Circus revealed that in the lightness and speed of anonymous bodies performing astonishing acrobatics without exhibitionism, it was pure spirit that appeared. This was a pointer to go beyond illustration to evocation, and I began to imagine a co-production with the Chinese. A year later, in New York, it was a ballet of Jerome Robbins that opened another door. A small group of dancers around a piano brought into fresh and magical life the same Chopin nocturnes that had always been inseparable from the trappings of tutus, painted trees and moonlight. In timeless clothes, they just danced. These pointers encouraged a burning hunch that, somewhere, an unexpected form was waiting to be discovered.

I talked this over with Trevor Nunn, director of the Royal Shakespeare Theatre, who said for this season he had created a young company who could in no time learn anything that was needed. It seemed too good to be true, especially as the Chinese Circus acrobats started their training at the age of five.

So we began with only the conviction that if we worked long, hard and joyfully on all the aspects of the play, a form would gradually appear. We started preparing the ground to give this form a chance. Within each day we improvised the characters and the story, practised acrobatics and then passing from the body to the mind, discussed and analysed the text line by line, with no idea of where this was leading us. There was no chaos, only a firm guide, the sense of an unknown form calling us to continue.

Through freedom and joy, Alan Howard as Oberon not only found very quickly that he could master the art of spinning a plate on a pointed stick but that he could do so on a trapeze without losing any of the fine nuances of his exceptionally sensitive verse-speaking. His Puck, John Kane, did the same, while mastering walking on stilts. In another register, a very talented and tragically short-lived young actor, Glynne Edwards, discovered that all the accepted ideas of Thisbe's lament over Pyramus's death being a moment of pure farce were covering a true depth of feeling. This suddenly turned the usually preposterous attempts at acting of the 'mechanicals' in the palace into something true and even moving. The situation was reversed and the smart and superior sniggering of the cultivated spectators well deserved the Duke's rebuke:

> For never anything can be amiss
> When simpleness and duty tender it.

Then, for the first time, we used a practice that we can no longer do without. In the middle of rehearsals, we invited a group of kids into our rehearsal room; then later we asked an *ad hoc* crowd in a Birmingham social club, so as to test what we were doing. Immediately, strengths and lamentable weakness were pitilessly exposed. We saw the trap of rehearsal jokes—everything that made the company fall about with laughter fell flat. It was clear that some embryonic forms could be developed and others discarded, although in the process nothing was lost. One thing can always lead to another. On French level crossings there is an apt warning: 'One train can conceal another.' This can have a hopeful reading: 'Behind a bad idea a good one can be waiting to appear.'

Gradually, the jigsaw began to fit, yet the very first preview was a disaster. My old friend Peter Hall took me by the arm and expressed his regret at the bad flop that was on its way. But at this point in the process a shock was needed. What to do? Peter Hall's close collaborator John Barton said, 'The problem is at the start. The way you begin doesn't prepare us for the unexpected approach that follows. As it is now, we just can't get into it.' Thanks to John, we found a way of starting the play literally with a bang. With an explosion of percussion from the composer Richard Peaslee, the whole cast literally burst onto the stage, climbed up the ladders and swarmed across the top level of the set with such joy and energy that they swept the audience along with them. After this, they could do no wrong. The presence of the audience in a week of previews and a high-pressured re-examination of every detail allowed at last the latent form to appear. Then, like the well-cooked meal, there was nothing to fiddle with, just to taste and enjoy. Often, after an opening, one has to go on working day after day, never satisfied, but this time we could recognise it. Miraculously it had fallen into place.

When the production had played across the world, there were many proposals to film it. I always refused because the essence of designer Sally Jacobs's imagery was a white box. The invisible, the forest, even the darkness of night were evoked by the imagination in the nothingness that had no statement to make and needed no illustration. Unfortunately, the cinema of the day depended entirely on celluloid, and after the first screenings more and more scratches would appear. In any event, photography is essentially naturalistic and a film based only on whiteness, least of all a soiled and blotchy one, was unthinkable. Of course, a play can be filmed, but not literally. I've attempted this many times, and always a new form had to be found to correspond with a new medium. It can never be a literal recording of what the audience in the theatre once saw. Here I felt that nothing could reflect the zest and invention of the whole group. This truly was a live event.

Then the production was invited to Japan. Everyone was eager to go. As the costs were so high, could I agree to it being tele-recorded in performance so that it could be shown all over Japan and so contribute to their expenses? If we all agreed, they promised the recording would be destroyed in the presence of the British Consul. I discussed this with the cast, who had all been with me in refusing filming. This time it seemed impossible for us to say 'No'.

A few weeks later, I received a bulky parcel from Japan. It contained a set of large discs. 'This,' wrote one of the producers, 'is a copy of the recording. We feel that you should have it.'

I found a player and discovered to my amazement that it looked very good. I sent a cable to Japan, telling them not to destroy the master. At once a telegram returned. 'This morning, in the presence of the British Consul, as you requested, the recording and the negative have been burned.'

Only later did I realise that this was a valuable reminder to stay with my own convictions. The life of a play begins and ends in the moment of performance. This is where author, actors and directors express all they have to say. If the event has a future, this can only lie in the memories of those who were present and who retained a trace in their hearts. This is the only place for our *Dream*. No form nor interpretation is for ever. A form has to become fixed for a short time, then it has to go. As the world changes, there will and must be new and totally unpredictable *Dreams*.

Today, more than ever, I am left with a respect for the formless hunch which was our guide, and it has left me with a profound suspicion of the now much-used word 'concept'. Of course, even a cook has a concept, but it becomes real during the cooking, and a meal is not made to last. Unfortunately, in the visual arts, 'concept' now replaces all the qualities of hard-earned skills of execution and development. In their place, ideas are developed as ideas, as theoretical statements that lead to equally intellectual statements and discussions in their place. The loss is not in words but in the draining away of what only comes from direct experience, which can challenge the mind and feeling by the quality it brings.

A used carpet placed over a mass of old, used shoes won international prizes. It was considered enough to express the tragedy of emigrations, of displaced people and their long march. This made an admirable piece of political correctness, but its impact was negligible when compared with Goya, Picasso or many shockingly intense photographs. A single light bulb going on and off won an important award because it expressed all of life and death. In fact, it only expressed the 'idea' of life and death. These have been prize-winning concepts, but would not Alexander Korda rightly have said, 'Come back when you have put your idea into a powerful form'?

A form exists on every visible and invisible level. Through the quality of its development, then in the way its meaning is transformed. It is an understandable difficulty for actors, directors and designers facing a play of Shakespeare not to ask, 'What should we do with it?' So much has been done already and so often filmed, recorded or described that it is hard not to begin by searching for something striking and new. A young director's future may depend on the impact he or she makes. It is hard to have to play characters like Rosencrantz and Guildenstern without looking desperately for an idea. This is the trap opening under the feet of every director. Any scene in Shakespeare can be vulgarised almost out of recognition with the wish to have a modern concept. This easily leads to spicing the words by having a drunk say them into a mobile phone or else peppering the text with obscene expletives. This is no exaggeration. I saw the videotape of an actor trying vainly to find a new way of saying 'To be or not to be'. As a last resort, one evening he set out to see whether alcohol might not be the answer. So he set up a camera, put a bottle of whisky on a table beside him, also a clock, and at planned intervals during the night recorded himself doing the soliloquy again and again as he gradually poured the contents of the bottle down his throat. The result needs no comment. Fortunately, there is another way. Always, an ever-finer form is waiting to be found through patient and sensitive trial and error. Directors are

asked, 'What is your concept?' The critics write about 'a new concept' as though this label could cover the process. A concept is the
result and comes at the end. Every form is possible if it is discovered by probing deeper and deeper into the story, into the words and
into the human beings that we call the characters. If the concept is
imposed in advance by a dominating mind, it closes all the doors.

We can all have an idea, but what can give the dish its substance
and its taste?

ADAPTATIONS

ROBERT COX

From The Merry Conceited Humours of
Bottom the Weaver[†]

Enter BOTTOME *the Weaver,* QUINCE *the Carpeuter,* SNUG *the Ioyner,* ELUTE *the Bellows mender,* SNOUT *the Tinker, and* STARVELING *the Taylor.*

BOTTOME   Come Neighbours let me tell you, and in troth I have spoke like a man in my daies, and hit right too, that if this business do but displease his Graces fancy, we are all made men for ever.

QUINCE   I believe so too neighbour, but is all our company here?

BOTT.   You had best to call them generally man by man according to the Scrip.

QU.   Here is the scrowl of every mans name which is thought fit through all *Athens,* to play in our enterlude between the Duke and the Dutchess on his Wedding day at night.

BOTT.   First good *Peter Quince* say what the Play treats of, then read the names of the Actors, and so grow on to a point.

QU.   Marry our play is the most Lamentable Comedy, and most cruel death of *Pyramus* and *Thisbe.*

BOTT.   A very good piece of work I assure you, and a merry; now good *Peter Quince* call forth your Actors by the Scrowl, Masters spread your selves.

QU.   Answer as I call you, *Nicolas Bottome* the Weaver.

BOTT.   Ready, name what part I am for, and proceed.

QU.   You *Nic. Bottome* are set down for *Pyramus.*

BOTT.   Wat is *Pyramus,* a Lover or a Tyrant?

QU.   A Lover that kills himself most gallantly for Love.

BOTT.   That will ask some tears in the true performing of it, If I do it, let the audience look to their eyes: I will move storms, I will condole in some measure, to the rest, yet my chief humour is for a Tyrant. I could play *Eroles* rarely, or a part to tear a cat in two, make all split, the raging Rocks, and shivering shocks shall break the locks of Prison gates, and *Phibbus* carre shall shine from far, and make and marre, the foolish fates: Now name the rest of the Players. This is *Eroles* reigne, a Tyrants reigne, a Lover is more condoling.

QU.   *Francis Flute* the Bellowes-mender.

FLUT.   Here *Peter Quince.*

QU.   You must take *Thisbe* on you.

---

† From *The Merry Conceited Humours of Bottom the Weaver* (London: Printed for F. Kirkman and H. Marsh, 1661). Punctuation has been lightly corrected.

FLUT.   What is *Thisbe* a wandering Knight?

QU.   It is the Lady that *Pyramus* must love.

FLUT.   Nay faith, let not me play a woman, I have a beard coming.

QU.   Thats all one, you shall play it in a mask and you may speak as small as you will.

BOTT.   And I may hide my face, let me play *Thisbe* too. I'le speak in a monstrous little voice *Thisne Thisne,* ah *Pyramus* my lover deare thy *Thisbe* deare and lover deare.

QU.   No no, you must play *Pyramus,* and *Flute* you *Thisbe.*

BOTT.   Well proceed.

QU.   *Robbin Starveling* the Taylor.

STAR.   Here *Peter Quince.*

QU.   *Robbin Starveling* you must play *Thisby's* mother. *Tom Snout* the Tinker.

SNO.   Here *Peter Quince.*

QU.   You *Pyramus* father, my self *Thisby's* father, *Snug* the Joyner you the Lyons part; and I hope theres a play fitted.

SNUG.   Have you the Lyons part written? Pray you if it be, give it me for I am slow of study.

QU.   You may do it *Ex tempore* for it is nothing but roaring.

BOTT.   Let me play the Lyon too, I will Roare that I will do any mans heart good to hear me, I will roare that I will make the Duke say let him roare again let him roare again.

QU.   If you should do it too terribly, you would fright the Dutchesse and the Ladyes that they would shrike and that were enough to hang us all.

ALL.   That would hang every mothers Son.

BOTT.   I graunt you freinds that if they should fright the Laydes out of their witt, they would have no more discretion but to hang us, but I will aggravate my voice so that I will roare you as gentle as any Sucking Dove, I will roare and twere any Nightingale.

QU.   You can play no part but *Pyramus,* for *Pyramus* is a sweetfaced man a proper man as one shall see in a Summers day, a most lovely Gentleman like man, therefore you must needs play *Pyramus.*

BOTT.   Well I will undertake it, what beard had I best play it in?

QU.   Why what you will.

BOTT.   I will discharge it either in your straw coloured beard, your Orange Tawny beard, your purple in graine beard, or your French crown coloured beard, your perfect Yellow.

QU.   Some of your French crowns have no haire at all and then you'l play barefaced. But maisters here are your parts and I am farther to entreat you, request you and desire you, to con them by tomorrow night, & meet me in the Palace Wood a mile without the Town by moonlight, there we will rehearse, for if we meet in

the City we shall be doggd by company and our devices known;
in the mean time I will draw a bill of properties such as our play
wants? I pray fail mee not.

BOTT.　We will meet and there we may rehearse more obscenely
and Couragiously. Take pain. Be perfect. Adieu.

QU.　At the Dukes Oake we meet?

BOTT.　Enough hold or cutt Bowstrings—

Exeunt.

　　　Enter OBERON *King of the Fayries and* PUGG *a Spirit.*

OB.　I am resolved and I will be revenged
　Of my proud Queen *Titania*'s injury,
　And make her yeild me up her beloved page;
　My gentle Pugg come hither thou Rememberest
　Since that I sat upon a Promontory,
　And heard a Mermaid on a Dolphins Back
　Uttering such dulcet and harmonious breath,
　That the rude Sea grew civil at her Song;
　And certain States shot madly from their Spheares,
　To hear the Sea-maids musick.

PUG.　I remember.

OB.　That very time I saw (but thou couldest not)
　Flying between the cold Moon and the earth
　Cupid all armed a certain aime hee took,
　At a faire Vestal throned by the west;
　And loo'st his love-shast smartly from his bow,
　As it should peirce a hundred thousand hearts:
　But I might see young *Cupids* fiery shaft
　Quench in the chast beames of the watry Moon,
　And the Imperial Votress passed on
　In maiden meditation fancy free,
　Yet markt I where the bolt of *Cupid* fell
　It fell upon a litle westerne flower
　Before milk white now purple with loves wound,
　And maidens call it *love in Idleness*;
　Fetch me that flower the hearb I shew'd thee once
　The juice of it on sleeping eye lids laid
　Will make or man or woman madly Dote
　Upon the next live Creature that it sees;
　Fetch me this hearb and be thou here again
　Ere the Leviathan can swim a league.

PUG.　I'le put a Girdle about the earth in forty minutes. *Exit.*

OB.　Having once this juyce;
　I'le watch *Titania* when she is a sleep
　And drop the liquor of it in her eyes,
　The next thing when she waking looks upon

(Be it on Lyon, Bear or wolfe or Bull
On medling Monkey or on busy Ape)
She shall persue it with the soul of love
And ere I take this Charme from off her sight
(As can take it with another hearb)
I'le make her render up her page to me.
Welcom wanderer, what ar't returned with it?

PUG.　I there it it is.

OB.　Come give it me?
　There is a bank *Titania* useth of
　In nights to sleep on, but see where she comes
　　　Enter QUEEN *and* FAIRES. *Exit* PUG.
　I'le stand aside you may depart.

QU.　Come now a Roundel and a fairy song
　To please my eye first then intice me sleep
　Then to your offices and let me rest.
　　　FAYRIES *first Dance and then sings 1.*
　You Spotted Snakes with double tongue,
　Thorny Hedghoges be not seen,
　Newts and blind worms do no wrong,
　Come not neare our Fairy Queen.
　Philomele with melody
　Singing your sweet Lullaby,
　Lulla lulla lullaby lulla lulla lullaby.
　Nere harme, nor spell nor Charme
　Come our lovely Lady by
　So good-night with lullaby.

2 FAIRY　Weaving spiders come not here.
　Hence you longlegd spinners hence.
　Beetles black approach not neare;
　Worme nor snayle do no offence:
　Philomele with melody. &c.

1 FAIRY　Hence away now all is well,
　One a loofe stand Centinell.

　　　　　　　　　　　　　　　　　Exeunt FAIRES.

OB.　What thou seest when thou dost wake
　　　OBERON *comes to her and touches her eye lids.*
　Do it for thy true love take,
　Love and languish for his sake;
　Be it Ounce or Catt or Beare
　Pard or Bore with Bristled hair
　In thine eye that shall appear,
　when thou awakest it is thy dear
　Wake then some vile thing is neere.

　　　　　　　　　　　　　　　　　　　　　Exit.

Enter Bottome Quince Snug Flute Snoute and Starveling

BOTT.   Are we all met?

QUIN.   Pat pat, and heres a marvellous convenient place for our rehearsal. This green Plot shall be our stage, This hauthorne Brake our tyring house, and we will do it in action as we will do it before the Duke.

BOTT.   *Peter Quince.*

QU.   What sayst thou *Bully Bottome*?

BOTT.   There are things in this Comedy of *Pyramus* and *Thisby* that will never please, first *Pyramus* must draw a Sword to kill himself which the Ladyes can't abide, how answer you that?

SNOUT.   Berlaken a parlous feare.

STAR.   I believe we must leave the killing out, when all's done.

BOTT.   Not a whit, I have advice to make all well. Write me a Prologue, and let the Prologue seem to say we will do no harme with our swords, and that *Pyramus* is not killed indeed: and for the more better assurance tell them that I *Pyramus* am, nor *Pyramus*, but *Bottome* the weaver, this will put them out of feare.

QU.   Well, we will have such a Prologue and it shall be written in eight and six.

BOTT.   No make it two more let it be written in eight and eight.

SNOUT.   Will not the Ladyes be afraid of the Lyon?

STAR.   I fear it I'le promise you.

BOTT.   Masters we ought to consider with ourselves to bring in (God sheild us) a Lyon among Ladies is a most dreadful thing, For there is not a more fearfull wild-foule then your Lion living, and we ought to look to it.

SNOUT.   Therefore another Prologue must tell he is not a Lyon.

BOTT.   Nay, You must name his name, and halfe his face must be seen through the Lions Neck, and he himself must speak through saying thus, or to the same effect, Ladyes or faire Ladyes, I would wish you, or I would request you, or I would intreat you not to tremble; my life for yours, if you think I come hither as a Lyon it were pitty of my life, no, I am no such thing I am a man as other men are, and there indeed let him name his name and tell plainly I am *Snug* the Joyner.

QU.   Well it shall be so: But there is two hard things, that is to bring the moon light into a Chamber, for you know *Pyramus* and *Thisbe* met by moonlight.

SNUG.   Doth the moon shine that night we play our play.

BOTT.   A Calender, a Calender, look in the Almanack find out moon-shine find out moonshine.

QU.   Yes, it doth shine that night?

BOTT.   Why then may you leave a casement of the great Chamber window where we play open, and the Moon may shine in at the Casement.

QUI. I, or else one must come with a bunch of Thornes and a Lanthorne, & say he comes to disfigure, or to present the person of
Moon-shine. Then there is another thing, we must have a wall in
the great Chamber, for *Pyramus* and *Thisbe* (saies the story) did
talk through the Chink of a wall.

SNUG. You can never bring in a Wall, what say you *Bottom*?

BOTT. Some man or other must present Wall, and let him have
some Plaister, or some Lome, or some Rough cast about him to
signifie Wall, or let him hold his fingers thus, and through that
Crany shall *Pyramus* and *Thisbe* whisper.

QUI. If that may be then all is well, come sit down every mothers
son and rehearse your parts, *Pyramus* you begin, when you have
spoken your speech enter into that Brake, and so every man
according to his Cue—

    Enter PUG.

PUG. What Hempen Home-spuns have we swaggering here so
neer the Cradle of the Fayry Queen. What? A play toward? I'le be
an Auditor, and Actor too perhaps if I see cause.

QUIN. Speak *Pyramus Thisby* stand forth.

PYRA. *Thisby*, the flowers of Odious savours sweet.

QUIN. Odours, Odours.

PIRA. Odours savours sweet, so hath thy breath my dearest *Thisbe*
dear. But hark a voice: stay thou but here a while, and by and by
I will to thee appear.

PUG. A stranger *Piramus* then ere plaid here.

                           Exit. PYR. *Exit after him*

THIS. Must I speak now?

QUIN. I marry must you. For you must understand that he goes
but to see a Noyse that he heard, and is to come again.

THIS. Most Radiant *Pyramus,* Most Lilly white of hue. Of colour
like the red Rose on triumphant Bryer. Most Brisky Juvenal, and
the most lovely Jew. As true as truest Horse that never yet would
Tyre. I'le meet thee *Pyramus* at *Ninus* Tombe.

QUI. *Ninus* Tombe man: why, you must not speak that yet; That
you answer to *Piramus*: you speak all your part at once Cues and
all, *Piramus* enter, your Cue is past, it is, never Tire.

THIS. O as true as truest Horse that yet would never Tire.

PIR. If I were faire *Thisby* I were only thine.

QUINCE O monstrous! O strange! we are haunted; pray masters
fly-Masters help.

                              Exeunt the CLOWNES

PUG. I'le follow you, I'le lead you about a round. Through Bog,
through Bush, through Brake, through Bryar. Sometimes a Horse
I'le be, sometimes a Hound, a Hogge, a headlesse Beare; sometimes

a Fire, and Neigh, and Bark, and Grunt, and Roare, and Burn, like
horse, hound, hog, beare, fire, at every turne.

    Enter BOTTOME *with an Asses head.*

BOTT.   Why do they run away, this is knavery of them to make me
afeard.

    Enter SNOUT.

SNO.   O *Bottome* thou art changed, what do I see on thee?

BOTT.   What do I see? you see an Asses head of your own do you?

    Enter PETER QUINCE

QUIN.   Blesse thee *Bottome,* blesse thee, thou art translated.

                                      Exeunt

BOTT.   I see their knavery, this is to make an asse of me, and fright
me if they could, but I will not stir from this place do they what
they can, I will walk up and down here, and will sing, that they
shall hear I am not afraid.

    he sings

The Woosel cock so black of hew,
with Orange Tawny bill.
The Thros'le with his note so true,

    QUEEN *of Fairy wakes and looks upon him.*

the Wren and little quill.

TITA.   What Angel wakes me from my flowry bed?

BOTT.   The Finch, the Sparrow, and the Lark.
The Plain-song Cuckow Gray,
whose note full many a man doth Mark,
and dare not answer Nay.
For indeed who should set his wit to so foolish a bird? who would
give a bird the lye though he should cry Cuckow never so.

TITA.   I pray thee gentle mortal sing again,
Mine eare is much enamoured of thy note.
On the first view to say, to sweare I love thee,
So is mine eye enthralled to thy shape
And thy faire vertues force (perforce) doth move me.

BOTTA.   Me thinks (Mistresse) you should have little reason for that,
and yet to say truth, reason and love keep little company together
now adayes. The more the pitty that some honest neighbours will
not make them freinds. Nay I can Gleek upon occasion.

TITA.   Thou art as wise as thou art beautifull.

BOTT.   Not so neither: but if I had wit enough to get out of this
Wood, I have enough to serve my own t[. . .]ne.

TITA.   Out of this wood do not desire to go.
Thou shalt remaine here whether thou wilt or no.
I am a spirit of no common fare,
The summer still doth tend upon my state,

And I do love thee, therefore go with me.
I'le give thee Fairies to attend on thee,
And they snall fetch thee jewels from the Deep,
And sing while thou on pressed flowers dost sleep,
And I will purge thy mortall grosseness so,
That thou shalt like a Ayery spirit go.

> *Enter* PEASEBLOSSOME, COBWEB, *and* MUSTARSEED *three*
> FAIRIES

FAIR. Ready and I, and I, and I, where shall we go.
TITA. Be kind and curteous to this Gentleman,
Hop in his walks and Gambol in his eyes.
Feed him with apricots and Dewberries,
With purple Grapes, Green Figs, and Mulberries.
The honey bags steale from the humble Bees,
And for white tapers crop their waxen thighs,
And light them at the fiery glow-wormes eyes
To have my love to bed and to arise,
And pluck the wings from painted Butterflies
To Fan the Moon-beames from his sleeping eyes.
Nod to him Elves, and do him Curtesies.
1. *Fai.* Haile mortal Haile.
2. *Fai.* Haile.
3. *Fai.* Haile.
BOTT. I cry your worships heartily mercy. I beseech your worships
name.
COB. Cobweb.
BOTT. I shall desire you of more acquaintance good Master *Cob-
web,* if I cut my finger, I shall make bold with you. Your name
honest Gentleman?
PEAS. Pease-blossome.
BOTT. I pray commend me to Mrs. *Squash* your Mother and to
Master *Pease-cod* your Father, I shall desire of you more acquain-
tance too. Your name I beseech you Sir.
MUS. *Mustard-seed.*
BOTT. Good Mr. *Mustard-seed,* I know your patience well? That same
cowardly Giant-like Ox-Beefe hath devoured many a Gentleman of
your house; I promise your kindred have made my eyes water ere
now. I desire you more acquaintance good Master *Mustard-seed.*
TITA. Come waite upon him, lead him to my Bower.
The Moon me thinks looks with a warry eye,
And when she weeps, weep every little Flower:
Lamenting some enforced chastity.
Tye up my lovers tongue, bring him silently.

Exeunt

Enter OBERON *King of Fairies Solus.*

OB.   I wonder if *Titania* he awaked.
   Then what it was that next came in her eye,
   Which she must dore on in extremity.
        Enter PUGG.
   Here comes my messenger, now now Mad spirit
   What night-rule now about this haunted Grove?
PUG.   My Mistresse with a Monster is in love
   Near to her Close and consecrated bower,
   Whiles she was in her dull and sleeping hower
   A Crew of Patches, rude Mechanicals,
   That work for bread upon *Athenian* stalls,
   Were met together to rehearse a play
   Intended for great *Theseus* Nuptial day.
   The shallowest Thick-skin of that barren sort,
   Who *Piramus* presented in their sport.
   Forsook his Scene, and entred in a brake
   Where I did him at this advantage take;
   An Asses Nose I fixed on his head,
   Anon his *Thisby* must be answered,
   And forth my mimick comes when they him spy,
   As Wild-geese that the creeping Fowler eye;
   Or russet-pated Choughs many in sort
   (Rising and cawing at the Guns report)
   Sever themselves, and madly sweep the sky,
   So at his sight away his fellows fly,
   And at our stamp ore and ore one falls
   He murther cryes, and help from Athens calls.
   Their sense thus weak lost with their fear thus strong
   Made senceless things begin to do them wrong.
   For Bryars and Thornes at their apparel snatch
   Some sleeves, some hats, from Yeilders all things catch.
   I led them on in this distracted feare,
   And left sweet *Pyramus* translated there.
   When in that moment so it came to passe
   Titania wak'd, and straight-way lov'd an asse.

                                                      Exit

OB.   This fall out better then I could devise,
   I shall now be avenged upon my Queen.
   But see she comes, I'le stand aside.
        Enter QUEEN, BOTTOME, FAIRIES.
TITA.   Come sit thee down upon this Flowry bed,
   While I thy aimable Cheeks do coy,
   And stick musk Roses on thy sleek smooth head,
   And kiss thy faire large eares, my gentle Joy.
BOTT.   Where's *Pease-blossome*?

PEAS. Ready.

BOTT. Scratch my head *Pease-blossome*, where's Monsieur *Cobweb.*

COB. Ready.

BOTT. Monsieur *Cobweb,* good Monsieur get your weapons in your hand, and kill me a red humble Bee on the top of a Thistle, and good Monsieur bring me the honey bag. Do not fret your self too much in the action Monsieur, and good Monsieur have a care the honey bag break not, I would be loath to have you ore flown with a honey bag Signior. Where's Monsieur *Mustard-seed.*

MUS. Ready.

BOTT. Give me your newfe Monsieur *Mustard-seed.*

Pray leave your Curtesie good Monsieur.

MUS. What's your will?

BOTT. Nothing good Monsieur, but to help Cavaliero *Cobweb* to scratch; I must to the Barbers Monsieur, for me thinks I am marvaillous hairy about the face, and I am such a Tender asse if my hair does but tickle me I must scratch.

TITA. What wilt thou hear some musick my sweet love?

BOTT. I have a reasonable good eare in musick, let us hear the Tong and the bones.

Musick Tongs Rurall Musick.

TITA. Or say sweet love what thou desirest to eate?

BOTT. Truly a peck of provender, I could maunch your good dry Oates, me thinks I have a great desire to a bottle of hay, good hay, sweet hay hath no fellow.

TITA. I have a ventrous Fairy

That shall seek the Squirils hoard

And fetch the new Nuts.

BOTT. I had rather have a handfull or two of dried pease. But I pray let none of your people stirr me, I have an exposition of sleep come upon me.

TITA. Sleep thou and I will winde the in my armes.

Fairies begon and be allwaies away,

So doth the wood bind the sweet Honisuckle

Gently entwist, the female Ivy so

Enrings the barky fingers of the Elme.

O how I love thee? How I dote on thee?

OB. Welcome good *Pug.*

OBERON *approaches*

Seest thou this sweet sight?

Enter PUG,

Her dotage now do I begin to pitty,

For meeting her of late behind the wood,

Seeking sweet favours for this hateful fool,

I did upbraid her and fall out with her,

For she his hairy temples then had rounded
With Coronet of fresh and Fragrant flowers,
And that same Dew which some time on the buds
Was wont to swell like round and orient pearl;
I stood now within the pretty flouriers eyes
Like teares that did there own disgrace bewaise,
And she in mild terms begd my patience.
I then did aske of her her Changeling child,
Which streight she gave me and her fairy sent
To beare him to my bower in Fairy land.
And now I have the boy I will undo
This hateful imperfection of her eyes,
And gentle *Pug* take this transformed Scalpe
From off the head of this Athenian swain,
That he awaking may returne to Athens
And thinke no more of this nights accidents
But as the sierce vexation of a dream.
But first I will release my fairy Queen.
Bee thou as thou was wont to be
See thou as thou was wont to see,
Dians bud or Cupids Flower
Hath such force and blessed power.
Now my *Titania* wake you my sweet Queen.

TIT.   My *Oberon* what visions have I seen!
Me thought I was inamored of an asse.

OB.   There lies your love.

TIT.   How came these things to pass?
Oh how mine eyes do loath this visage now.

OB.   Silence a while. *Pug* take thou off his head
            He puls off his asses head

PUG.   When thou awakes with thine own fools eyes peep.
                                                        Exeunt.

        After a while BOTTOME *wakes.*

BOTT.   When my cue comes call me, and I will answer, my next is
    most faire *Pyramus* hei ho. *Peter Quince, Flute* the bellowes
    mender? *Snout* the Tinker? *Starveling?* Gods my life stolne hence
    and left me asleep, I have had a most rare vision, I had a dream
    past the witt of man to say what dream it was. Man is but an Asse
    if he go about to expound this dream, me thought I was thers no
    man can tell what me thought I was, and me thought I had, but a
    man is but a patched fool if he will offer to say what me thought
    I had, the eye of man hath not heard, the eare of man hath not
    seen, mans hand is not able to cast, his tongue to conceive, not
    his heart report what my dream, was. I will get *Peter Quince* to
    write a Ballad of this dream, it shall be called *Bottomes* dream

because it hath no Bottom and I will sing it in the later end of the Play before the Duke, peradventure to make, it the more gratious I will sing it at her death.

Exit

Enter QUINCE, FLUTE, THISBY, SNOUT *and* STARVELING.

QU.   Have you sent to *Bottoms* house? is he come yet?

STAR.   He cannot be heard of, out of doubt he is transported.

FLUTE.   If he come not then the play is marrd, it goes not forward doth it?

QU.   It is not possible, you have not a man in all *Athens* able to discharge *Pyramus* but he.

FLUT.   Noe: He hath simply the best wit of any handycrafts man in *Athens*.

QU.   Yea and the best person too, and he is a very Paramour for a sweet voice.

FLU.   You must say Paragon, a Paramour is God blesse us a thing of naught.

Enter SNUG *the Ioyner.*

SNUG.   Masters, the Duke is now coming from being married at the Temple, oh if our sport had gone forward, we had all been made men.

FLU.   O sweet Bully *Bottome*, thou hast lost six pence a day during his life, he could not have scaped six pence a day, and the Duke had not given him sixpence a day for playing *Pyramus*. I'le be hang'd, he would have deserved sixpence a day in *Pyramus* or nothing.

Enter BOTTOME.

BOTT.   Where are these lads? Where are these hearts?

QU.   *Bottome*! O most couragious day! oh most hapy hour.

BOTT.   Masters I am to discourse wonders, but aske me not what, for if I tell you I am no true *Athenian,* I will tell you every thing as it fell out.

QU.   Let us hear, sweet *Bottome.*

BOTT.   Not a word of me, all that I will tell you is that the Duke hath dined, get your apparel together, good strings to your beards, new Ribbands to your Pumps, meet presently in the Pallace every man look over his part for the short and the long is, our play is preferred, in any case let *Thisby* have clean linnen: and let not him that plaies the Lyon pare his Nailes for they shall hang out for the Lyons clawes, and most dear actors eate no Onions nor Garlick, for we are to utter sweet breath and doubt not to hear them say it is a sweet Comedy. No more words away: go away.

Exeunt.

Enter DUKE, DUTCHESS *and two* LORDS.

EGAEUS   May all things prove propitious to this match,
And heavens power down whole showers of joy to waite

Within your Royal walkes your Board, your bed.
DUKE   Thanks kind *Egaeus,* but what pleasant maskes,
   What dances, have we now to weare away
   This long age of three hours which yet we have
   To spend ere bed time?
1. LORD   And't please your grace, there is a scene
   Tedious yet breif to be presented of
   The love of *Pyramus* and *Thisbe*
   Mirth very Tragical.
DUKE   Merry and Tragical? tedious and brief. That is hot Ice, and wondrous
   Strange snow? how shall we find a concord in this discord?
2. LORD   A play there is my Lord, some ten words long
   Which is as briefe as I have known a play,
   But by ten words my Lord it is too long,
   Which makes it tedious, For in all the play
   Theres not one word apt, one player fitted;
   And Tragical my noble Lord it is,
   For *Pyramus* therein doth kill himself,
   Which when I saw rehearst I must confess
   Made my eyes water but more merry tears
   The passion of loud laughter never shed.
DUKE   What are they that do play it?
1. LORD   Hard handed men that worke in *Athens* here,
   Which never laboured in their minds till now,
   And now have toyled their unbreathed memories
   With this same play against your Nuptials.
DUKE   And we will hear it, let them approach.
     They take their seates, Enter Prologue.
PRO.   If we offend it is with our good will.
  That you should think we come not to offend
  But with good will, To shew our simple skill,
  That is the true beginning of our end.
  Consider then, we come but in despite,
  We do not come as minding to content you
  Our true intent is. All for your delight
  We are not here. That you should here repent you
  The actors are at hand, And by their show
  You shall know all that you are like to know.
DUKE   This fellow doth not stand upon points.
1. LORD   He hath read his prologue like a Rough Colt, he knowes
   not the Stop. A good moral my Lord. It is not enough to speak,
   but to speak true.
DUTCH   Indeed he hath plaid on his Prologue like a Child on the
   recorder, a sound but not in government.

DUKE   His speech was like a tangled chaine nothing impaired but
    all disordered. Who is the next?

   Enter PYRAMUS, THISBE, WALL, MOONSHINE *and* LYON.

PROLO.   Gentels perchance you wonder at this show;
 But wonder on till truth doth make all things plain:
 This man is *Pyramus* if you would know;
 This beauteous Lady *Thisbe* is certain.
 This man with Lime and Rough-cast doth present
 Wall the vile Wall which did these lovers sunder,
 And through Walls chink (poor soules) they are content
 To whisper, at the which let no man wonder.
 This man with Lanthorne Dog, and bush of Thorne
 Presenteth Moon-shine; for if you will know,
 By Moon-shine did these lovers think no scorne
 To meet at *Ninus* Tombe, there there to woe.
 This Grisly beast (which Lyon height by name)
 The trusty *Thisbe* coming first by night
 Did scare away, or rather did affright,
 And as she sled her mantle she did fall,
 Which Lyon vile with bloody mouth did staine;
 Anon comes *Pyramus* sweet youth and tall,
 And finds his gentle *Thisbie*'s mantle slaine,
 Whereat with blade, with bloody blameful blade
 He bravely broach't his bloody boiling breast,
 And *Thisbe* tarrying in Mulberry shade
 His Dagger drew and dyed. For all the rest
 Let *Lyon, Moon-shine, Wall,* and Lovers twaine
 At large discourse, while here they do remaine.

         Exeunt all but WALL.

DUKE   I wonder if the Lyon be to speak?
2. LOR.   No wonder my Lord, one Lyon may, when many Asses do.
WALL   In this same enterlude it doth befall
 That I one *Snug* (by name) present a wall,
 And such a wall as I would have you think
 As had in it a crannied hole or chink,
 Through which the Lovers *Pyramus* and *Thisbe,*
 Did whisper often very secretly.
 This loame, this rough-cast, and this stone doth show
 That I am that same wall the truth is so,
 And this the Cranny is right and sinister,
 Through which the fearful lovers are to whisper.
DUKE   Would you desire lime and haire to speak better.
2. LOR.   It is the wittiest partition that ever I heard discourse my Lord.
DUKE   *Pyramus* draws near the wall, Silence—

Enter PYRAMUS

PYRA.   O Grim lookt night! O night with hue so black!
O night which ever art when day is not.
O night, O night, alack, alack, alack
I fear my *Thisbie*'s promise is forgot;
And thou O wall, thou sweet and lovely wall,
That stands between her fathers ground and mine,
Thou Wall, O Wall, O sweet and lovely Wall
Shew me thy Chink to blink through with mine eyes.
Thanks Curteous Wall; *Iove* shield thee well for this.
But what see I? No *Thisby* do I see.
O witched Wall through whom I see no blisse:
Curst be thy stones for thus deceiving me.

DUKE   The Wall me thinks being sensible should curse againe.

PYRAM.   No in truth Sir he should not, *Deceiving me* Is *Thisbies*
Cue, she is to enter, and I am to spy her through the Wall, you
shall see it will fall.

Enter THISBY.

Pat as I told you; yonder she comes.

THISB.   O Wall full often hast thou heard my moanes
For parting my faire *Pyramus* and me.
My Cherry lips have often kist thy stones,
Thy stones with Lime and Haire knit up in thee.

PYRA.   I hear a voice, Now will I to the Chink
To spy if I can see my *Thisbies* face. *Thisby.*

THIS.   My love, thou art my love I think.

PYRA.   Think what thou wilt I am thy lovers Grace,
And like *Limander* am I trusty still.

THIS.   And I like *Helen* till the fates me kill.

PIRA.   Not *Thafalus* to *Procrus* was so true.

THIS.   As *Shalafus* to *Procrus* I to you.

PIRA.   O kisse me through the hole of this vile Wall.

THIS.   I kisse the Wall hole, not your lips at all.

PIRA.   Will thou at *Ninnies* tombe meet me straight way?

THIS.   Tide life ride death I'le come without delay.

Exeunt PIR. *and* THISBY

WALL   Thus have I Wall my part discharged so.

Exit WALL

DUKE   Now is the Moral downe between the two neighbours.

2. LOR.   No remedy my Lord when Walls are so wilfull.

DUTCH   This is the silliest stuffe that ever I heard.

DUKE   The best in this kinde are but shaddows, and the worst no
worse, if imagination amend them.

DUTCH   It must be your imagination then, not theirs.

DUKE   If we imagine no worse of them then they of themselves,
they may passe for excellent men. Here comes two noble Beasts
in, a Man and a Lyon.

  Enter LYON *and* MOON-SHINE.

LYON   You Ladies, you whose gentle hearts do fear
the monstrous Mouse that creeps on floore;
May now perchance both quake and tremble here,
When Lyon rough in wildest rage doth roare.
Then know that I one *Snug* the Joyner am,
A Lyon fell, nor else no Lyons damme,
For if I should as Lyon come in strife
Into this place, t'were pitty of my life.

DUKE   A very gentle beast, and of a good conscience.

2. LOR.   The very best at a beast my Lord that ever I saw.

1. LOR.   This Lyon is a very Fox for his valour.

DUKE   True, and a Goose for his discretion.

2. LOR.   Not so my Lord, for his valour cannot carry his discretion,
and the Fox carries the Goose.

DUKE   His discretion I am sure cannot carry his valour, for the Goose
carries not the Fox. It is well, leave it to his discretion.

MOON   This Lanthorne doth the horned Moon present.

2. LOR.   He should have worne the horns on his head.

DUKE   He is no Crescent, and his horns are invisible within the
circumference.

MOON   This Lanthorne doth the horned Moon present; my self
the man ith Moon doth seeem to be.

DUKE   This is the grearest error of all the rest, the man should be
put in the Lanthorne, how is he else the man in the Moon.

2. LOR.   He dares not come in there for the Candle, for you see 'tis
already in snuffe.

DUTCH   I am weary of this moon, would he would change,

DUKE   It appears by his small light of Discretion that he is in the
Waine: but yet in curtesie in all reason we muststay the time.

1. LOR.   Proceed Moon?

MOON   All that I have to say is, to tell you that the Lanthorne is the
Moon; *I* the man in the Moon, this thorne-Bush my bush, and
this Dog my Dog.

2. DOR.   Why, all these should be in the Lanthorne, for they are in
the Moon. But silence, here comes *Thisbe*.

  Enter THISBE

THIS.   This is old *Ninnies* tombe: where is my love.

LYON   Oh—

  The LYON *roares,* THISBY *runs off*

1. LOR.   Well roar'd *Lyon*.

DUKE   Well run *Thisby*.

DUTCH   Well shone Moon. Truly the moon shines with a good grace.

DUKE   Well mouz'd Lyon

2. LORD   And then came *Pyramus*.

1. LORD   And so the Lyon vanish.

     Enter PYRAMUS

PYR.   Sweet moone I thank thee for thy sunny beames,
   I thank the moon for shining now so bright,
   For by thy gratious golden glittering Streames
   I trust to tast of truest *Thisbes* sight.
   But stay: O spight! but marke poor knight
   What dreadful dole is here?
   Eyes do you see! How can it be!
   O dainty Duke! O deare!
   Thy mantell good; what stain'd with blood
   Approach you furies fell.
   O Fates come come, cut thred and thrum
   Quail, crush, conclude and quell.

DUKE   This passion and the death of a dear freind would go
   neere to make a man look sad.

DUT.   Beshrew my heart but I pity the man.

PYR.   O wherefore nature didst thou Lyons stame?
   Since Lyon wild hath here defloured my deare,
   Which is, no no, Which was the fairest Dame
   That livd, that loved, that liked, that look'd with cheere
   Come teares confound, out sword and wound
   The pap of *Pyramus*.
   I that left pap where heart doth hap
   Thus eye I thus thus thus.
   Now am I dead, now am I fled, my soul is in the sky
   Tongue loose thy light moon take thy flight.

                         Exit MOONSHINE

   Now dye, dye, dye, dye, dye.

2. LORD   No dye but an ace for him for hees but one.

1. LORD   Less then an ace man for hees dead hees nothing.

DUKE   With the help of a Surgeon he might yet recover and prove
   an Asse.

DUTCH   How chance moonshine is gon before.

     THISBE *comes back and finds her slain lover. Enter* THISBE

DUKE   She finds him by starlight
   Here She comes and her passion ends the play.

DUT.   Me thinks she should not use a long one, for such a *Pyramus*
   I hope she will be brief.

2. LOR.   A Moth will turn the ballance, which *Pyramus*, which *Thisbe*
   is the better.

1. LOR.   She hath spyed him already with those sweet eyes.

2. LOR.   And thus she means. *Videlicet.*

THIS.   Asleep my love? What dead my dove?
      O *Pyramus* arise,
      Speak, Speak. Quite dumbe? Dead, dead? a tombe
      Must cover thy sweet eyes.
      These lilly lips, this cherry nose.
      These yellow Cowslip cheeks
      Are gone, are gone, lovers make moane,
      His eyes were as green as leeks.
      O Sisters three, come come to me
      With hands as pale as milk,
      Lay them in gore, since you have shore
      With sheares, his thred of silk.
      Tongue not a word; Come trusty Sword,
      Come blade my breast imbrue,
      And farewell freinds, thus *Thisbe* ends.
      Adieu Adieu Adieu.

DUKE   *Moon-shine* and *Lyon* are left to bury the Dead.

2. LOR.   I and Wall too.

BOTT.   No *I* assure you, the wall is down that parted their Fathers.
      Will it please you to see the Epilogue, or to hear a Burgo-mask
      dance between two of our company.

DUKE   No Epilogue pray you, for your play needs no excuse, never
      excuse. For when the Players are all Dead, there need none to be
      blamed. Marry if he that writ it had playd *Pyramus,* and hung
      himself in *Thisbies* Garter, it had been a fine Tragedy, and so it is
      truly, and very notably discharged; but come, your Burgo-mask,
      let your Epilogue alone.

                    After a Dance, Exeunt Omnes.

HENRY PURCELL AND ELKANAH SETTLE

The Fairy-Queen[†]

THE PROLOGUE

      What have we left untry'd to please this Age,
      To bring it more in liking with the Stage?
      We sunk to Farce, and rose to Comedy;
      Gave you high Rants, and well-writ Tragedy.
      Yet Poetry, of the Success afraid,

[†] *The Fairy-Queen: An Opera. Represented at the Queen's-Theatre By Their Majesties Servants* (London, Printed for Jacob Tonson, 1692). Purcell wrote the songs and music; Settle wrote the libretto.

Call'd in her Sister Musick to her aid.
And, lest the Gallery should Diversion want,
We had Cane-Chairs to Dance 'em a Courant.
But that this Play may in its Pomp appear;
Pray let our Stage from thronging Beaux be clear.
For what e're cost we're at, what e're we do,
In Scenes, Dress, Dances; yet there's many a Beau,
Will think himself a much more taking show.
How often have you curs'd these new Beau-skreens,
That stand betwixt the Audience and the Scenes?
I ask'd one of 'em t'other day—Pray, Sir,
Why d'ye the Stage before the Box prefer?
He answer'd—Oh! there I Ogle the whole Theatre,
My Wig—my Shape, my Leg, I there display,
They speak much finer things than I can say.
These are the Reasons why they croud the Stage;
And make the disappointed Audience rage.
Our Business is, to study how to please,
To Tune the Mind to its expected ease.
And all that we expect, is but to find,
Equal to our Expence, the Audience kind.

ACT I. SCENE I, *A PALACE.*

Enter DUKE *and* ATTENDANTS *at one door.* EGEUS, HERMIA,
LYSANDER, *and* DEMETRIUS *at the other.*

DU.   Now, good Egeus, what's the News with thee?
EG.   Full of Vexation come I, and Complaint,
   Against my Child, my Daughter Hermia.
   Stand forth Demetrius, my Gracious Lord,
   This Man has my Consent to Marry her.
   Stand forth, Lysander; this, most Noble Duke,
   This, has Bewitch'd the Bosom of my Child.
   Thou, thou Lysander, thou hast given her Spells,
   In Bracelets of thy Hair, Rings, Lockets, Verses.
   (Arts that prevail on unexperienc'd Youth)
   With cunning thou hast stoln my Daughter's Heart.
   Turn'd her Obedience (which is due to me)
   To Stubborness: If therefore, (Royal Sir)
   My Daughter does not here before your Grace,
   Consent to Marry with Demetrius,
   Let the stern Law punish her Disobedience,
   And Cage her in a Nunnery.
DU.   Be advis'd, Fair Hermia,
   To you your Father should be as a God,

The Maker of those Beauties; yes, and one
To whom you are but as a Form in Wax,
By him Imprinted, and within his Pow'r,
To leave the Figure, or to race it out.

HER.   O would my Father look'd but with my Eyes.

DU.   No, no; your Eyes must with his Judgment look.

HER.   Let me intreat you, Sir, to Pardon me.
I know not by what Power I am made bold,
Nor how it may concern my Modesty,
In such a Presence to unfold my thoughts.
But I beseech your Grace, that I may know
The worst that may befal me in this case,
If I refuse to Wed Demetrius.

DU.   You must Abjure
Forever the Society of Men.
Therefore, Fair Hermia, question your Desires,
Know of your Youth, examine well your Blood,
Whether (if you refuse your Father's Choice)
You can indure the Habit of a Nun,
To be immur'd forever in a Cloister.

HER.   Is there no Mean? No other Choice, my Lord?

DU.   None, Hermia, none.
Therefore prepare to be Obedient,
Or like a Rose to wither on the Tree.
Consider well; take till to morrow Morning,
And give me then your Resolution.

DE.   Relent, sweet Hermia; and Lysander yield
Your doubtful Title, to my certain right.

LY.   You have her Father's Love, Demetrius,
Let me have Hermia's; Marry, marry him.

EG.   Scornful Lysander, true he has my Love.
And what is mine my Love shall render him;
And she is mine, and all my right in her
I give, and settle on Demetrius.

LY.   I am, my Lord, as Nobly Born, as he;
My Fortune's every way as great as his.
And (without boast) my Love is more than his.
But what is more than all these boasts can be,
I am Belov'd of Beautious Hermia.
Why should this Faithless Man Invade my Right?
He who solicited Old Nedar's Daughter,
And won her Love; The Beautious Hellena,
Tho' she's neglected; she poor Lady dotes
Upon this spotted and inconstant Man.

DU.   'Tis true, Lysander, I have heard as much.

Hermia, resolve to be obedient.
Or, as the Law ordains it, you must take
An everlasting Farewel of the World.
To Morrow in the Morning give your answer: so farewell.

[*Ex. all but* HER. *and* LY.

LY.   O my true Hermia! I have never found
   By Observation, nor by History,
   That Lovers run a smooth, and even course:
   Either they are unequal in their Birth—
HER.   O cross too high to be impos'd on Love!
LY.   Or if there be a Simpathy in choice,
   War, Sickness, or pale Death lay Siege to it,
   Making it momentary as a sound,
   Swift as the Lightning in the blackest night;
   That at one Instant shews both Heav'n and Earth.
   Yet e'er a man can say, behold the Flame,
   The jaws of darkness have devour'd it up;
   So quick even brightest things run to Confusion.
HER.   If then true Lovers have been ever cross'd,
   It stands as a Decree in Destiny.
   Then let us teach each other Patience,
   Because it is a customary thing.
LY.   'Tis well advis'd, my Hermia,
   Pray hear me. I have an Aunt, a Widow,
   She has no Child, and is extreamly rich;
   She chose me, loves me, bred me as her Son,
   Has setled all her Fortune upon me.
   To her we'll fly; and there, (my sweetest Hermia)
   There (if you give consent) I'll marry you.
   And thither this Inhuman, Cruel Law
   Cannot pursue us. If thou lov'st me then,
   Steal from thy Father's House this very night,
   And in the Wood, a mile without the Town,
   Near the great spreading Oak, I'll stay for thee,
   And at some little distance from that place
   Have all things ready to convey thee thence.
HER.   Oh my Lysander!
   I swear to thee by Cupid's strongest Bow,
   By his best Arrow with the Golden Head,
   By all the Oaths which ever Men have broke,
   (In number more than ever Women spoke)
   I will, where thou appoint'st, meet my Lysander.
LY.   Enough, my Love: look here comes Hellena.
      Enter HELLENA.
HER.   Welcome, fair Hellena.

HEL.   You mock me, Hermia, when you call me fair;
  'Tis you are fair, 'tis you Demetrius loves.
  Sickness is catching, oh were Beauty so,
  I'd catch your Graces, Hermia, e'er I go;
  My Ear should catch your Voice, my Eye your Eye,
  My Tongue should catch your Tongue's sweet Harmony.
  O teach me how you look, and with what art
  You charm and govern my Demetrius's Heart?

HER.   I frown upon him, yet he loves me still.

HEL.   Oh that your frowns could teach my smiles such Skill!

HER.   I give him Curses, when he gives me Love.

HEL.   Oh that my Prayers could such Affection move!

HER.   His Folly, Hellena, is none of mine.

HEL.   No, 'tis your Beauty; wou'd that Fault were mine.

HER.   Take comfort, he no more shall see my Face.

LY.   To you, fair Hellena, we'll disclose our minds.
  This very night, when Luna does behold
  Her Silver Visage in the Watry Glass,
  Decking with liquid-Pearl the bladed-Grass,
  (A time propitious to unhappy Lovers)
  We from this cursed Town will steal away.

HER.   And in the Wood, where often you and I
  Upon faint Primrose Beds have laid us down,
  Emptying our Bosoms of our secret thoughts.
  There my Lysander and myself shall meet
  To seek new Friends, new Habitations.

LY.   Madam, farewell. O may the Pow'rs above
  Make Hellen happy in Demetrius's Love.

                      [*Exeunt* LYSANDER *and* HERMIA.

HEL.   Oh why should she be more belov'd than I?
  My Beauty is as much extol'd as hers:
  But what of that? Demetrius thinks not so;
  He will not see that which all others do.
  Love looks not with the Eyes, but with the Mind,
  Therefore the God of Love is painted blind.
  Love never had of Judgment any Taste;
  Wings, and no Eyes, must figure thoughtless Haste.
  For the same reason Love is call'd a Child,
  Because so often in his choice beguil'd.
  As Boys ev'n at their Sports themselves forswear;
  So the Boy Love is perjur'd everywhere.
  Before Demetrius saw fair Hermia's Eyes,
  He swore his Heart was made my Beauty's Prize.
  But when from Hermia new heat he felt,
  His frozen Oaths did in an Instant melt.

I'll to Demetrius, tell him of their flight,
The place they meet at by the Moon's pale light:
Then to the Wood he will pursue the Maid;
And if he thanks me, I am overpaid.   [*Exit.*

>   *Enter* QUINCE *the Carpenter,* SNUG *the Joyner,* BOTTOM *the*
>   *Weaver,* FLUTE *the Bellows-mender,* SNOUT *the Tinker, and*
>   STARVELING *the Taylor.*

QU.   Is all our Company here?

BO.   You had best call 'em generally, Man by Man, according to the
      Scrip.

QU.   Here is the Scrowl of every Man's Name, who is thought fit
      through all the Town to play in our Enterlude before the Duke, at
      the Marriage of Lysander and Hermia, or Demetrius and Her-
      mia, no matter which.

BO.   First, Peter Quince, say what the Play treats on; then read the
      Names of the Actors, and so go on to appoint the Parts.

QU.   Marry, our Play is the most lamentable Comedy, and most
      cruel Death of Pyramus and Thisbe.

BO.   A very good piece of work, and a merry. Now, good Peter Quince,
      call forth the Actors. Masters spread your selves.

QU.   Answer as I call you. Nick Bottom the Weaver.

BO.   Ready. Name what part I am for, and proceed.

QU.   You Nick Bottom, are set down for Pyramus.

BO.   What is Pyramus? A Lover, or a Tyrant?

QU.   A Lover that kills himself most Gallantly for Love.

BO.   That will ask some tears in the true performance of it. If I do
      it, let the Ladies look to their Eyes; I will move stones. I will con-
      dole in some measure. [*To the rest.*] yet my chief humour is for a
      Tyrant, I could play Ercles rarely, or a part to make all split. The
      raging Rocks, and shivering Shocks, shall break the Locks of
      Prison-Gates; and Phoebus Carr shall shine from far, and make
      and mar the foolish Fates. This was Lofty. Now name the rest of
      the Players, This is Ercle's vain, a Tyrant's vain, a Lover's is more
      condoling.

QU.   Francis Flute the Bellows-mender.

FL.   Here, Peter Quince.

QU.   You must take Thisbe on you.

FL.   What is Thisbe? A wandring Knight?

QU.   It is the Lady that Pyramus must love.

FL.   Nay faith, let not me play a Woman, I have a beard come.

QU.   That's all one, you shall play it in a Mask, and you may speak
      as small as you will.

BO.   And I may hide my face, let me play Thisbe too; I'll speak in a
      monstrous little voice, Thisbe, Thisbe; ah! Pyramus, my Lover dear,
      and Thisbe dear, and Lady dear.

QU.   No, no, you must play Pyramus, and I'll play Thisbe, and Flute, Thisbe's Father.

BO.   Well, proceed.

QU.   Robin Starveling the Taylor.

ST.   Here, Peter Quince.

QU.   Robin Starveling, you must play Thisbe's Mother. Tom Snout the Tinker.

SN.   Here, Peter Quince.

QU.   You, Pyramus's Father: Snug the Joyner, you the Lion's part, and I hope there is a Play fitted. Snug. Have you the Lion's part written? Pray if it be, give it me, for I am slow of Study.

QU.   You may do it extempore, for it is nothing but roaring.

BO.   Let me play the Lion too, I will roar that it will do any Man's heart good to hear me; I will roar, that I will make the Duke say, let him roar again, let him roar again.

QU.   If you should do it too terribly, you would fright the Ladies, and they would shriek, and that were enough to hang us all.

ALL   I, I, that would hang every Mothers Son of us.

BO.   I grant you friends, if I should fright the Ladies out of their wits, they might have no more discretion but to hang us, but I will aggravate my voice so, that I will roar you as gently as any sucking Dove; I will roar you as 'twere any Nightingale.

QU.   You can play no part but Pyramus; for Pyramus is a sweet fac'd Youth, as proper a Man as one shall see in a Summers Day; a most lovely Gentleman-like man, therefore you must needs play Pyramus.

BO.   I will undertake it then. But hark you, Peter Quince.

QU.   What say'st thou, Bully Bottom?

BO.   There are things in this Comedy of Pyramus and Thisbe, will never please; first, Pyramus must draw a Sword to kill himself, which the Ladies cannot abide. How answer you that?

SNUG   Berlaken, a parlous fear.

STA.   I believe we must leave killing out, when all's done.

BO.   Not a whit, I have a device to make all well; write me a Pro- logue, and let the Prologue say we will do no harm with our Swords, and that Pyramus is not kill'd indeed; and for the better assurance, tell 'em that I Pyramus am not Pyramus, but Nick Bottom the Weaver, and that will put 'em out of all fear.

QU.   Well, we will have such a Prologue.

SNO.   Will not the Ladies be afraid of the Lion?

STA.   I promise you I fear it.

BO.   Masters, you ought to consider with your selves. To bring in (God bless us) a Lion among Ladies, is a most dreadful thing! for there is not a more fearful Wild-fowl than the Lion living, and we ought to look to it.

SNUG   Therefore we must have another Prologue to tell 'em he is
not a Lion.

BO.   Nay, you must name his name, and half his face must be seen
thro' the Lion's neck, and he himself must speak thro' it, saying
thus, or to the same defect; Ladies, or fair Ladies, I would wish
you, or I would request you, or I would intreat you, nor to fear,
nor to tremble, my life for yours: if you think I come hither as a
Lion, it were pity of my life; no, I am no such thing, I am a Man
as other Men are. And there in deed let him Name his Name,
and tell 'em plainly he is Snug the Joyner.

QU.   Well, it shall be so. But there are two hard things in our Comedy, to bring the Moon-shine into a Chamber, for you know Pyramus and Thisbe met by Moon-light.

SNUG   Does the Moon shine that Night we play our Play?

BA.   A Callender, a Callender. Look in the Almanack; find out
Moon-shine, find out Moon-shine.

FL.   Yes, it does Shine that Night.

BO.   Why then you may leave a Casement of the great Hall Window (where we play our Play) open, and the Moon may shine in at
the Casement.

QU.   Or else, one may come in with a Bush of Thorns, and a Lanthorn, and say he comes to disfigure, or to present the Person of
Moon-shine. Then there is another thing, we must have a Wall in
the great Room; for Pyramus and Thisbe, (as says the Story) did
talk thro' the chink of a Wall.

STA.   You can never bring in a Wall. What say you Bottom?

BO.   Some Man or other must present Wall, and let him have some
Plaster, and some Lome, and some rough-cast about him, to sig-
nifie Wall; and let him hold his Fingers thus, and thro' that
Cranny shall Pyramus and Thisbe whisper.

QU.   If that may be, then all's well; here my Masters, here are your
Parts; and I am to intreat you, request you, and desire you, to Con
'em against Night, and meet in the Palace-Wood, a Mile without
the Town, by Moon-light; there we will Rehearse; for if we meet
in the City, we shall be dogg'd with Company, and our Devices
known; in the meantime, I will get your Properties ready, and all
your Habits, that every Man may Dress, to Act it in Form; and
pray fail me not.

BO.   We will meet, and there we may Rehearse more obscenely,
and couragiously. Take pains, and be perfect. Adieu.

QU.   At the Duke's Oak we meet.

ALL   Enough, enough.   [*Exeunt.*

ACT II. SCENE I, *A WOOD, BY MOON-LIGHT*

Enter a FAIRY *at one door,* ROBIN GOODFELLOW *at the other.*

ROB.   Tell me Fairy, where's our Queen?
   And where have you been wandering?

FA.   Over Hill, over Dale, thro' Bush, thro' Bryer,
   Over Park, over Pale, thro' Flood, thro' Fire,
   I wander swifter than the Moon's bright Sphere.
   I serve the Mighty Fairy-Queen,
   Sprinkle her Circles on the Green.
   The Cowslips tall, her Pentioners be;
   Spots in their Gold Coats you see.
   Those be Rubies, Fairy-Favours,
   In those freckles live their savours;
   I must gather Dew-drops here,
   And hang a Pearl in every Cowslips Ear.
   Farewell Lob-Spirit, I'll be gone,
   The Queen and all her Elves come here anon.

ROB.   The King will keep his Revels here to Night,
   Take heed the Queen comes not within his Sight.
   For Oberon is passing fell and wrath,
   Because that she for her Attendant hath
   A Lovely Boy, stoln from an Indian-King,
   She never had so fair a Changling.
   The Jealous Oberon would have the Child,
   But she perforce with-holds the Lovely Boy.
   And now they never meet in Grove, or Green,
   By Fountain, or by Star-light, are they seen:
   But as they quarrel, all their Elves for fear,
   Creep into Acorn-Cups, and hide 'em there.

FA.   Either I mistake your shape, and making quite,
   Or else you are that shrewd, and Knavish Spright,
   Call'd Robin Good-Fellow; are you not he
   Fright Village-Maids and pinch each Sluttish she?
   Skim Milk, and sometimes labour in the Quern,
   And bootless make the breathless Huswife Chern?
   And sometimes make the Drink to bear no Barm?
   Mislead Night-wanderers, laughing at their harm?
   Those that Hobgoblin call you, and kind Puck,
   You sweep their Houses, send 'em all good luck;
   Are you not he?

ROB.   Yes, yes, thou speak'st aright,
   I am that Merry Wanderer of the Night.
   I jest to Oberon, and make him smile.
   Sometimes I hide me in a Gossips Bowl,

Just in the likeness of a Roasted Crab;
And when she drinks, against her Lips I bob;
And on her wither'd Dew-lap pour the Ale,
The wisest Wife, telling the saddest Tale.
She for a Three-leg'd Stool mistaketh me,
Then slip I from her Bum, down toples she.
Look yonder, Fairy, here comes Oberon!

FA.   Titania meets him, would we two were gone.

> *Enter* OBERON, *and* TRAIN *at one Door.* TITANIA, *and her*
> TRAIN *at the other.*

OB.   Now proud Titania I shall find your Haunts.

TIT.   What, Jealous Oberon! Faries away,
I have forsworn his Bed, and Company.

OB.   Tarry, rash Woman, am not I thy Lord?

TIT.   And am not I your Lady too? Remember
When you did steal away from Fairy-Land,
And in the shape of Corin sat all day
Playing on Oaten-Pipes, and Singing Love
To Amorous Philida. Why are you here
Come from the farthest Verge of India?
But that some Lusty Pair, some Wedding's near,
And you must Sport, and Revel with the Bride,
And give their Bed Joy and Prosperity.

OB.   How canst thou thus for shame, Titania,
Reflect on my past scapes? when well thou know'st,
I have pursu'd you to this very place,
Where you retir'd, to Wanton with a Boy
You lately stole from a Fair Indian.

TIT.   These are the Forgeries of Jealousie.
And never since the middle of the Summer,
Met we on Hill, or Dale, Forrest, or Mead,
By Streaming Fountain, or by Rushy Brook,
Or on the beached Margent of the Sea,
To Dance in Circles to the Whistling Wind;
But with thy brawls thou hast disturb'd our Sport.

OB.   Do you amend it'then, it lies in you;
Why should Titania cross her Oberon?
I only beg a little Changling Boy,
Give me him, we are Friends.

TIT.   Let this suffice,
All Fairy-Land buys not the Child of me:
His Mother was a Votress of my Order,
And for her sake I breed the pretty Boy,
And for her sake, I will not part with him.

OB.   How long within this Wood mean you to stay?

TIT. 'Till you have Grac'd your Lover's Nuptial Day.
   If you will patiently Dance in our Round,
   And see our Midnight Revels, go with us;
   If not, avoid my Haunts, as I will yours.
OB. Give me the Boy, and I will go with you.
TIT. Not for the Wealth of India, come away.
   We chide down-right, if I should longer stay. [*Exit* TIT. *and* TRAIN.
OB. Well, go thy ways, thou shalt not from this Grove,
   'Till I Torment thee for this Injury.
   My gentle Puck come hither, thou remembrest
   Since when I sat upon a Promontory,
   And heard a Mearmaid, on a Dolphin's back,
   Sing with such Sweet, with such Harmonious breath,
   That the Rude Sea grew Civil at her Song,
   And Twinkling Stars shot madly from their Sphears,
   To hear the Sea-Maid's Musick.
ROB. I well remember it.
OB. That very time I say (thou couldst not see it)
   Flying between the cold Moon, and the Earth,
   I saw young Cupid in the Mid-way hanging,
   At a Fair Vestal Virgin taking aim;
   Let flye his Love-Shaft smartly from his Bow,
   As it would pierce a hundred thousand Hearts:
   But when it came beneath the watry Moon,
   The Chast Beams of Diana quench'd its heat,
   And the Imperial Virgin passed on,
   In Maiden Meditation, free from harm.
ROB. What's this to me?
OB. Observe me, Puck.
   I look'd, and mark'd the place where the Bolt fell;
   It fell upon a little western Flower,
   Before Milk white, now Purple, with Love's wound,
   And Maidens call it, Love in Idleness:
   Fetch me that Flower, thou know'st I shew'd it thee.
   The juice of it on Sleeping Eye-lids laid,
   Will make a Man or Woman madly Dote
   Upon the next Live Creature that it sees.
   Fetch me this Herb, go, and be here again,
   E'er the Leviathan can swim a League.
ROB. I'll compass the whole Earth in forty minutes. [*Exit.*
OB. When I have this Juice,
   I'll find Titania where she lies asleep,
   And drop some of the Liquor in her Eyes.
   The next Live Thing she waking looks upon,
   (Be it on Lion, Bear, or Wolf, or Bull,

The medling Monkey, or the busie Ape)
She shall (with all the eagerness of Love)
Pursue; and e're I take the Charm away,
(As I can take it with another Herb)
I'll make her render up her Page to me.
But who comes here? I am invisible;
I'll stay and over-hear their Conference.
        Enter DEMETRIUS, *and* HELENA *following him.*
DEM.   Why do you follow him who Loves you not?
  Where is Lysander? and Fair Hermia?
  You told me they were stoln into this Wood.
  I seek, but cannot find her. Hence, be gone.
HEL.   You draw me, you hard-hearted Adamant;
  And yet I am not Iron, yet you draw me.
DE.   Do I intice you? do I speak you fair?
  I rather tell you an ill-manner'd Truth,
  Tell you I do not, nor I cannot love you.
HEL.   And even for that I love Demetrius more.
  Ah! what am I reduc'd to? like a Spannel,
  The more you beat, the more I fawn on you.
  Use me most barbarously, strike me, spurn me,
  Neglect me, scorn me; only give me leave,
  Unworthy as I am, to follow you.
DE.   You throw a scandal on your Modesty,
  To leave the City, and commit your self
  Into the hands of one who loves you not:
  To trust the opportunity of Night,
  And the ill Counsel of a Desart place,
  With the rich purchase of your Virgin Treasure.
HEL.   Your Virtue is my Guard, Demetrius:
  It is not night when I behold that Face,
  Nor can this Wood want Worlds of Company,
  For you, my Love, are all the World to me,
  Then how can I be said to be alone,
  When all the World is here to guard my Virtue.
DE.   I'll run from thee, and hide me in the Brakes,
  And leave thee to the Mercy of Wild Beasts.
HEL.   The wildest Beast has not a Heart like you:
  Run when you will, the Story shall be chang'd;
  Apollo flies, Daphne pursues the God;
  The Dove chases the Vulture; the mild Hind
  Makes haste to catch the Tyger; prepostrous Chace,
  When Cowardise pursues, and Valour flies.
DE.   Plague me no more, return e'er 'tis too late.
  Follow me not, for fear my Rage should tempt me

To some unmanly Act, and mischief thee. [*Ex.* DE.

HEL.   Ay, in the Temple, in the Town, and Field,
You do me mischief everywhere, Demetrius:
Such Wrongs will be a scandal to your Sex.
I'll follow if he rids me of my Woe,
I'll kiss the hand that gives the fatal blow. [*Ex.* HEL.

OB.   Poor Nymph, farewell. Before he leaves this Grove
Thou shalt fly him, and he shall seek thy Love.

        Enter ROBIN-GOOD-FELLOW.

Welcome my Puck; hast thou the Flow'r?

ROB.   'Tis here.

OB.   Give it me Puck.
I know there is a bank where wild Time blows,
Where Ox-lips, and the nodding Violet grows,
All over Canopied with Woodbine sweet,
Where Eglantine, and where Musk-Roses meet.
There my Titania Sleeps, lull'd in Delights,
And tyr'd in Dancing with her Fairy Sprights.
'Tis there the Snake casts her Enammell'd skin,
Too large a Robe to cloathe a Fairy in.
There with this wondrous Juice I'le streak her Eyes.
Take some of it; you'l find within this Grove,
A most Unhappy Nymph, who is in Love
With a disdainful Youth; anoint his Eyes;
But do it, that the next thing he espies
May be that Lady; thou shalt know the Man,
By the Embroider'd Garment he has on.
Do it, and meet me at the Crystal Lake.

ROB.   I will; and bring the Nymph when he shall wake.

OB.   What different Passions in her Soul will move?
To see his former Hatred, turn'd to Love.

                                            [*Exeunt.*

        Enter TITANIA, *and her* TRAIN.

TIT.   Take Hands, and trip it in a round,
While I Consecrate the ground.
All shall change at my Command,
All shall turn to Fairy-Land.

*The Scene changes to a Prospect of Grotto's, Arbors, and delightful
Walks: The Arbors are Adorn'd with all variety of Flowers, the Grotto's supported by Terms, these lead to two Arbors on either side of
the Scene, of a great length, whose prospect runs toward the two
Angles of the House. Between these two Arbors is the great Grotto,
which is continued by several Arches, to the farther end of the
House.*

Now Fairies search, search everywhere,
Let no Unclean thing be near.
Nothing Venomous, or Foul,
No Raven, Bat, or hooting Owle.
No Toad, nor Elf, nor Blind-worm's Sting.
No Poisonous Herb in this place Spring.
Have you search'd? is no ill near?
All. Nothing, nothing; all is clear.
Tit. Let your Revels now begin,
Some shall Dance, and some shall Sing.
All Delights this place surround,
Every sweet Harmonious Sound,
That e're Charm'd a skilful Ear,
Meet, and Entertain us here.
Let Eccho's plac'd in every Grot,
Catch, and repeat each Dying Note.

A PRELUDE.

Then the First SONG.

Come all ye Songsters of the Sky,
Wake, and Assemble in this Wood;
But no ill-boding Bird be nigh,
None but the Harmless and the Good.
May the God of Wit inspire,
The Sacred Nine to bear a part;
And the Blessed Heavenly Quire,
Shew the utmost of their Art.
While Eccho shall in sounds remote,
Repeat each Note,
Each Note, each Note.
CHORUS.   May the God, &c.
Now joyn your Warbling Voices all,
Sing while we trip it on the Green;
But no ill Vapours rise or fall,
Nothing offend our Fairy Queen.
CHORUS. Sing while we trip, &c.
   At the end of the first Stanza, a Composition of Instrumental
   Musick, in imitation of an Eccho. Then a Fairy Dance.
TIT.   Come Elves, another Dance, and Fairy Song;
   Then hence, and leave me for a while alone.
   Some to kill Kankers in the Musk-Rose-Buds;
   Some War with Rere-mice for their Leathern Wings,
   To make my small Elves Coats. And some keep back
   The clamarous Owl, that hoots, and wonders at us.

Each knows her Office. Sing me now to Sleep;
And let the Sentinels their Watches keep. [*She lyes down.*

2. *Song.*

Enter NIGHT, MYSTERY, SECRESIE, SLEEP; *and their*
ATTENDANTS. NIGHT *Sings.*

NI.   See, even Night herself is here,
  To favour your Design;
  And all her Peaceful Train is near,
  That Men to Sleep incline.
  Let Noise and Care,
  Doubt and Despair,
  Envy and Spight,
  (The Fiends delight)
  Be ever Banish'd hence.
  Let soft Repose,
  Her Eye-lids close;
  And murmuring Streams,
  Bring pleasing Dreams;
  Let nothing stay to give offence.
  See, even Night, &c.

MYS.   I am come to look all fast,
  Love without me cannot last.
  Love, like Counsels of the Wise,
  Must be hid from Vulgar Eyes.
  'Tis holy, and we must conceal it,
  They profane it, who reveal it.
  I am come, &c.

SE.   One charming Night
  Gives more delight,
  Than a hundred lucky Days.
  Night and I improve the tast,
  Make the pleasure longer last,
  A thousand thousand several ways.
  Make the pleasure, &c.

SL.   Hush, no more, be silent all,
  Sweet Repose has clos'd her Eyes.
  Soft as feather'd Snow does fall!
  Softly, softly, steal from hence.
  No noise disturb her sleeping sence.
  Rest till the Rosie Morn's uprise.

CHORUS   Hush, no more, &c.

A Dance of the Followers of Night.

Enter OBERON.

OB.   What thou seest when thou dost wake,
For thy Lover thou must take,
Sigh, and Languish, for his sake.
Be it Ounce, or Wolf, or Bear,
Pard, or Boar with bristel'd Hair,
In thy Eye what first appear,
Make that Beastly thing thy Dear,
Wake, when some vile Creature's near. [*Ex.* OB.

     Enter LYSANDER, *and* HERMIA.

LY.   You faint, my Sweet, with wandring in the Wood,
I fear, my Hermia, we mistook our way.
Let us lye down, and rest, if you think good,
And tarry for the comfort of the Day.

HER.   Let it be so, Lysander,
Go, lay thee down; and so good-night, dear Friend,
Our Loves ne're alter, till our Lives shall end.

LY.   Amen to that sweet Pray'r, my Charming Love.
May my Life end, when I inconstant prove. [*They lye down at a distance.*

     Enter ROBIN-GOOD-FELLOW.

ROB.   Through the Forrest I have gone,
But a Stranger find I none,
With Embroider'd Garment on;
On whose Eyes I might approve,
This Flow'r's force in Moving Love.
Night, and silence! who is here?
He does such a Garment wear.
This is he, my Master said,
Scorn'd and dispis'd the lovely Maid.
Here's the Virgin sleeping sound,
On the Dank, and dewy Ground.
Churl, upon thy Eyes I throw,
All the pow'r this Charm does owe.
At the first Cock wake, and spy,
She who Loves thee very nigh.
Farewel Lovers, I am gone;
I must now to Oberon. [*Exit.*

ACT III.

     Enter HELENA.

HEL.   I am out of breath with following him so fast
O happy Hermia, wheresoe'er she is!

How her attractive Eyes still draw him on!
How came her Eyes so bright? not with salt tears;
If so, my eyes are oftner wash'd than hers.
Ha! who lies here? Lysander on the Ground!
I hope he is not dead! Lysander, speak.
    [LY. *wakes.*

LY.   Ha, Helen! fairest of all Womankind!
More lovely than the Grecian Beauty was,
Who drew so many Kings to wed her Cause.
Ah, false Demetrius! when e'er we meet,
This Sword shall punish thy Ingratitude.

HEL.   O say not so, Lysander! though he loves
Your Mistress, kill him not; pray be content,
Be satisfy'd, your Hermia loves you still.

LY.   Content with Hermia! no, I now repent
Each tedious minute I have spent with her.
'Tis Helena, not Hermia, I love:
Who wou'd not change a Raven for a Dove?
No growing things are ripe before their Season;
Time and Experience only ripens Reason.
When I saw Hermia first, I was unripe,
Raw, green, and unacquainted with the World;
But time and you have taught me better Skill,
For now my Reason over-rules my Will.
I find new Charms when on your Eyes I look,
And read Love's Stories in Love's fairest Book.

HEL.   What spightful Planet reign'd when I was born?
What have I done deserves this Mockery?
But fare you well; I thought you better natur'd.
Must I, because I am by one refus'd,
Be by the rest of all Mankind abus'd! [Exit.

LY.   She sees not Hermia. Sleep, sleep for ever;
Never come nearer to Lysander more.
For as a Surfeit of the sweetest things,
Creates a greater loathing in the Stomach.
Thou art my Surfeit, and I hate thee most:
O may I never, never see thee more;
Helen the Goddess I must now adore. [*Ex.* LY.

HER.   Help me, Lysander, quickly! help me here, [HER. *wakes.*
To pluck this crawling Serpent from my Breast:
Oh all ye Powers! what a Dream had I?
Methought a Serpent eat my Heart away,
And yet sat smiling at his cruel Prey:
Lysander; what, remov'd? where are you? speak.

No sound! no word! O I shall die with fear!
Who are these coming hither? Let me fly!
My Fears will vanish, if Lysander's nigh. [*Ex.* HER.
     Enter BOTTOM, QUINCE, SNUG, FLUTE, SNOUT, *and* STARVELING.
BOT.   Are we all met?
QU.   All, all, and drest in the same Habits we intend to act in
before the Duke; and here's a marvellous convenient place for
our Rehearsal; this Plat shall be our Stage; behind these Trees
our retiring Room: and we will do it in action, as we will do it
before the whole Court.
     Enter ROBIN-GOOD-FELLOW.
RO.   What home-spun Fellows have we swagg'ring here,
So near the Grotto of the Fairy-Queen?
QU.   Now every Man retire, and enter according to his Cue.
Prologue, stand ready, you begin.
RO.   What, a Play toward? I'll be an Auditor;
An Actor too, perhaps, as I see cause.
     Enter PROLOGUE.
PRO.   If we offend, it is with our good Will
That you should think we come not to offend:
But with good will to shew our simple Skill,
That is the true beginning of our end.
Consider then we come but in despight;
We do not come as minding to content you.
Our true intent is all for your delight:
We are not here that you should here repent you.
The Actors are at hand, and by their show,
You shall know all that you are like to know.
BO.   He has rid his Prologue like a rough Colt, he knows no stop;
'Tis not enough to speak, but to speak true.
     Enter WALL.
WALL.   In this same Interlude it doth befal,
That I, Starveling (by name) present a Wall:
And such a Wall as I would have you think,
That had in it a crannied hole or chink.
Through which the Lovers, Pyramus and Thisbe,
Did whisper often very secretly.
This Loam, this Rough-cast, and this Stone doth show,
That I am that same Wall, the Truth is so;
And this the Cranny is, right and sinister,
Through which the fearful Lovers are to whisper.
RO.   Who wou'd desire Lime and Hair to speak better? 'Tis the wit-
tiest Partition I ever saw.
     Enter PYRAMUS.

PY.   O grim-look'd Night! a Night with hue so black!
O night! which ever art when day is not!
Oh night! oh night! alack! alack! alack!
I fear my Thisbe's Promise is forgot.
And thou, oh Wall; thou sweet and lovely Wall,
That stands between her Father's Ground and mine,
Shew me thy Chink to blink through with my eyn.
Thanks, courteous Wall, Jove shield thee well for this.
But what see I? no Thisbe do I see:
O wicked Wall, through whom I see no Bliss!
Curst be thy Stones for thus deceiving me.

RO.   Methinks the Wall being sensible, shou'd curse again.

BO.   No, but he shou'd not: Deceiving me is Thisbe's Cue.
Therefore hold your prating there.

    Enter THISBE.

TH.   O Wall, full often hast thou heard my Moans;
For parting my fair Pyramus and me.

PY.   I hear a Voice; now will I to the Chink,
To spy if I can see my Thisbe's Face. Thisbe!

TH.   My Love thou art; my Love, I think.

PY.   Think what thou wilt, I am thy Lover's Grace;
And like Limander am I trusty still.

TH.   And I like Helen, till the Fates me kill.

PY.   Not Shafalus to Procrus was so true.

TH.   As Shafalus to Procrus, I to you.

PY.   O kiss me through the Hole of this vile Wall.

TH.   I kiss the Wall's Hole, not thy Lips at all.

PY.   Wilt thou at Ninny's Tomb meet me straightway?

TH.   Tide Life, tide Death; I come without delay. [*Exeunt* PYRAMUS
and THISBE *several ways.*

WALL   Thus have I Wall, my part discharged so,
And being done, thus Wall away does go. [*Ex.* WALL.

    Enter LION *and* MOONSHINE.

LYON   You Ladies, you (whose gentle Hearts do fear
The smallest monstrous Mouse that creeps on Floor)
May now perchance both quake and tremble here.
When Lion rough in wildest Rage doth roar,
Then know that I one Snug the Joyner am;
No Lion fell, nor else no Lion's Dam.
For if I shou'd as Lion, come in strife
Into this place, 'twere pity of my Life.

RO.   Upon my word, a very gentle Beast.

MOON   This Lanthorn does the horned Moon present,
My self the Man i'th' Moon do seem to be.

RO.   Make an end, good Moon-shine.

MOON. All I have to say is to tell you, that the Lanthorn is the
Moon, I the Man in the Moon, this Thorn-bush my Thorn-bush,
and this Dog my Dog.
  Enter THISBE.
TH. This is old Ninny's Tomb; where is my Love?
LION Oa, Oa, Oa. [*Exit* THISBE *running, the* LION *after her.*
RO. Well roar'd Lion, and well run Thisbe too.
  Enter PYRAMUS.
PY. Sweet Moon, I thank thee for thy Sunny Beams:
I thank thee, Moon, for shining now so bright:
For by thy Gracious, Golden, Glittering Streams,
I trust to taste of truest Thisbe's sight.
But stay. O spight!
But mark; poor Knight!
What dreadful dole is here?
Eyes do not see,
How can it be?
O dainty Duck! O dear!
Thy Mantle slain? what stain'd with Blood?
Approach, you Furies fell:
O Fates! come, come.
Cut, thread, and thrum,
Quail, crush, conclude, and quell.
RO. If this wont move the Ladies, poor Pyramus will take pains to
little purpose.
PY. O wherefore, Nature, did'st thou Lions frame?
Since Lion vile has here deflour'd my Dear.
Which is—no, no, which was the fairest Dame
That liv'd, that lov'd, that lik'd, that look'd with chear,
Come Tears confound!
Out Sword, and wound
The Pap of Pyramus:
Ay, that left Pap,
Where Heart doth hop,
As Bird doth hop in Cage.
Thus die I, thus, thus, thus.
Now am I dead,
Now am I fled,
My Soul is in the Sky.
Tongue lose thy light,
Eyes take your flight,
Now die, die, die, die.
  Enter THISBE.
TH. Asleep, my Love?
What dead, my Dove?

O Pyramus arise!
Speak, speak! quite dumb?
Dead, dead! a Tomb
Must cover my sweet Eyes.
These Lilly-Lips, this Cherry-Nose,
These yellow Cowslip-Cheeks,
Are gone, are gone,
Lovers make moan,
His Eyes are green as Leeks.
Tongue not a word,
Come trusty Sword,
Come Blade, my Breast imbrue.
Now farewell Friends,
Thus Thisbe ends,
Adieu, adieu, adieu.
        They all come in.

SNOUT   Come, get up Pyramus and Thisbe, and let me speak the
Epilogue.

RO.   No, no; I'll be the Epilogue.
Robin runs in amongst them.

QU.   O monstrous! we are haunted!
Pray Masters, fly Masters.

ALL   Help, help, help!   *Exeunt, running several ways.*

RO.   I'll follow you;
I'll lead you such a round.
Through Bog, through Bush, through Brake, through Brier;
Sometimes a Horse I'll be, sometimes a Hound;
A Hog, a headless Bear; sometimes a Fire.
And neigh, and grunt, and bark, and roar, and burn,
Like Horse, Hog, Hound, Bear, Fire, at every turn.   [*Ex.* ROB.
        Enter BOTTOM, *with an Ass's Head on.*

BOT.   Why do they run away? This is a piece of Knavery among
'em, to make me afraid.
        Enter SNOUT.

SN.   O Bottom! Thou art chang'd.
What's that I see on thee?

BOT.   What do you see?
You see an Ass-head of your own, that you see.
        Enter PETER QUINCE.

QU.   Bless thee, Bottom, bless thee! thou art translated. [*Exeunt*
SNOUT *and* QUINCE.

BOT.   I find their Knavery; they would fain make an Ass of me, and
fright me if they could. But I won't stir from this place, do what they
can. I will walk up and down here, and I will sing, that they may
hear I am not afraid.

Sings.

The Woosel-Cock, so black of hue,
With Orange-tawny Bill;
The Thrustle, with his Note so true,
The Wren with little Quill.

  TITANIA *wakes.*

TIT. What Angel wakes me from my Flowry Bed.

BOT. The Finch, the Sparrow, and the Lark,
The One-tun'd Cuckow gray;
Whose Note most Married Men do mark;
And dare not answer, Nay.
For indeed, who wou'd set his wit to so foolish a Bird? who
wou'd give a Bird the lie, tho' he cry Cuckow never so often?

TIT. I pray thee, lovely Mortal, sing again:
My Ear is much enamour'd with thy Note.
My Eye is fix'd on thy Majestick Shape.
Oh, how thy Graces charm me! I am forc'd,
At the first sight to say, to swear I love thee.

BOT. Methinks, Mistress, you should have little Reason for that;
and yet to say Truth, Reason, and Love, keep little Company
together now a days; the more the pity, that some honest
Neighbour will not make 'em Friends. Nay I can break a Jest on
occasion.

TIT. Thou art as wise as thou art beautiful.

BOT. Not so neither; but if I had Wit enough to get out of this
Wood, I have enough to serve my own turn.

TIT. Out of this Wood never desire to go;
Here you shall stay whether you will or no.
I'll purge your grossness, you shall never die,
But like an airy Spirit, you shall fly.
Where are my Fairy Spirits?

  Enter 4 FAIRIES.

1 FA. I am here.

2 FA. And I.

3 FA. And I.

4 FA. And I.

ALL What shall we do?

TIT. Attend this Charming Youth.
Dance as he walks, and gambole in his Eye.
Feed him with Apricooks, and Dew-berries;
With purple Grapes, ripe Figs, and Mulberries.
The Hony-Bags steal from the Humble-bees.
For his Night-Tapers crop their waxen thighs,
And light 'em at the fiery Glow-worms Eyes.

And pluck the Wings from painted Butter-flies,
To fan the Moon-beams from his sleeping Eyes.
Bow to him Elves, do Homage to my Love.

1 FA.   Hail, Mortal, hail.

2 FA.   Hail.

3 FA.   Hail.

4 FA.   Hail.

TIT.   Come, wait upon him, lead him to my Bower.
The Moon, methinks, looks with a watry Eye;
And when she weeps, then every little Flower
Laments for some lost Virgin's Chastity:
Tye up my Love's Tongue; bring him silently.   [*Exeunt.*

      Enter OBERON.

OB.   By this time my Titania should be wak'd;
I long to know what came first to her Eye.

      Enter ROBIN-GOOD-FELLOW.

Here comes my Messenger. Welcome, mad Spright:
What pranks have you been playing in the Grove?

ROB.   My Lady with a Monster is in love.
I led sweet Pyramus through the Fairy Pass,
And plac'd him just before the sleeping Queen;
She wak'd, and saw him, and straight lov'd the Ass,
His comly Visage, and his graceful Meen.

OB.   'Tis as I wish'd (my Puck) but tell me now,
How fares the scornful Youth?

ROB.   That's finish'd too.
I found 'em sleeping on a Bed of Brakes;
I streak'd his eyes, he sees her when he wakes.
Demetrius and Hermia cross the Stage.

OB.   Stand close, they come. Now hate her if you can.

ROB.   This is the Woman, but not that the Man.

OB.   What hast thou done? thou hast mistaken quite,
And laid the Juice on the true Lover's sight.

ROB.   Then Fate o'er-rules; where one Man keeps his Troth,
A thousand fail, by breaking Oath on Oath.

OB.   About the Wood, go swifter than the Wind.
You shall the poor despairing Helen find;
By some Illusion train, and bring her here,
I'll charm his Eyes. And when the Damsel's near,
We'll wake Demetrius.

ROB.   I go, I go,
Swift as an Arrow from a Tartar's Bow.   [*Ex.* ROB.

      Enter TITANIA, BOTTOM, *and* FAIRIES.

TIT.   Come, lovely Youth, sit on this flowry Bed,

While I thy amiable looks survey;
Garlands of Roses shall adorn thy Head,
A thousand Sweets shall melt themselves away,
To charm my Lover till the break of day.
Shall we have Musick sweet?

BOT.   Yes, if you please.

TIT.   Away, my Elves; prepare a Fairy Mask
To entertain my Love; and change this place
To my Enchanted Lake.

*The Scene changes to a great Wood; a long row of large Trees on
each side: A River in the middle: Two rows of lesser Trees of a different kind just on the side of the River, which meet in the middle, and
make so many Arches: Two great Dragons make a Bridge over the
River; their Bodies form two Arches, through which two Swans are
seen in the River at a great distance.*

Enter a Troop of FAWNS, DRYADES *and* NAIDES.

A Song in two Parts.

If Love's a Sweet Passion, why does it torment?
If a Bitter, oh tell me whence comes my content?
Since I suffer with pleasure, why should I complain,
Or grieve at my Fate, when I know 'tis in vain?
Yet so pleasing the Pain is, so soft is the Dart,
That at once it both wounds me, and tickles my (Heart.
I press her Hand gently, look Languishing down,
And by Passionate Silence I make my Love known.
But oh! how I'm Blest when so kind she does prove,
By some willing mistake to discover her Love.
When in striving to hide, she reveals all her Flame,
And our Eyes tell each other, what neither dares Name.

*While a Symphany's Playing, the two Swans come Swimming on
through the Arches to the bank of the River, as if they would Land;
there turn themselves into Fairies, and Dance; at the same time the
Bridge vanishes, and the Trees that were Arch'd, raise themselves
upright.*

Four SAVAGES *Enter, fright the* FAIRIES *away,
and Dance an Entry.
Enter* CORIDON, *and* MOPSA.

CO.   Now the Maids and the Men are making of Hay,
We have left the dull Fools, and are stol'n away.

Then Mopsa no more
Be Coy as before,
But let us merrily, merrily Play,
And Kiss, and Kiss, the sweet time away.

MO.   Why how now, Sir Clown, how came you so bold?
I'd have you to know I'm not made of that mold.
I tell you again,
Maids must Kiss no Men.
No, no; no, no; no Kissing at all;
I'le not Kiss, till I Kiss you for good and all.

CO.   No, no.

MO.   No, no.

CO.   Not Kiss you at all.

MO.   Not Kiss, till you Kiss me for good and all.
Not Kiss, &c.

CO.   Should you give me a score,
'T would not lessen the store,
Then bid me chearfully, chearfully Kiss,
And take, and take, my fill of your Bliss.

MO.   I'le not trust you so far, I know you too well;
Should I give you an Inch, you'd take a whole Ell.
Then Lordlike you Rule,
And laugh at the Fool.
No, no, &c.

A Song by a Nymph.

When I have often heard young Maids complaining,
That when Men promise most they most deceive,
Then I thought none of them worthy my gaining;
And what they Swore, resolv'd ne're to believe.
But when so humbly he made his Addresses,
With Looks so soft, and with Language so kind,
I thought it Sin to refuse his Caresses;
Nature o'recame, and I soon chang'd my Mind.
Should he employ all his wit in deceiving,
Stretch his Invention, and artfully feign;
I find such Charms, such true Joy in believing,
I'll have the Pleasure, let him have the pain.
If he proves Perjur'd, I shall not be Cheated,
He may deceive himself, but never me;
'Tis what I look for, and shan't be defeated,
For I'll be as false and inconstant as he.

A DANCE *of Hay-Makers.*

After the DANCE

CHORUS   A Thousand Thousand ways we'll find,
   To Entertain the Hours;
   No Two shall e're be known so kind,
   No Life so Blest as ours.

TIT.   Now I will Feast the Pallate of my Love,
   The Sea, the Air, the Earth I'll ransack for thee.
   Name all that Art or Nature e're produc'd,
   My Sprights shall fetch it instantly: O say
   What will you have to Eat?

BO.   A Peck of Provender, if your Honour please; I could munch
   some good dry Oats very heartily; I have a great exposition of
   Sleep upon me, would some of your Attendants would shew me a
   necessary place for that same purpose.

TIT.   I'll lead thee to a Bank strew'd o'er with Violets,
   With Jessamine, and cooling Orange Flowers,
   There I will fold thee in my tender Arms,
   As the sweet Woodbine, of the Female Ivy,
   Circles the Barky Body of the Elm.
   Well Sport away the remnant of the Night,
   And all the World shall envy my Delight.   [*Exeunt.*

ACT IV.

Enter OBERON *and* ROBIN-GOOD-FELLOW

OB.   I Squese this Flower of Purple die,
   Hit with Cupid's Archery,
   On the Apple of his Eye;
   When the mournful Helen's nigh,
   She shall shine as gloriously,
   As yonder Venus in the Sky.
   Thou shalt wake when she is by,
   And beg her pardon for thy Cruelty.

ROB.   Lord of all the Fairy Land,
   All is done at thy Command;
   Helena is here at hand,
   And the Youth mistook by me,
   Pleading for a Lover's Fee.
   Shall we their fond Pageants see?
   Lord, what Fools these Mortals be!

OB.   Be careful, or the noise they make
   Will cause Demetrius to awake.

ROB.   Then will two one Damsel court,

That must needs be pleasant sport.
I am always pleas'd to see
Things fall out prepostrously.
     Enter LYSANDER *and* HELENA:

LY.   Why should think you that I would woo in scorn?
   Scorn and Derision never come in Tears.
   How can these watry Eyes seem Scorn to you?
   Wearing Love's Livery to prove 'em true.

HEL.   You but advance your cunning more and more,
   When truth kills truth, 'tis the Devil's holy War.
   These Vows are Hermia's, they belong to her.

LY.   I had no Judgment when to her I swore.

HEL.   And now much less, if now you give her o'er.

LY.   Demetrius loves her, and loves not you.
     DEMETRIUS *wakes.*

DE.   Oh Helen! Goddess! Angel! all Divine!
   To what shall I compare those charming Eyes?
   The Stars are dim, Crystal is muddy too.
   How ripe, how tempting ripe those Lips appear!
   Those two Twin-Cherries kissing as they grow?
   The purest Snow holds no comparison,
   With that white lovely Breast. O let me kiss
   That hand, that hoard of Sweets, that Seal of Bliss.
   I am Love's Convert, Helena; I see,
   And I repent my former Heresie.

HEL.   O! utmost spight! I see you all are bent,
   All set against me for your merriment.
   Can you not hate me? as I know you do;
   Must you contrive, and joyn to mock me to?
   If you are Men? as Men you are in show,
   You wou'd not use a harmless Virgin so;
   To vow, and swear, and over-praise each part,
   When I am sure you hate me in your Heart.
   You both are Rivals, both love Hermia,
   And now both Rivals to mock Helena.
     Enter HERMIA.

HER.   Dark night that from the Eye distinction takes,
   The Ear more quick of apprehension makes.
   'Twas my Ear guided me to find you out.
   But why, Lisander, did you leave me so?

LY.   Impertinent! Love summon'd me to go.

HER.   What Love could call Lysander from my side?

LY.   The Love of Helena, whose brighter Eyes
   Darken the Starry Jewels of the Night;
   They take from her, not from the Sun their light.

HER.   You speak not as you think; it cannot be.

HEL.   Oh Heav'n! she's one of the Confederacy.
   Injurious Hermia! ungrateful Maid!
   Have you conspir'd to deride me too?
   What though I am not beautiful as you,
   Though I am most unhappy in my Love?
   You ought to pity, not despise me for't.
   But fare you well; I know the fault's my own;
   And either Death, or Absence, soon shall end it.

LY.   Stay, lovely Maid; by Heav'n I swear to thee,
   Thou art my Eyes, my Life, my Soul, fair Helen.

DE.   I love thee more, much more than he can do.

LY.   Words, words: let us withdraw, and prove it too.

DE.   Follow me then.

HER.   Hold, hold, Lysander; to what tends all this?

LY.   Away, you Ethiop.

DE.   Ay, ay, seem to break loose.
   Struggle as if you meant to follow me,
   But come not. You may let the tame Man go.

LY.   What can I do? would'st have me beat her from me?
   No; though I hate her, yet I cannot harm her.

HER.   How can you do me greater harm than this?
   Hate me? wherefore? ah me! my dearest Love!
   Am not I Hermia? are not you Lysander?
   Or am I alter'd since you saw me last?
   This night you lov'd me, and this night you fly me.
   Have you forsaken me? (oh Heav'n forbid)
   Come tell me truly; do you hate me now?

LY.   Ay, by my Life,
   And wish I never may behold thee more.
   Let this remove all doubt, for nothing's truer,
   Than I hate thee, and love fair Helena.

HER.   O then 'tis you, you Jugler, Canker-blossom,
   You Thief of Love, you who have come by Night,
   And stoln Lysander's Heart.

HEL.   Indeed 'tis fine.
   Have you no Modesty? no touch of Shame?
   No Bashfulness? let not this Pigmie tear
   Impatient answers from my milder Tongue.

HER.   Pigmie! why so? Ay, that way goes the Game.
   Now I perceive she has made Comparisons
   Between our Statures; she has urg'd her height,
   Her Manly Presence, and tall Personage.
   And are you grown so high in his Esteem,
   Because I am so Dwarfish, and so low?

How low am I? thou painted May-Pole, speak.
How low am I?

LY.   Be not afraid, she shall not hurt thee, Sweet.

DE.   No, Sir, she shall not, though you take her part.

HEL.   When she is angry, she's a very Shrew:
She was a Vixen when she went to School,
And though she is but little, she is fierce.

HER.   Little again? nothing but low and little?
'Tis you encourage her t' abuse me thus.
Let me come at her?

LY.   Away, you Dwarf.

DE.   You are too officious.

LY.   Now she holds me not.
Now follow if thou dar'st; and let us try
Which of has most right to Helena.

DE.   Follow? nay I'll go with you; yes, before you.   [*Ex.* LY. & DE.

HER.   You Mistress; all this stir is about you.
Nay, go not back.

HEL.   I dare not trust you, Hermia.
Your hands I know, are quicker for a Fray:
My Legs are longer tho', to run away.
                              [*Ex.* HEL. *running, and* HER. *after her.*

OB.   This is thy negligence; still thou mistak'st,
Or else committ'st thy Knaveries willingly.

ROB.   Believe me, King of Shadows, I mistook.
Did you not tell me I should know the Man,
By the Embroider'd Garment he had on?
If he had made to the right Woman court,
We had had no Divertisement, no Sport.

OB.   Thou see'st these Lovers seek a place to fight;
Haste, Robin, haste; and overcast the Night.
These furious Rivals you must lead astray,
Be sure they come not in each others way.
Now like Lysander, now Demetrius,
Call here and there; mis-lead and tire 'em thus.
Till o'er their Eyes, Death's Counterfeit, sound Sleep,
With Leaden Legs, and Batty Wings shall creep.
Then crush this Herb into Lysander's Eye:
The Liquor has this virtuous property,
It will remove the Errors of this night,
And bring his Eye-Balls to their own true sight.
When next they wake, all that has past shall seem
A meer Illusion, a Fairy Dream.
While I in this Affair do thee employ,
I'll to my Queen, and get her Indian Boy.

Then from the Charm I will her eye release,
Send home the Clown, and all shall be at peace.

ROB.   This must be done with speed, I must not stay,
For with her Dragons Wings Night flies away:
See yonder shines Aurora's Harbinger,
At whose approach, Ghosts wandring here and there;
Troop home to Churchyards, Damned Spirits all,
That in Cross-ways and Floods have Burial:
Already to their Wormy-Beds are gone,
For fear Bright Day their shames should look upon.
They wilfully Exile themselves from Light,
And must forever wander in the Night.

OB.   But we are Spirits of another sort;
Can anywhere, at any time resort.
I have more work for thee, make no delay,
We must effect this Business yet e're day. [*Ex.* OB.

ROB.   Up and down, up and down, I will lead 'em up and down. I
am fear'd in Field and Town; Goblin lead 'em up and down,
here comes one.

    Enter LYSANDER.

LY.   Where art thou, proud Demetrius? answer where?

ROB.   Here Villain; drawn, and ready, where art thou?

LY.   I shall be with you straight.

ROB.   Follow me then to evener ground. [*Leads* LYSANDER *out, and
returns.*

    Enter LYSANDER. *He leads him in.*

LY.   He goes before me, and still dares me on,
When I come where he calls me, he is gone.
'Tis very dark, the way uneven too;
I'm tyr'd with running, here I'll lay me down,
And wait with patience the approach of day,
Then if I meet him, we will end our Fray. [*Sleeps.*

    Enter ROBIN, *and* DEMETRIUS.

ROB.   Speak Coward, answer me; why com'st thou not?

DE.   Stay Villain, if thou dar'st.
Thou run'st before me, shifting every place.
Stand, if thou art a Man, and meet me fairly.
Where art thou?

ROB.   I am here.

DE.   I see thee not, answer me where?

ROB.   Here, here.

DE.   Now thou derid'st me, thou shalt buy this dear,
When I thy Coward face by day-light see.
My faintness forces me to rest a while,
To measure out my length on this cold ground,

Thou wilt not with the breaking Day be found.   [*Sleeps.*
    Enter HELENA.

HEL.   Oh weary, tedious Night abate thy Hours;
    Shine from the East that I may fly to Town,
    From those who my poor Company detest.
    And sleep that sometimes shuts up Sorrows Eye,
    Steal me a while from my own Company.   [*Sleeps.*

ROB.   There's yet but three, come one more;
    Two of both kinds make up four.
    Here she comes pevish and sad.
    Cupid is a Knavish Lad,
    Thus to make poor Maidens mad.
    Enter HERMIA.

HER.   Never was Maid so weary, and so wrong'd,
    Wet with cold Dew, and torn with cruel Briars.
    I can scarce crawl, I can no farther go;
    My Legs can keep no pace with my desires.
    Here I will rest the remnant of the Night.
    Heav'n guard Lysander, if they meet and fight.   [*Sleeps.*
    Enter OBERON.

Thou hast perform'd exactly each Command.
    Titania too has given me the sweet Boy.
    And now I have him, I will straight undo
    The hated imperfection of her Eyes.
    And gentle Puck, take thou the Asses Head,
    From the transform'd Clown she doated on.
    That he awaking when the others do,
    May with his Fellows to their Homes repair.
    And think no more of this Night's Accidents,
    Than of the fierce vexation of a Dream,
    But first, I will release the Fairy Queen.
    Be, as thou wert wont to be;
    See, as thou wert wont to see.
    Cinthia's Bud, and Cupid's Flow'r,
    Has such force, and Blessed Pow'r.
    Now my Titania, wake.   [*She rises.*

TIT.   My Oberon! What Visions have I seen?
    Methought I was enamour'd of an Ass.

OB.   There lies your Love.

TIT.   How came these things to pass?
    How I detest that hateful Visage now!

OB.   Robin, take from the Fool the Ass's head.

ROB.   Hark, thou King of Shadows, hark!
    Sure I hear the morning Lark.

OB.   Let him warble on, I'll stay,

And bless these Lover's Nuptial Day.
Sleep, happy Lovers, for some Moments, sleep.
ROB.   So, when thou wak'st with thy own Fools Eyes, peep.
        [*He takes off the Ass's Head.*
OB.   Titania, call for Musick.
TIT.   Let us have all Variety of Musick,
All that should welcome up the rising Sun.

*The Scene changes to a Garden of Fountains. A Sonata plays while
the Sun rises, it appears red through the Mist, as it ascends it dissi-
pates the Vapours, and is seen in its full Lustre; then the Scene is
perfectly discovered, the Fountains enrich'd with gilding, and adorn'd
with Statues: The view is terminated by a Walk of Cypress Trees
which lead to a delightful Bower. Before the Trees stand rows of
Marble Columns, which support many Walks which rise by Stairs to
the top of the House; the Stairs are adorn'd with Figures on Pedestals, and Rails and Balasters on each side of 'em. Near the top, vast
Quantities of Water break out of the Hills, and fall in mighty Cas-
cades to the bottom of the Scene, to feed the Fountains which are on
each side. In the middle of the Stage is a very large Fountain, where
the Water rises about twelve Foot.*

    Then the 4 SEASONS *enter, with their several* ATTENDANTS.
    One of the ATTENDANTS *begin.*
NOW the Night is chac'd away,
All salute the rising Sun;
'Tis the happy, happy Day,
The Birth-Day of King Oberon.
Two others sing in Parts.
Let the Fifts, and the Clarions, and shrill Trumpets (sound,
And the Arch of high Heav'n the Clangor resound.
        A Machine *appears, the Clouds break from before it, and*
        PHOEBUS *appears in a Chariot drawn by four Horses; and
        Sings.*
When a cruel long Winter has frozen the Earth,
And Nature Imprison'd seeks in vain to be free;
I dart forth my Beams, to give all things a Birth,
Making Spring for the Plants, every flower, and each Tree.
'Tis I who give Life, Warmth, and Being to all,
Even Love who rules all things in Earth, Air, and Sea;
Would languish, and fade, and to nothing would fall,
The World to its Chaos would return, but for me.
CHORUS   Hail! Great Parent of us all,
    Light and Comfort of the Earth;
    Before thy Shrine the Seasons fall,

Thou who givest all Beings Birth.
Spring. Thus the ever Grateful Spring,
Does her yearly Tribute bring;
All your Sweets before him lay,
Then round his Altar Sing, and Play.
Summer. Here's the Summer, Sprightly, Gay,
Smiling, Wanton, Fresh, and Fair;
Adorn'd with all the Flowers of May,
Whose various Sweets perfume the Air.
Autumn. See my many Colour'd Fields,
And loaded Trees my Will obey;
All the Fruit that Autumn yields,
I offer to the God of Day.
WINTER   Now Winter comes Slowly, Pale, Meager, and Old,
First trembling with Age, and then quiv'ring with Cold;
Benum'd with hard Frosts, and with Snow cover'd o're,
Prays the sun to Restore him, and Sings as before.
CHORUS   Hail Great Parent, &c.

A DANCE *of the Four Seasons.*

OB.   Now my Puck this Herb apply
To the Mistaken Lover's Eye;
The powerful Juice will clear his Sight,
Make 'em Friends, and set all right.
TIT.   Come, my Lord, and tell me how?
How I sleeping here was found,
With these Mortals; on the Ground. [*Ex. All but* PUCK.
ROB.   On the Ground, sleeping sound,
I apply to your eye, gentle Lover, Remedy.
When thou wak'st, then thou tak'st
True Delight in thy former Lady's sight;
And the Country Proverb known,
That every Man should take his own,
In your waking shall be shown.
Jack shall have Gill, nought shall go ill,
The Man shall have his Mare again, and all shall be well. [*Exit.*

ACT V.

Enter DUKE, EGEUS, *and* TRAIN.
DU.   GO one of you, find out the Forrester,
I long to hear the Musick of my Hounds,
They shall uncouple in the Western Vally.
EG.   I mark'd it lately, 'twas a gallant chiding,
Beside the Groves, the Hills, and distant Vales,

    The Skies, the Fountains, every Region near,
    Seem'd all one mutual cry. I never heard
    So Musical a discord; such sweet Thunder.
DU.   My Hounds are bred out of the Spartan kind;
    So flew'd, so sanded; and their Heads are hung,
    With Ears that sweep away the morning dew!
    Crook-kneed, and Dew-lapt, like Thessalian Bulls,
    Slow in pursuit, but match'd in Mouth like Bells,
    Each under each; a cry more tunable,
    Was never hollow'd too, nor cheer'd with Horn!
    Judg when you hear. But soft, what Nymphs are these?
EG.   My Leigh, this is my Daughter here asleep!
    And this Lysander; this Demetrius!
    This Helena, how came they here together?
DU.   No doubt,
    They rose to grace our Solemn Hunting here.
    But speak, Egeus, is not this the Day,
    Hermia should give her answer?
EG.   It is my Leige.
DU.   Go bid the Huntsmen wake 'em with their Musick.
    A Composition in imitation of Hunting, at the end of it a Shout,
      the Lovers wake.
    God morrow friends; Saint Vallentines is past,
    How came these Wood-birds but to couple now?
LY.   Pardon me, gracious Sir.
DU.   Stand up, Lysander.
    I know you two are Rival Enemies,
    How comes this noble Concord in the World?
    That hatred is so far from Jealousie,
    To sleep by hate?
LY.   Sir I shall answer you amazedly,
    I do not sleep, yet scarce am half awake,
    I do not truly know how I came hither!
    But as I think (for I would truly speak)
    Yes, now I think I can remember it.
    Hither I came with beauteous Hermia,
    Our intent was to fly from hence, and so
    Evade the danger of your Cruel Law.
EG.   Enough (most Noble Duke) he owns enough:
    I ask your Justice for this breach of Law.
    They would have stol'n away; they would Demetrius.
    They meant to have defeated you, and me;
    You of your Wife, and me of my Consent.
DE.   All this fair Helen told me, my good Lord;
    And hither I in Fury follow'd 'em;

Hither, the too kind Helen follow'd me:
And here, by some strange pow'r (I know not how)
My Love to Hermia melted like the Snow:
And now she seems but as an idle Toy,
Which in my Infancy I doted on:
And all my Faith, the Vertue of my Heart,
Joy of my Life, and Pleasure of my Eye,
Is only Helena's. I was (my Lord)
Betroth'd to her, e're I saw Hermia:
But then, my sickly Palate loath'd its Food.
Now I'm in Health, come to my natural tast,
And now I wish, I love, I long for it;
And will be ever true to Helena.

DU.   Then we came hither in a happy time:
Egeus, I must over-rule your Will;
For in the Temple, when our Hunting's done,
These Lovers shall eternally be joyn'd.
Egeus, I will be a Father too,
And give fair Helen to Demetrius,
Then feast these Lovers Royally: away. [*Ex. all but the* LOVERS.

LY.   How have I dream'd, and thought I was awake?
And now I am awake, think I dream still.

HEL.   I never was so happy when awake:
Nay, pray disturb me not; let me dream on.

DE.   These things seem strange, and undistinguishable,
Like Mountains far, far off, turn'd into Clouds.

HER.   Methinks I see 'em with a parted Eye,
Where everything seems double.

HEL.   I think so too:
And I have found Demetrius like a Jewel
Long sought for, hardly credited when found.

DE.   Pray Heaven we dream not still.
Did you not think the Duke himself was here?

HER.   Yes, and my Father.

HEL.   And bid us follow him.

LY.   Ay, to the Temple.

HEL.   And said, he'd give me to Demetrius.
And feast us Royally.

LY.   Nay then we are awake; let's follow him.
And as we go, let us recount our Dreams. [*Exeunt.*
        [*A noise of Hunting at a distance,* BOTTOM *wakes.*

BOT.   When my Cue comes, call me, and I will answer. My next
is—most fair Pyramus—hey, ho! Peter Quince, Snout the Tinker,
Starveling? 'Ods my life, stoln hence, and left me asleep. I have had
a most rare Vision. I had a Dream, past the Wit of Man to say

what Dream it was; Man is but an Ass, if he go about to expound
this Dream: Methought I was! no Man can tell what. Methought
I was, and methought I had—but that Man is an arrant Fool, who
will offer to say what methought I had. I will get Peter Quince to
write a Ballad of this Dream; it shall be called Bottom's Dream,
because it has no bottom; And I will sing it my self, at the latter
end of our Play, before the Duke.

     Enter QUINCE, FLUTE, SNOUT, STARVELING.

QU.   I have sought far and near, and cannot find him.

ST.   So have I. Out of doubt he is Translated.

QU.   If we find him not, our Play is marr'd; it cannot be done without him: He has simply the best Wit of any Handicraft Man in
the whole Town.

QU.   Yes, and the best Person too: then he is a very Raven for a
sweet Voice.

     Enter SNUG.

SNUG   O Masters! the Duke's going to the Temple! the Lords and
the Ladies are to be Married this Morning. If our Play had gone
forward, we had been all made Men.

SNOUT   Ah sweet Bully Bottom; thou hast lost God knows what.
An the Duke had not given him God knows what for Playing
Pyramus, I'll be hang'd.

BOT.   O are you here? my Lads, my hearts of Iron?

QU.   He's here! he's here! Bottom's here! O most couragious day! O
happy day!

BOT.   Masters, I am to discourse wonders to you, but ask me not
what; for if I tell you, I am no true man. For I will tell everything
as it fell out.

QU.   Let us hear it then, sweet Bottom.

BOT.   Not a word, all I will tell you is, Get your Apparel together,
good strings to your Beards, new Ribbons, Powder, and Wash, and
meet presently at the Palace. Our Play shall be preferr'd. Let
Thisbe have clean Linnen, and let not him that Plays the Lion,
pare his Nails; they shall hang out for the Lion's Claws. And let no
man eat Onions, or Garlick, for we must utter most sweet breath.
No more words; but away.

                                   [*Exeunt.*

     Enter DUKE, EGEUS, LOVERS, *and* ATTENDANTS.

EG.   Are not these Stories strange, my Gracious Lord?

DU.   More strange than true. I never could believe,
These Antick Fables, nor these Fairy toys.
Lovers, and Lunaticks have pregnant brains.
They in a moment by strong fancy see
More than cool reason o're could comprehend.
The Poet, with the mad-man may be joyn'd.

He's of imagination all made up,
And see's more Devils, than all Hell can hold.
Can make a Venus of an Ethiop.
And as imagination rolls about,
He gives the airy Fantasms of his Brain,
A Local habitation, and a name.
And so these Lovers, wandring in the night,
Through unfrequented ways, brim full of fear,
Hoe easie is a Bush suppos'd a Bear!
> [*While a short Simphony Plays,* Enter OBERON, TITANIA,
> ROBIN-GOOD-FELLOW, *and all the* FAYRIES.

I hear strange Musick warbling in the Air.

OB.   'Tis Fairy Musick, sent by me;
To cure your Incredulity.
All was true the Lovers told,
You shall stranger things behold.
Mark the wonders shall appear,
While I feast your eye and ear.

DU.   Where am I? does my sence inform me right?
Or is my hearing better than my sight?

TIT.   When to Parlors we retire,
And Dance before a dying fire.

OB.   Or when by night near Woods, or Streams,
We wanton by the Moons pale beams.
Then gross shades, and twinkling light,
Expose our Shapes to mortal sight.
But in the bright and open day,
When in Sol's Glorious beams we play,
Our bodies are, in that fierce light,
Too thin and pure for humane sight.

TIT.   Sir, then cast your eyes above:
See the Wife of mighty Jove.

Juno appears in a Machine drawn by Peacocks.

OB.   Juno, who does still preside,
Over the Sacred Nuptial Bed:
Comes to bless their days and nights,
With all true joys, and chaste delights

*While a Symphony Plays, the Machine moves forward, and the Pea-
cocks spread their Tails, and fill the middle of the Theater.*

JUNO *sings.*

Thrice happy Lovers, may you be
For ever, ever free,

From that tormenting Devil, Jealousie.
From all that anxious Care and Strife.
That attends a married Life:
Be to one another true,
Kind to her as she to you.
And since the Errors of this Night are past,
May he be ever Constant, she be ever Chast.
The Machine ascends.
Ob. Now my gentle Puck, away,
Haste, and over-cast the Day.
Let thick Darkness all around,
Cover that Spot of Fairy Ground;
That so the gloomy Shades of Night
May usher in a glorious Light.

While the Scene is darken'd, a single Entry is danced; Then a Symphony is play'd; after that the Scene is suddainly Illuminated, and discovers a transparent Prospect of a Chinese Garden, the Architecture, the Trees, the Plants, the Fruit, the Birds, the Beasts, quite different from what we have in this part of the World. It is terminated by an Arch, through which is seen other Arches with close Arbors, and a row of Trees to the end of the View. Over it is a hanging Garden, which rises by several ascents to the top of the House; it is bounded on either side with pleasant Bowers, various Trees, and numbers of strange Birds flying in the Air, on the Top of a Platform is a Fountain, throwing up Water, which falls into a large Basin.

      A CHINESE *Enters and Sings.*
Thus the gloomy World
At first began to shine,
And from the Power Divine
A Glory round it hurl'd;
Which made it bright,
And gave it Birth in light.
Then were all Minds as pure,
As those Etherial Streams;
In Innocence secure,
Not Subject to Extreams.
There was no Room for empty Fame,
No cause for Pride, Ambition wanted aim.
      A CHINESE WOMAN *Sings.*
Thus Happy and Free,
Thus treated are we
With Nature's chiefest Delights.
CHORUS   Thus happy, &c.

We never cloy
But renew our Joy,
And one Bliss another Invites.
CHORUS   We never, &c.
  Thus wildly we live,
  Thus freely we give,
  What Heaven as freely bestows.
CHORUS   Thus wildly, &c.
  We were not made
  For Labour and Trade,
  Which Fools on each other impose.
CHORUS   We were not &c.
    A CHINESE MAN *Sings.*

Yes, Xansi, in your Looks I find
The Charms by which my Heart's betray'd;
Then let not your Disdain unbind
The Prisoner that your Eyes have made.
She that in Love makes least Defence,
Wounds ever with the surest Dart;
Beauty may captivate the Sence,
But Kindness only gains the Heart.
    SIX MONKEYS *come from between the Trees, and Dance.*
    TWO WOMEN *Sing in Parts.*
1 WO.   Hark how all Things with one Sound rejoyce,
  And the World seems to have one Voice.
2 WO.   Hark how the Echoing Air a Triumph Sings,
  And all around pleas'd Cupids clap their Wings.
1 WO.   Sure the dull God of Marriage does not hear;
  We'll rouse him with a Charm. Hymen appear!
CHORUS   Appear! Hymen appear!
BOTH   Our Queen of Night commands you not to stay.
CHORUS   Our Queen, &c.
    Enter HYMEN.
HY.   See, see, I obey.
  My Torch has long been out, I hate
  On loose dissembled Vows to wait.
  Where hardly Love out-lives the Wedding-Night,
  False Flames, Love's Meteors, yield my Torch no Light.
    Six Pedestals of China-work rise from under the Stage;
    they support six large Vases of Porcelain, in which are six
    China-Orange-trees.
BOTH WO.   Turn then thy Eyes upon those Glories there,
  And Catching Flames will on thy Torch appear.
HY.   My Torch, indeed, will from such Brightness shine:
  Love ne'er had yet such Altars, so divine.

The Pedestals move toward the Front of the Stage, and the Grand Dance begins of Twenty four Persons; then HYMEN *and the* TWO WOMEN *sing together.*

They shall be as happy as they're fair;
Love shall fill all the Places of Care:
And every time the Sun shall display
His Rising Light,
It shall be to them a new Wedding-Day;
And when he sets, a new Nuptial-Night.
    A CHINESE MAN *and* WOMAN *dance.*
    THE GRAND CHO   They shall be, &c.
    All the DANCERS *join in it.*

OB.   At Dead of Night we'll to the Bride-bed come,
  And sprinkle hallow'd Dew-drops round the Room.

TIT.   We'll drive the Fume about, about,
  To keep all Noxious Spirits out:
  That the Issue they create,
  May be ever fortunate.

OB.   Stay; let us not, like very foolish Elves,
  Take care of others, and neglect our selves.
  If these should be offended, we are lost;
  And all our Hopes, and future Fortunes cross'd.

TIT.   It is below the Fairy-Queen to fear.
  Look there: Can there be any Danger near,
  When Conquering Beauty fills that Heavenly Sphear

OB.   But here are Wits, and Criticks and 'tis said,
  Their Adders Tongues can sting, or hit us dead.

TIT.   Away: Let not the Name of Wits alarm us;
  They are so very few, they cannot harm us.

OB.   Consider; Sharpers, Beau's, the very Cits,
  All either are, or else they would be Wits.

TIT.   Well, let 'em all be Wits; and if they shou'd
  Blast us, or nip us in the very Bud,
  The Loss will be their own another Day.
  Are we not in a very hopeful Way
  To make 'em all amends—if they will stay.

OB.   They are impatient, and their Stomachs keen;
  They will not be postpon'd, 'tis you're Fifteen.

TIT.   Well, If their Appetites so fiercely crave,
  We'll give 'em all the Ready that we have.
  First, Losing Gamesters, Poets, Railing Wits;
  Some Basset-Ladies, and all Broken Cits;
  (Who live by what from others they purloyn)
  We'll lend 'em mighty Sums—in Fairy-Coin.

OB.   Ladies in Dreams shall have their Fortunes told;

The Young shall dream of Husbands, and the Old
Their Youthful Pleasures shall each Night repeat.
TIT.   Green-Sickness Girls, who nautiate wholesom Meat,
How they their Parents, and themselves may cheat.
OB.   Widows, who were by former Husbands vex'd,
Shall dream how they may over-reach the next.
TIT.   Each separate Lady, to supply her Want,
Shall every Night dream of a new Gallant.
OB.   Those Beau's, who were, at Nurse, chang'd by my Elves.
TIT.   Shall dream of nothing, but their pretty selves.
OB.   We'll try a Thousand charming Ways to win ye.
TIT.   If all this will not do, the Devil's in ye.

FINIS.

Selected Bibliography

•indicates works included or excerpted in this Norton Critical Edition

•Barber, C. L. *Shakespeare's Festive Comedy.* Princeton UP, 2011.
 Bell, William. *Shakespeare's Puck and His Folklore.* Richards, 1852.
•Boose, Lynda E. "The Father and the Bride in Shakespeare." *PMLA*, vol. 97, no. 3, 1992, pp. 325–47.
•Brook, Peter. *The Quality of Mercy: Reflections on Shakespeare.* Nick Hern Books, 2013.
 Brown, John R. "Free Shakespeare." *Shakespeare Survey: An Annual Survey of Shakespeare Studies and Production,* vol. 24, 1971, pp. 127–35.
•Bullough, Geoffrey. *Narrative and Dramatic Sources of Shakespeare: Volume I: Early Comedies, Poems, Romeo and Juliet.* Routledge and Kegan Paul, 1964.
 Calderwood, James L. "*A Midsummer Night's Dream*: Anamorphism and Theseus' Dream." *Shakespeare Quarterly,* vol. 42, no. 4, 1991, pp. 409–430.
 Chamberlain, Stephanie. "The Law of the Father: Patriarchal Economy in *A Midsummer Night's Dream*." *Journal of the Wooden O Symposium,* vol. 11, 2011, pp. 28–40.
•Coleridge, Samuel Taylor. *Coleridge's Essays & Lectures on Shakespeare & Some Other Old Poets & Dramatists,* edited by Ernest Rhys. J. M. Dent & Sons; E. P. Dutton & Co., 1907.
 Colthorpe, Marion. "Queen Elizabeth I and *A Midsummer Night's Dream*." *Notes and Queries,* vol. 34, no. 2, 1987, pp. 205–207.
 Crystal, Ben. *A Midsummer Night's Dream: Before/During/After.* Arden Shakespeare, 2013.
 Dent, R. W. "Imagination in *A Midsummer Night's Dream*." *Shakespeare Quarterly,* vol. 15, no. 2, 1964, pp. 115–29.
 Desmet, Christy. "Disfiguring Women with Masculine Tropes: A Rhetorical Reading of *A Midsummer Night's Dream*." *A Midsummer Night's Dream: Critical Essays,* edited by Dorothea Kehler. Garland, 1998. pp. 299–329.
 Foakes, R. A., ed. *A Midsummer Night's Dream.* Cambridge UP, 2003.
 Forey, Madeleine. "'Bless Thee, Bottom, Bless Thee! Thou Art Translated!': Ovid, Golding, and *A Midsummer Night's Dream*." *Modern Language Review,* vol. 93, no. 2, 1998, pp. 321–329.
 Garner, Shirley N. "*A Midsummer Night's Dream*: 'Jack Shall have Jill/Nought Shall Go Ill'." *A Midsummer Night's Dream: Critical Essays,* edited by Dorothea Kehler. Garland, 1998, pp. 128–43.
 Griffiths, Trevor. "Tradition and Innovation in Harley Granville-Barker's *A Midsummer Night's Dream*." *Theatre Notebook: A Journal of the History and Technique of the British Theatre,* vol. 30, 1976, pp. 78–87.
 Gurr, Andrew. "The First Plays at the New Globe." *Theatre Notebook: A Journal of the History and Technique of the British Theatre,* vol. 51, 1997, pp. 4–7.
 Halio, Jay. "The Staging of *A Midsummer Night's Dream*." *Shakespeare's Universe: Renaissance Ideas and Conventions, Essays in Honour of W. R. Elton,* ed. John M. Mucciolo Scolar Press, 1996, pp. 155–72.

Hattaway, Michael. "'Enter Cælia, the Fairy Queen, in Her Night Attire': Shakespeare and the Fairies." *Shakespeare Survey: An Annual Survey of Shakespeare Studies and Production*, vol. 65, 2013, pp. 26–41.

•Hazlitt, William. *Characters of Shakespear's Plays*. Taylor & Hessey, 1818.

•Hendricks, Margo. "'Obscured by dreams': Race, Empire and Shakespeare's *A Midsummer Night's Dream*." *Shakespeare Quarterly*, vol. 47, no. 1 1996, pp. 37–60.

Hodgdon, Barbara. "Gaining a Father: The Role of Egeus in the Quarto and the Folio." *The Review of English Studies*, ns. 37, 1986, pp. 534–42.

Holland, Norman N. "Hermia's Dream." *The Dream and the Text: Essays on Literature and Language*, edited by Carol S. Rupprecht and Norman N. Holland. State U of New York P, 1993, pp. 178–99.

Holland, Peter. "Theseus' Shadows in *A Midsummer Night's Dream*." *Shakespeare Survey: An Annual Survey of Shakespeare Studies and Production*, vol. 47, 1994, pp. 139–51.

Hunt, Maurice. "The Voices of *A Midsummer Night's Dream*." *Texas Studies in Literature and Language*, vol. 34, 1992, pp. 218–38.

Ioppolo, Grace. *Revising Shakespeare*. Harvard UP, 1991.

———. *Dramatists and Their Manuscripts in the Age of Shakespeare, Jonson, Middleton and Heywood*. Routledge, 2006.

Kehler, Dorothea, editor. *A Midsummer Night's Dream: Critical Essays*, Garland, 1998.

•Knight, G. Wilson. *The Shakespearean Tempest*. Oxford UP, 1932.

•Kott, Jan. *Shakespeare Our Contemporary*. Trans. Bolesław Taborski. W. W. Norton & Co., 1974.

Lamb, Mary E. "Taken by the Fairies: Fairy Practices and the Production of Popular Culture in *A Midsummer Night's Dream*." *Shakespeare Quarterly*, vol. 51, no. 3, 2000, pp. 277–312.

Levine, Laura. "Rape, Repetition, and the Politics of Closure in *A Midsummer Night's Dream*." *Feminist Readings of Early Modern Culture: Emerging Subjects*, edited by Valerie Traub, M. Lindsay Kaplan, and Dympna Callaghan. Cambridge UP, 1996, pp. 210–28.

Mahood, M. M. "*A Midsummer Night's Dream* as Exorcism." *Essays on Shakespeare in Honour of A. A. Ansari*, edited by T. R. Sharma. Shalabh Book House, 1986, pp. 136–49.

Montrose, Louis A. "*A Midsummer Night's Dream* and the Shaping Fantasies of Elizabethan Culture: Gender, Power, Form." *Rewriting the Renaissance: The Discourse of Sexual Difference in Early Modern Europe*, edited by Margaret W. Ferguson, et al. U of Chicago P, 1986, pp. 65–87.

Muir, Kenneth. "Pyramus and Thisbe: A Study in Shakespeare's Method." *Shakespeare Quarterly*, vol. 5, no. 2, 1954, pp. 141–53.

Richmond, Hugh M. "Shaping a Dream." *Shakespeare Studies*, vol. 17, 1985, pp. 49–60.

———. "Peter Quince Directs *Romeo and Juliet*." *Shakespeare and the Sense of Performance: Essays in the Tradition of Performance Criticism in Honor of Bernard Beckerman*, edited by Marvin Thompson, Ruth Thompson, and Jay L. Halio. U of Delaware P–Associated UPs, 1989, pp. 219–27.

Schleiner, Winfried. "Imaginative Sources for Shakespeare's Puck." *Shakespeare Quarterly*, vol. 36, no. 1, 1985, pp. 65–68.

Shell, Alison. "Delusion in *A Midsummer Night's Dream*." *Shakespeare and Early Modern Religion*, edited by David Loewenstein, Michael Witmore, and Brian Cummings. Cambridge UP, 2015, pp. 81–95.

•Swinburne, Algernon. *Shakespeare*. Henry Frowde, 1909.

Traub, Valerie. "The Homoerotics of Shakespearean Comedy." *Shakespeare, Feminism and Gender*, edited by Kate Chedgzoy. Palgrave, 2001, pp. 135–60.

Turner, Robert K., Jr., "Printing Methods and Textual Problems in *A Midsummer Night's Dream* Q1." *Studies in Bibliography*, vol. 15, 1962, pp. 33–55.

Warner, Marina. *From the Beast to the Blonde: On Fairy Tales and Their Tellers.* Chatto & Windus, 1994.

Warren, Roger. "Staging *A Midsummer Night's Dream*: Peter Hall's Productions, 1959–2010." *Shakespeare Survey: An Annual Survey of Shakespeare Studies and Production*, vol. 65, 2013, pp. 147–54.

Wells, Stanley. "*A Midsummer Night's Dream* Revisited." *Critical Survey*, vol. 3, no. 1, 1991, pp. 14–29.

Wilson, John Dover. "'they Sleepe all the Act'." *Review of English Studies: A Quarterly Journal of English Literature and the English Language*, vol. 4, no. 14, 1928, pp. 191–93.

•——— and Arthur Quiller-Couch, editors. *A Midsummer Night's Dream by William Shakespeare*. Cambridge UP, 1924.